The Institution of Criticism

The Institution of Criticism

Peter Uwe Hohendahl

Cornell University Press

Ithaca and London

THIS BOOK HAS BEEN PUBLISHED WITH THE AID OF A GRANT FROM
THE HULL MEMORIAL PUBLICATION FUND OF CORNELL UNIVERSITY.

First published 1982 by Cornell University Press.
Published in the United Kingdom by Cornell University Press Ltd.,
Ely House, 37 Dover Street, London W1X 4HQ.

International Standard Book Number 0-8014-1325-7
Library of Congress Catalog Card Number 81-15188
Printed in the United States of America
Librarians: Library of Congress cataloging information
appears on the last page of the book

ACKNOWLEDGMENTS

With the exception of the introduction, all essays in this volume have been translated from the German. Henry J. Schmidt and Ronald Smith translated the three studies that first appeared in my essay collection *Literaturkritik und Öffentlichkeit* (Munich, R. Piper & Co. Verlag, 1974), and are presented here as essays 1, 3, and 5. Their original titles are: "Literaturkritik und Öffentlichkeit" (first published in *Lili: Zeitschrift für Literaturwissenschaft und Linguistik*, Vol. 1, 1971); "Das Ende einer Institution? Der Streit über die Funktion der Literaturkritik" (first published in *Revolte und Experiment: Die Literatur der sechziger Jahre in Ost und West*, Heidelberg, 1972); "Promoter, Konsumenten und Kritiker: Zur Rezeption des Bestsellers" (first published in *Popularität und Trivialität*, Vol. 4, Wisconsin Workshop, edited by Reinhold Grimm and Jost Hermand, Frankfurt, 1974). Schmidt and Smith also translated essay 2, "Kunsturteil und Tagesbericht: Zur ästhetischen Theorie des späten Heine," which was originally published in *Heinrich Heine: Artistik und Engagement*, edited by Wolfgang Kuttenkeuler (Stuttgart, 1977). I am indebted to J. B. Metzlersche Verlagsbuchhandlung for permission to reprint.

Three essays appeared in *New German Critique:* "The Task of Contemporary Literary Criticism," in no. 7 (Winter 1976), translated by David Bathrick; "Prolegomena to a History of Literary Criticism," in no. 11 (Spring 1977), translated by Jeannine Blackwell; and "Critical Theory, Public Sphere, and Culture: Jürgen Habermas and His Critics," in no. 16 (Winter 1979), translated by Marc Silverman. All these essays have been amended slightly for this edition. I am grateful to the editors of the journal for permission to reprint. Unless otherwise indicated, the translations of quotations are those of the translators or, in the case of the introduction, mine.

In the final preparation of the manuscript I was assisted by Philip Brewster and Richard Bean, who helped me to revise the translations. I am grateful for their advice. Finally, I thank Carol Rosenzweig for typing the manuscript.

P.U.H.

Ithaca, New York

CONTENTS

The Institution of Criticism

INTRODUCTION

The recognition that a literary text is embedded in a historical context that can be defined in cultural, political, and social terms has been common knowledge for some time. This insight, however, has not been fully appreciated in the examination of various forms of literary criticism—scholarly books and articles, journalistic essays, book reviews in newspapers, and the like. Yet studies that deal with literary works in one way or another should also be recognized as literary texts and should be seen against their own background. Literary criticism, to borrow a definition from Ernst Robert Curtius, is that form of literature which is concerned with literature. The task of this introduction, seen in these terms, is to define and unfold the literary, cultural, and political context of the seven essays collected in this volume. They were written between 1970 and 1977—years that mark striking changes in the history of literary criticism in Europe and the United States. These changes are particularly evident in the West German situation, to which my essays refer primarily. The literary system of West Germany (the German Democratic Republic is excluded from the following considerations, since the East German situation is for a number of reasons fundamentally different) was going through a crisis that affected all its aspects: the production of literature was questioned no less than its distribution and reception. During these years of turmoil there was no agreement on the task of criticism and especially not on the method and function of aesthetic evaluation. For a number of years the crisis was so severe that the system itself appeared beyond repair. During the first half of the 1970s it was almost impossible for the critical observer to follow traditional paths of literary criticism and write just another scholarly book or concentrate critically on the latest novel or play. It would have been a problematical pretense to insist on perpetuating the tradition of the discipline. Academic critics were literally besieged when students protested against conventional literary studies and occupied the seminar rooms and libraries. And journalists who earn their living by writing reviews for newspapers, contributing essays to literary magazines, and lecturing on the cultural programs of public broadcasting were confronted with outspokenly polemical criticism. Their more polite antagonists asked them to review their professional commitment and in particular to reflect on their highly elitist concern with questions of aesthetic evaluation, while their more radical opponents told them to keep quiet unless they were willing to address more important issues. The conventional attitude that kept literary and social issues separate became suspicious, to say the least. Moreover, the German literary tradition, the canon of classical authors from Gotthold Ephraim Lessing to Thomas Mann, came under critical scrutiny. In the early seventies it became a hazardous task to defend the cultural heritage of Weimar and Jena, which had been the focus of German studies since the 1850s.

These unusual circumstances suggested a more radical approach to the discipline of literary criticism. The following essays are an attempt to come to terms with the crisis of criticism. They address themselves, from different perspectives, to the crucial question of what the task of criticism could be in the context of an advanced capitalistic industrial society. The traditional discourse on the method and the history of literary criticism has more or less ignored this aspect, emphasizing instead aesthetic or theoretical issues. The history of criticism would thus appear to be the history of a self-contained discipline with its own sets of intrinsic problems. This approach presupposes that there are institutions like the university and the press which can serve as the basis for the production and distribution of literary criticism. My approach, although by no means indifferent to questions of aesthetic norms and problems of evaluation, is more concerned with the institutional side—that is, the social models which guide and control the activity called literary criticism.

Since these essays focus on the mediation between the literary and the sociocultural spheres, the position of their author must be taken into consideration. They do not merely deal with the problems of the sixties and early seventies; they are themselves part of those struggles and the controversy. Therefore, writing now in a significantly different social and political climate, I have not tried to revise and update them. I have refrained from this accustomed academic practice because it reflects a notion of linear scholarly progress which these essays question in various ways and forms. Where this idea of progress—the notion that the results of scholarship are just building blocks for future scholarship—is dominant, a more challenging sense of historicity, emphasizing the commitment of the author, is repressed. In contrast to the German situation, there might be the chance that these essays could suggest new ways of looking at the discourse of criticism in this country precisely because this discipline has been problematized in recent years. Although most of the material dealt with in my essays is taken from the literary and social history of Germany, and therefore some of the observations and results cannot be generalized immediately, it is obvious that West Germany is an advanced industrial society, part of the Western world, and both politically and culturally closely related to other European and American industrial societies. I do not wish to downgrade national traditions, which certainly play a significant role in the practice of literary criticism; yet it has to be noted that the essential problems are common to all advanced industrial societies, although they are expressed in various forms.

Insofar as these essays refer to an individual national culture—that is, the literary life of Germany—they make a number of assumptions that may not be immediately evident to the American reader. The term "literary criticism" has a decidedly different connotation from the German term *Literaturkritik*. A discussion of the past and present status of *Literaturkritik* is not the same as an analysis of literary theory or critical methods. In this country "literary criticism" is used to describe the work of academic writers, but the German term includes both the academic and popular modes. If there is any bias in the use of the word, it is toward the kind of literary criticism one refers to as book reviewing.

Since the late nineteenth century, German usage has distinguished between *Literaturwissenschaft* as the form of literary criticism situated in the academy, and *Tageskritik* or *Buchkritik,* which is closely connected with a mass medium like the press. *Literaturwissenschaft,* especially in this period, devoted its efforts to the literature of the past, while the task of *Literaturkritik* in the narrow sense of the word has been to describe and evaluate the literature of its own time. Yet there is more involved than the distinction between two fields of research. The academic critic and the journalist are molded by divergent literary institutions: the university and the press. Academic critics are expected to perform according to the rigorous rules of scholarship; journalists, on the other hand, address themselves to a general audience that is unfamiliar with the technical terms of literary analysis and usually uninterested in the professional disputes and disagreements that are an important aspect of academic criticism. The distinction, in other words, is clearly reflected in both the critics' role models and their modes of discourse.

This division between the academy and the press is not unknown in the United States and has at least to some extent shaped the mode of American literary criticism. Yet this impact has been less forceful, since the literary critic as a journalist is a model that has been less successful here than in Europe. The academic critic has assumed many of the functions that are exercised by the free-lance critic, the publicist, in France or Germany. Reviewers for the *New York Review of Books* are usually university professors at more or less distinguished institutions. They may appreciate receiving an honorarium for their contributions, but this is rarely an essential part of their income. In Germany, on the other hand, free-lance criticism has been and still is an established profession and is clearly distinguished from that of the university professor. The division is so obvious that it is considered self-evident. It hardly occurs to the general public that this distinction is not natural but the result of a notable shift that occurred in German literary criticism during the latter half of the nineteenth century. Before 1850 public and academic criticism were cut from the same patterns. The major literary histories that were written between 1830 and 1865, the works of Georg G. Gervinus, Julian Schmidt, and Hermann Hettner, were not intended primarily for the students of the university or secondary school. Their audience was drawn from the educated general reading public. Literary history was not a specialized professional field; rather, the historians embarked on their voluminous projects because they wanted to inform the educated reader about the German cultural tradition. The writing of literary history was intimately connected with the paramount task of the nineteenth-century critic: defining the national cultural identity. And this question, especially in the case of Germany, was closely related to the problem of political identity.

The rift between academic and public criticism emerged after 1850 when the burgeoning German universities acknowledged modern German studies (*Literaturgeschichte*) as a proper academic field, and separate professorial chairs were created for German literary history. Still, during the two decades following the Revolution of 1848 the discipline of literary criticism to a large degree maintained its public function. The most influential literary historian of this period, Julian Schmidt, was not an academic, but a journalist. His literary histories were based on essays he wrote for *Die Grenzboten,* one of the most prominent and influential literary magazines of his time.

One generation later, in the heyday of Positivism, academic criticism had established itself as a proper discipline that could prove its legitimacy by a rigorous professional method—philology. At the same time, however, it had lost its impact on the general public. When academic critics, under the spell of Positivism, insisted on scientific objectivity, they began to exclude contemporary literature from their discipline. This field was left to the journalists, because it could supposedly not be treated objectively. By accepting this task as an important function of criticism, journalists exposed themselves to the reproach of *Unwissenschaftlichkeit.*

This constellation was not changed by the new critical paradigm that emerged around 1900. The attempt to redefine literary criticism as part of the *Geisteswissenschaften* (humanities)—initiated by Wilhelm Dilthey and then propagated by such influential critics as Rudolf Unger and Oskar Walzel—left the institutional structure untouched. The new school of criticism that superseded Positivism developed a new theory and methodology, yet at the same time its critique of Positivism reinforced the hiatus between academic and public criticism because it had to emphasize its allegiance to the idea of *Wissenschaftlichkeit,* which had dominated the era of Positivism.

The new generation of scholars continued to insist on objectivity, so that the field of contemporary literature was again left to the newspapers and the literary magazines. It is interesting to note that Wilhelm Dilthey from the very beginning privileged the past over the present. His influential essays, later collected in *Das Erlebnis und die Dichtung* (1905), dealt with such authors as Lessing, Novalis, Goethe, and Hölderlin, who had, with the exception of Hölderlin, already reached canonical status when Dilthey became interested in them.

During the 1870s, under the impact of the new mass media, we find a new mode of literary criticism in the public sphere. Its practitioners concentrated on contemporary literary life. They reviewed the latest novels of popular authors; they reported on the theater, and informed the public on cultural life in general. The locus for this form of criticism was the *feuilleton* of the press—that is, the cultural supplement of the daily newspaper. Following the French example, the leading German newspapers began to add a feuilleton section to their daily editions as early as 1850. By 1870 this practice was so well established that the critic who wrote principally for the daily press was easily labeled a feuilletonist. To be sure, this label was not a compliment when used by members of the academic community. The feuilleton had a reputation for triviality and subjectivity compared to the rigor of academic studies. It goes without saying that the journalists, reacting to the criticism, made fun of the cumbersome language of academic criticism.

This attitude of mutual dislike, still visible even today in Germany, reflects the growing rift between academic and public criticism. Their modes of discourse were not compatible, and it became increasingly difficult for any individual to participate in both. The discourse of journalistic criticism was shaped by the structure of the new mass media. After the foundation of the Second Empire, when the German press was dominated by publishers who were primarily interested in profit and therefore began to build large corporations, the cultural section of the newspapers, the feuilleton, underwent a significant transformation. It was adapted to the taste of a mass audience that consisted of heterogeneous social groups. While the critic of the early nineteenth century was addressing a fairly homogeneous reading public, the journalist of the late nineteenth century was writing for an audience that could not be expected to be truly familiar with its own national literary heritage. These changes were reflected in the language of criticism. The leading literary critics of the 1850s, men like Rudolf Gottschall, Julian Schmidt, and Hermann Marggraff, used the same style to discuss past and contemporary literature. The language of their reviews was basically identical with that of their literary histories. By 1880 it was taken for granted that the journalist and the academic critic followed different stylistic patterns.

A good example of this difference is Theodor Fontane's review of Otto Brahms's study on Gottfried Keller. Fontane pointed out that Brahms's book failed to offer what a good review ought to provide for its readers. The way Fontane disagreed with Brahms makes it obvious that he himself belonged to the tradition of the nonacademic feuilleton:

> An impressive apparatus is set up in order to prove, with a stupendous amount of scholarship, to what extent this or that author, in our case Gottfried Keller, was influenced by Jean Paul or Goethe, by the Romantics or the Swabian School. On top of this [there is] a rigorous count of individual words and expressions, a comparison of major and minor characters, similarities and oppositions, subjective and objective—and all this according to statistics prepared in the form of tables, which are used to report on compulsory school attendance of children and headaches of women.[1]

Obviously, this criticism makes fun of the methodological rigidity of Positivism. Fontane argues that this mode of criticism, which defines its subject by historical comparison and statistical analysis, misses the essential elements: first of all the aesthetic structure of the work of art, and second, the interests of the average reader, who wants to be informed about the content of the work in question. Brahms followed the requirements of academic discourse as it was established by Wilhelm Scherer. Fontane sensed that this mode of criticism, with its insistence on being scientific, fails to do justice to the task of literary criticism as it was defined in the early nineteenth century. At that time the emphasis was placed on the dialogue between the critic and the

[1] Theodor Fontane, *Aufsätze zur Literatur*, ed. Kurt Schreinert (Munich, 1963), p. 268.

audience. On the other hand, scientific discourse, the method of Brahms, is fundamentally indifferent to the expectations of the general public and is governed by rules of methodological purity and logical consistency. This problem, as we have seen, was not restricted to Positivism. When academic criticism began to follow Wilhelm Dilthey's example, and emphasized its distinct method, objectivity and rigorous analysis were still taken for granted. The language of Dilthey and his followers is not more popular than that of Scherer; rather, the opposite may be true. Methodological reflection on the process of understanding, an essential part of the hermeneutic tradition, usually results in a higher degree of complexity in the critic's language. Both Positivism and the hermeneutic tradition aimed at an objective method by which scholarly criticism could be clearly differentiated from the popular evaluations which the newspapers offer in their cultural supplements. By 1900 serious literary historiography had established itself as a professional, specialized discipline with its own rather limited audience. The exception was biographical criticism, which still reached the broad audience of the educated reader.

Popular literary criticism also experienced significant changes at this time. The emergence of the modern mass media, which have to satisfy the interests of a wide and heterogeneous audience, had a substantial impact on the form and the content of critical discourse. Because of the division of labor which assigned past literature to academic criticism, journalists found themselves alienated from the literary tradition, and in their attempt to respond to the work of art without mediation through the literary tradition, they turned to their own subjectivity. Critical appreciation became a form of expression in which the critic, without consideration of given aesthetic norms, articulated what he experienced when he read a novel or watched a theater performance. The normative judgment of older criticism was replaced by an expression of the critic's feelings. Instead of talking about the work of art, the critics, encouraged by the new model, talked about themselves.

In the history of German criticism it is Alfred Kerr (1867–1948) who brought about this radical transformation of its discourse. He introduced the subjective manner: his reviews are not meant to describe and analyze what he had seen or read;

they are records of what he experienced while seeing or reading. Thus Kerr blurred the traditional distinction between aesthetic and critical language, between criticism and the work of art. Explicitly, Kerr stressed that criticism is as much a part of poetic literature as poems and plays: "From now on we shall say: literature can be divided into the epical, the lyrical, the dramatic, and the critical genres."[2] By postulating that criticism is a genre of poetic literature (*Dichtung*), Kerr freed himself from the increasingly problematical notion of critical norms and general standards. When the literary public became more diffuse under the impact of the Industrial Revolution, the critic lost the well-defined reading public of an earlier generation. The traditional liberal model, which had conceived of criticism as a dialogue between the critic and the public, became an abstraction that could no longer navigate the course of practical reviewing. Thus critical discourse moved toward a monologue. "The isolated subjectivity in which the modern critic found himself was redefined as the virtue of the artist. Artistic privilege, on the other hand, permitted him to engage in polemics without constructing an objective basis; in the tradition of Romanticism, art was its own justification."[3] Kerr had to pay a high price for this radical impressionism, which does not clearly distinguish between life and art. As Russell Berman has pointed out, he lost the work of art as an aesthetic object, and by the same token lost his understanding of the historical context.[4] Criticism is grounded in experience, but the concept of experience reduces itself to the notion of a passive stream of life to which the critic can and must return. In that sense the emancipation of feuilleton criticism from the norms of Goethe's and Friedrich Schiller's aesthetic theories, and of literary tradition as well, marked the end of criticism as an autonomous discourse. This was noted by both Karl Kraus and Bertolt Brecht; the conservative critic of culture as well as the radical writer attacked Kerr as typical of decadent middle-class culture after that class had been irreversibly defeated.

The defeat of Imperial Germany in 1919 was obviously not the end of literary criticism in Germany, but was undoubtedly

[2]Alfred Kerr, *Die Welt im Drama* (Berlin, 1917), 1:vi.
[3]Russell Alexander Berman, "The Development of Literary Criticism in Germany: 1871–1914," dissertation, Washington University (St. Louis, 1979), p. 309.
[4]Ibid., p. 315.

the end of criticism as an unproblematical discipline. The transition from liberal to organized capitalism, which was completed in Germany during the 1920s, embraced the cultural sphere. The advent of organized commercial culture—the culture industry, as it was termed a decade later by the Frankfurt School—left its imprint on literary criticism as well, though more on the feuilleton of the newspapers than on academic criticism, which could retain a stronger affiliation with the literary tradition. The subjectivity of the feuilleton essay, which relied on the individual experience of the critic, turned into a cliché that became formulaic. This deficiency prefigured the crisis of the 1960s, when the institution of criticism as a whole was questioned. The decade following World War II witnessed a growing discrepancy between the institutionalized forms of criticism on the one hand and the restructured public sphere on the other. Literary criticism, and particularly its liberal variety, which insisted on the active participation of an educated audience, could be maintained only by divorcing it from social reality.

The work of Walter Benjamin in the 1920s and 1930s is an admirable example of the problems of an author who was unwilling to accept either the traditional role of the academic critic or the role of the accommodating journalist who sells his talents to the highest bidder. It is not accidental that Benjamin, then still trying to find a place in the academic community, chose to write his doctoral dissertation on Romantic criticism. In part this choice was probably influenced by the revival of Romanticism around the turn of the century. More specifically, however, Benjamin wanted to recapture a period of literary criticism which offered a theory of art far superior to that of his own time. Benjamin's final remarks in his dissertation make it very clear that his interest in the aesthetic philosophy of the Romantic period was more than an interest in history: "The status of the philosophy of art in Germany around 1800, as it is reflected in the theories of Goethe and the early Romantics, is still legitimate today."[5] It was not Benjamin's intention to restore Romantic criticism and Goethe's philosophy of art. In fact, Benjamin was

[5]Walter Benjamin, *Der Begriff der Kunstkritik in der deutschen Romantik*, in *Gesammelte Schriften*, ed. Rolf Tiedemann and Hermann Schweppenhäuser (Frankfurt am Main, 1974), 1/1:117.

convinced that they ultimately failed to solve the essential problems of criticism. Goethe's philosophy of art, according to Benjamin, does not allow us to offer a critical judgment of the work of art. The Romantics, on the other hand, came closer to his ideal; Friedrich Schlegel, in particular, developed a theory that contains a critical perspective. When Benjamin insisted that for Schlegel judgment was an *essential* component of literary analysis, he emphasized the element that was to become the center of his own program. The ideas that Benjamin outlined at the end of his dissertation evolved as the guidelines of his own work in the 1920s, when he began to practice literary criticism for newspapers and magazines. But the more he learned about the professional side of book reviewing, the give and take among publishers, newspaper owners, and journalists, the more he moved away from the idealist model of criticism which he had embraced in his dissertation, until he reached a position in which he saw himself in basic agreement with a Marxist perspective.

In the history of literary criticism, Benjamin's reflections on the institution of criticism occupy a central position. His first major attempt to establish himself as a literary critic outside the university grew out of his acquaintance with the publisher Guido Weiss, who encouraged him to found his own literary magazine. In 1921 Benjamin, who was still under the influence of the Romantic and Neoromantic tradition, conceived this magazine as a locus for literary criticism in the most uncompromising sense. The critical discourse of the *Angelus Novus,* as he wanted to call the journal, was not expected to appeal to a broad audience. Referring back to the *Athenäum* of the Schlegel brothers, Benjamin indicated in his prospectus that "the norms for authentic topicality cannot lie with the masses."[6] He argued: "Any journal, like this one [the *Athenäum*], unrelenting in its thinking, imperturbable in its expression, and utterly without regard for the public, if need be, ought to concentrate on that which, as truly topical, manifests itself beneath the barren surface of the unprecedented and the novel, the exploitation of which we leave to the daily press."[7] Benjamin explicitly distanced himself from the tradition of the feuilleton, but he also rejected the model

[6]Ibid., 2/1:241.
[7]Ibid., pp. 241–242.

2 1

of nineteenth-century *Literaturwissenschaft,* which tried to situate literary works through historical comparison and philological analysis. Instead Benjamin proposed, following Romantic theory, a mode of textual criticism which brings out—to use a later term of Theodor W. Adorno's—the truth content (*Wahrheitsgehalt*) of the work of art.

In 1921 Benjamin was convinced that literature and the arts were undergoing a severe crisis, but he still believed that a rigorous theory of criticism would be an adequate remedy. The social and political context of this crisis—that is, the commercialized culture of a mass society—was not essential to Benjamin's project, which defined its own radicalism in philosophical terms. The price Benjamin had to pay for his attempt to distance himself from the feuilleton of the daily press was esoteric individualism.

When the *Angelus Novus* project failed, Benjamin applied his ideas to his famous essay on Goethe's *Elective Affinities,* but he soon abandoned his purely philosophical definition of literary criticism. By 1925 he had considerably changed his project—without, however, sacrificing the rigor of his earlier program. When he realized that his second dissertation would not be accepted and he would therefore not be able to enter the upper echelon of the academic profession, and particularly when he began to face serious financial problems because his father was unable and unwilling to support him, the social and economic context of criticism came home to him. The esoteric stance was ultimately renounced.

In *Einbahnstrasse* (1929), a collection of short prose pieces, Benjamin defined the task of criticism in a rather different way. Now the interests and the needs of the masses find their place. In order to become effective, Benjamin argued, the critic "must nurture the inconspicuous forms that better fit its influence in active communities than does the pretentious, universal gesture of the books—in leaflets, brochures, articles, and placards. Only this prompt language shows itself actively equal to the moment."[8] This is clearly a decision in favor of the mass media that in 1921 were still considered uncouth. The program of criticism which Benjamin offers in *Einbahnstrasse* ultimately goes back,

[8]Benjamin, *Reflections,* ed. Peter Demetz, trans. Edmund Jephcott (New York, 1978), p. 61.

although not directly, to the liberal model of the nineteenth century. When he postulated that criticism should be essentially polemical, he moved toward the tradition of major criticis like Ludwig Börne and Heinrich Heine, who had molded and sharpened the German language for the task of polemical writing. The practice of criticism, Benjamin claimed, must be rescued from the type of historical appreciation which Dilthey and his school had established at German universities. It is supposed to have an immediate impact on literary life—by taking a clear-cut position, by fighting for or against the literary tendencies of its era. Yet in the way Benjamin defined the relationship between the critic and the work of art it becomes obvious that he was also aware of the problematics of this model. His twelfth thesis on criticism states: "The public must always be in the wrong but always have the feeling that it is represented by the critic."[9] The seventh thesis can be understood as a commentary on this argument: "For the critic, his colleagues are the final jurisdiction, not the public, and by no means posterity."[10] In 1929 he suggested that, first of all, literary criticism ought to be directed to the general public and, second, that the critic ought to be the spokesperson for this public.

It is interesting to note, however, that Benjamin—who at this time clearly wanted to restore the political element to literary criticism—defined the role of the public in much more negative terms than nineteenth-century liberalism. Benjamin's public does not have the attributes of intellectual maturity which Immanuel Kant had envisioned as the stepping stone on the way to enlightenment. Self-determination, according to Benjamin, is reached only in the judgment of authentic critics, who are endowed with the authority to critique the literary production of their time.

The radicalism of Benjamin's theses should not blind us to the fact that this program could no more solve the dilemma of criticism than could the project of 1921. Benjamin's new literary activism, the attempt to work out a political stance, remained abstract. When he became a journalist and wrote regularly for the *Frankfurter Zeitung* and *Die literarische Welt*, he became ex-

---

[9]Benjamin, *Gesammelte Schriften*, 4/1:109.
[10]Ibid., p. 108.

posed to the pressure of capitalist journalism. He had to realize that the political dimension of literary criticism could not be restored simply by revising the theory. His experiences with the *Frankfurter Zeitung* in particular, where Siegfried Kracauer was the editor in chief for the literary supplement, showed him the dependency of the free-lance critic, who does not own the means of production. The advocate of a rigorous program of criticism, he was occasionally forced to compromise if he wanted to be on good terms with those in power.

Benjamin the journalist learned to pay attention to the economic context of literary production. The essay "The Author as Producer," which later became so influential in the German student movement of the late 1960s, summarized views and arguments which Benjamin had articulated before in essays and reviews. In 1934—that is, after the rise of National Socialism in Germany—Benjamin criticized any form of political engagement which relied on the capitalist apparatus of the media. Furthermore, he postulated the identity of the writer and the audience, as it was reached, according to him, in the revolutionary press of the Soviet Union. It was the press, the very medium Benjamin had decried in 1921, which now became the focus of his attention. The newspaper in Russia evolved as the central medium for revolutionary literature. In Western Europe, on the other hand, the press was controlled by capitalism and was therefore hardly a useful instrument for Benjamin's program. He argued: "Since on the one hand, the newspaper, technically speaking, represents the most important literary position, but on the other hand, this position is controlled by the opposition, it is no wonder that the writer's understanding of his dependent position, his technical possibilities, and his political task has to grapple with the most enormous difficulties."[11] For Benjamin the notion of political criticism remains an illusion as long as the criticial intelligentsia does not control the apparatus of the mass media. It should be noted that his friends at the Institut für Sozialforschung did not exactly share this position. The more Benjamin stressed the importance of economic factors, the closer he moved to Brecht, who had come to the conclusion that the central issue of literary criticism was not the question of

[11]Benjamin, *Reflections,* pp. 225–226.

theory and method but the practical problem of control over the media.

During the thirties—and this applies to more than just his well-known essays "The Author as Producer" and "The Work of Art in the Age of Mechanical Reproduction"—Benjamin undertook to redefine the task of the writer (who at this point is almost identical with the critic) in such a way that Romantic concepts like the creative artist and the organic work of art were replaced by concepts more suitable for the industrial age. Like Brecht he concentrated on forms of didactic literature which would allow the audience to participate in the process of production. "What matters, therefore, is the exemplary character of production, which is able first to induce other producers to produce, and second to put an improved apparatus at their disposal. And this apparatus is better the more consumers it is able to turn into producers—that is, readers or spectators into collaborators."[12]

The model Benjamin had in mind was the epic theater of Brecht. The application of this model to criticism would imply that the educated critic, coming from a middle-class background, would seek solidarity with the proletariat. The task would be to look for works that would help the masses to define their goal, rather than screening the output of the publishing industry, as was the function of the feuilleton critic, who was paid by the newspapers to be the judge of the literary fashion show. This definition of the critic's role explains what has puzzled some observers: Benjamin's interest in odd books which escaped the eyes of the well-adjusted review editors, and his lack of interest in the "great authors" of his time.

In this context the collaboration between Benjamin and Brecht at least has to be mentioned. Their common concern with the politics and economics of literary criticism crystallized in the idea of bringing out a literary magazine together.[13] The title of the projected magazine, *Krise und Kritik* (Crisis and Criticism), is a good indication of their goals. The journal was to focus on the social and economic analysis of literary production, and especially of literary criticism. Although the project never materialized, Brecht and Benjamin continued to share a position that

---

[12]Ibid., p. 233.
[13]See Bernd Witte, *Der Intellektuelle als Kritiker* (Stuttgart, 1976), pp. 168–177.

was adamantly opposed to feuilleton criticism. For Brecht, Alfred Kerr in particular embodied all the vices of the journalist whose opinions are owned by the newspaper industry. His attacks on Kerr were relentless; he denounced him as the typical feuilletonist, for whom literature has only a culinary function:

> The style of today's literary criticism is culinary. Our critics take a consumer attitude, which does not mean, however, that they enjoy theater and use it in the interest of the public—that is to say, are on the side of the public, critically facing the theater as consumers; rather, together with the public and the theater, they consume the works that have come down to them as the so-called cultural goods of their class. One does not produce anymore, one consumes, enjoys, and legitimizes the given situation. According to this ritual, the final arbiter in matters of art is taste, in fact a taste that favors individualistic nuances, calling for variations.[14]

Here Brecht touched on a very sensitive area of feuilleton criticism. The concept of taste had a central function in eighteenth-century criticism, since it emphasized the subjective element that helped to defeat the inflexible rules of Classicism. Thus Brecht's critique captured not only the idiosyncrasies of the individual critic but also an essential element of the liberal model of criticism. Taste is defined as the consensus between the critic and the audience. By focusing his attack on the consumer attitude of the critic Brecht exploded the liberal notion that the critic functions independently in the public sphere. Brecht pointed out that the public sphere and thereby criticism did not have the autonomy which the liberal mind took for granted. Contrary to the idealist definitions that critics have used to safeguard their profession, the institution of criticism—and by this Brecht meant first and foremost criticism in newspapers and journals—is part of the apparatus which advanced capitalism had developed to disseminate culture. Brecht argued:

> The social role of today's bourgeois criticism is that of announcing entertainment. The theaters sell evening entertainment and the critics send the public to the theaters. . . . We have already indicated

[14]Bertolt Brecht, *Gesammelte Werke,* Edition Suhrkamp (Frankfurt, 1967), 18: 98.

why the critics represent the interests of the theaters more than those of the public. The answer is brief: because the theaters are organized, regulative economic enterprises which can thus exert influence and offer social privileges.[15]

Brecht's polemic owed its power to the application of economic categories to the cultural sphere. By laying bare the context of criticism, he showed that its crisis was the result of larger social and economic problems which could not be corrected simply by new styles or reform programs. For Brecht, ultimately only the abolition of the capitalist form of production could bring about an authentic mode of criticism.

Still, Brecht was not inclined to believe in the automatic collapse of capitalism. He stressed the usefulness of literary production under capitalism, and by the same token he favored new approaches to criticism. Criticism, he argued, should become sociological and scientific rather than aesthetic and culinary. Brecht's critic becomes the spokesperson for Brecht's literary program, the epic theater. The critic's function is to speak out for useful literary forms. The institution of criticism, in other words, is expected to familiarize the public with its true interest, "for the audience has to be taught and changed."[16] Thus Brecht proposed to redefine aesthetic problems, which the feuilleton critic discussed in terms of taste, as concrete social problems. It becomes the critic's task to analyze the correlation between these questions and the formal structures that articulate them in the aesthetic realm.

Brecht's critique of literary criticism emphasized two areas: first, he called for a rigorous sociology of criticism—that is, an analysis of the economic base, the class situation, and the social institutions which dominate criticism; second, he insisted on a scientific mode of criticism, by which he meant a method that deals with questions of form and structure in terms of their social and political function. This notion of criticism as a critique of ideology was at the center of the Frankfurt School's Critical Theory—Leo Lowenthal's and Adorno's early work comes to mind. Yet the difference between their position and that of

[15]Ibid., p. 109.
[16]Ibid., p. 112.

Brecht cannot be overlooked. Adorno, for instance, always refused to address aesthetic problems as functions of social questions. His later polemic against Jean-Paul Sartre and Brecht in his essay "Commitment" (1962) only confirmed his stance against any attempt to resort to a theory that grounds criticism in the concept of class struggle and thereby uses the distinction between economic base and cultural superstructure as the point of reference.[17] This disagreement between Brecht and the Frankfurt School (Adorno, Max Horkheimer) surfaced again in the late sixties when the student movement questioned established forms of criticism. The more radical the movement became, the closer it approached a Brechtian position, abandoning its initial roots in Critical Theory.

It is interesting to note, however, that these most advanced positions of the early thirties were completely buried under the impact of German Fascism. And when the Third Reich was finally defeated in 1945, there was no attempt to return to those positions. The substantive transformation of criticism which had been anticipated did not occur. There were changes, to be sure, but they were limited to the abolition of overtly fascist norms in criticism. Otherwise the restoration of criticism consisted of a return to a more traditional format. It would be an overstatement to say that academic criticism (*Literaturwissenschaft*) was searching its own past to uncover the reasons for its compromising alliance with National Socialism. Academic criticism tried, rather, to overcome these unpleasant questions by favoring a theory that stressed the intrinsic approach. Its methodology, which shared basic features with New Criticism, focused its attention on the aesthetic structure of the work of art, thus displacing the historical context in such a way that the political problematic disappeared. It was only in the mid-sixties that a younger generation began to ask critical questions about the tradition of German academic criticism and tried to trace its fascist elements back to the Romantic origins of *Germanistik*.[18] Even these investigations had no serious impact on the institution until 1966,

---

[17]Theodor W. Adorno, "Engagement," *Noten zur Literatur* (Frankfurt, 1965), 3:109–135. An English translation is available in *The Essential Frankfurt School Reader*, ed. Andrew Arato and Eike Gebhardt (New York, 1978), pp. 300–318.

[18]See Eberhard Lämmert et al., *Germanistik—eine deutsche Wissenschaft* (Frankfurt, 1968).

when the student movement more aggressively examined the background of German literary studies. This was also the time when Marxist theory finally reached German universities—as shown, on the one hand, by the political radicalization of Critical Theory by its second generation (Oskar Negt, Frank Wolf, Ekkehart Krippendorff, Claus Offe, Peter Brückner), and, on the other hand, by the rediscovery of Georg Lukács and Brecht, which would imply a revision of the attitude of the New Left toward East Germany.

For any analysis of the sixties and seventies it is crucial to understand the role of the Frankfurt School. Critical Theory, the only form of Marxist theory that was not repressed in Adenauer's Federal Republic, clearly helped to prepare the way for the opposition movement of the late sixties. Both Horkheimer and Adorno were highly visible figures in the cultural sphere after their return to Germany in the late forties. Their contributions to cultural magazines, newspapers, radio programs, and the like left a noticeable imprint on the intellectual development of West Germany. Nor was their prominence limited to the social sciences. The renewed controversy in 1961 about methodology between the Frankfurt and Cologne School, the so-called *Positivismusstreit*,[19] had repercussions far beyond the academic discipline of sociology. This methodological controversy was at the same time the opportunity for Jürgen Habermas to defend the position of Critical Theory against Neopositivism and thereby gain stature. By 1965, when the student movement began to appropriate Critical Theory, in particular under the guidance of Habermas, the impact of the Frankfurt School could be recognized in the political public sphere as well. The social and political criticism of the New Left owed its critical force initially to Horkheimer's and Adorno's *Dialectic of Enlightenment,* Habermas' *Strukturwandel der Öffentlichkeit,* and Herbert Marcuse's *One Dimensional Man.*

Literary criticism definitely came under the spell of Critical Theory, although it would be inappropriate to suggest that the Frankfurt Institute had any influence on university curricula or the decisions of newspaper editors. The function of Critical

---

[19]See Theodor W. Adorno et al., *The Positivist Dispute in German Sociology,* trans. Glyn Adey and David Frisby (New York, 1976).

Theory was that of a catalyst, stimulating and provoking the various ideological camps to articulate their positions. By 1967 literary criticism moved toward a situation which ultimately called for a new paradigm, yet it was by no means clear how this paradigm would be defined. Within the confines of academic criticism both traditional historicism and formalism (*Werkimmanenz*) had lost their appeal, mainly because of their close ties with the university establishment and its politics. Within a very short period, the discussion radicalized, polarizing the critics into antagonistic camps that were labeled "materialist" or "bourgeois." While the "bourgeois" camp consisted of conservatives and liberals, the materialist camp was made up of fairly divergent ideological groups, ranging from Critical Theory to Leninist Orthodoxy and Maoism.

The search for the new paradigm was carried out as a search for relevance.[20] The polemic against the literary establishment—and this is very similar to the American situation—emphasized that its attitude toward literature severed the aesthetic function from the social one, so that to praise the autonomy of a work of art implicitly or explicitly supported the social status quo. Therefore, the suggestion of semiotic criticism was to replace the concept of the work of art (*Kunstwerk*) by the concept of the text, a strategy that would allow the inclusion of literary forms heretofore neglected by traditional academic criticism. "Reception" theory, introduced by Hans Robert Jauss and Wolfgang Iser in West Germany, struggled with similar problems. The idea of replacing production aesthetics with reception aesthetics was motivated by the legitimation crisis of traditional literary history. At the same time, however—and this is most obvious in the original (1967) version of his program—Jauss understood his theory as a response to Marxist criticism. He meant to offer a critique of Leninist orthodoxy, thereby emphasizing reflection theory as the crucial feature of Marxism. It was symptomatic that Jauss identified Marxist criticism with Lukács rather than with Adorno

---

[20]For a more detailed account, see my essay "Politisierung der Kunsttheorie: Zur ästhetischen Diskussion nach 1965," in *Deutsche Literatur in der Bundesrepublik seit 1965*, ed. Paul Michael Lützeler and Egon Schwarz (Königstein, 1980), pp. 282–299.

or Marcuse. Only in 1970, in the third edition of "Literaturgeschichte als Provokation der Literaturwissenschaft," did Jauss
acknowledge that the question of Marxist criticism was somewhat
more complex than he had thought when he originally conceived it.[21] He now admitted the importance of critics like Karel
Kosik and tried to integrate Czech structuralism, which in the
thirties and forties had worked out some of the theoretical problems Jauss had claimed for his paradigm. By distancing himself
emphatically from production aesthetics, Jauss overlooked even
in 1970 the close similarity of his theory to the basic tenets of
Adorno's aesthetic theory. For Adorno innovation of form was
a central category in the analysis of historical processes. Reception theory, in spite of its emphasis on the reader, shared basic,
common assumptions with Adorno's production aesthetics. The
logic of formal innovation, which also underlies Russian Formalism, was grounded in the history of the avant-garde movements.
Not until 1972, when Jauss tried to reach beyond Modernism to
develop a theory of aesthetic experience, did he recognize this
common root, and then he explicitly distanced himself from
Adorno.[22]

A similar departure from Critical Theory could be detected
within the Marxist camp around 1970, though the reasons were
not the same. As soon as the New Left politicized Critical Theory
and carried its project into the streets, Adorno's position came
under attack. The hostile reception of his posthumous *Ästhetische
Theorie* (1970) was typical of the antagonism between the
Frankfurt School and the New Left. This negation should not be
construed as the dénouement of Adorno's influence, as the
Leninists liked to see it. Adorno's position was abandoned, but
his theory continued to be an important touchstone for the ensuing discussion. The polemical rejection of Adorno's aesthetic
theory was to a large extent caused by its close links to the great
authors of Modernism, writers like Franz Kafka, James Joyce,
and Samuel Beckett. Since Modernism and the avant-garde had
long been accepted in the canon of great books, the defense of

---

[21]Hans Robert Jauss, *Literaturgeschichte als Provokation* (Frankfurt am Main,
1970), pp. 144–207.
[22]Jauss, *Kleine Apologie der ästhetischen Erfahrung* (Constance, 1972).

this position by Adorno became a conservative strategy that ignored the increasing political tensions and social antagonisms in the Federal Republic. These became visible even to the average citizen when in 1967 the Christian Democrats, who had been in power since 1949, invited their opponents, the Social Democrats, to form a coalition government, thus leaving the task of opposition to the minority party—the Free Democrats.

In this situation, Critical Theory faced a political crisis that called for a more radical praxis than Horkheimer and Adorno were prepared to accept. It was precisely Adorno's overriding concern with literary and aesthetic questions which angered the student movement. Adorno's insistence on giving a lecture on Goethe's *Iphigenie* in Berlin in the summer of 1967, immediately after a clash between the students and the police which had resulted in the death of one student, became a turning point in the relationship between the Frankfurt School and the New Left. Another crucial event was a public lecture by Jürgen Habermas in which he compared leftist militancy with Fascism.[23] The ensuing heated discussions only widened the rift between the members of the Institute and the younger generation.

In spite of the growing tension, the Frankfurt School and the New Left shared basic theoretical positions, particularly during the first phase of the movement, which lasted from 1965 to 1970. Seen in theoretical terms, their antagonism was rooted in the ambivalence of Critical Theory toward the interpretation of advanced capitalism. Since Horkheimer and Adorno believed that monopoly capitalism was thoroughly in control of the Western World, they were not inclined to endorse grass-roots political movements. They clung to the notion of a liberal state which guaranteed civil liberties, and they openly criticized East European versions of Marxism. The more the radical students and the members of the Frankfurt School disagreed on political strategy, the more the students tended to dismiss Horkheimer, Adorno, and, to some extent, Habermas as liberals who had abandoned their earlier Marxist project.

Because this widely accepted explanation hardly does justice

[23] Wolfgang Abendroth et al., *Die Linke antwortet Jürgen Habermas*, ed. Oskar Negt (Frankfurt, 1968), pp. 5–15.

to the complex theoretical issues that fueled the debates of the seventies, the position of the Frankfurt School has to be restated briefly before we turn to the second phase of the opposition movement, which lasted until approximately 1975.[24]

Adorno's theory of art places equal emphasis on the aesthetic and the social nature of the work of art. Both aspects are grounded in the process of historical evolution. His insistence on historicity applies both to the material of the work of art under discussion and the theoretical subject. The philosophy of art, Adorno argued, has to reflect its own locus within the historical process. The historical approach, far from being a form of historicism, serves to unfold the truth content (*Wahrheitsgehalt*) in the work of art. To put it differently, the examination of a work of art situates the text within its social and political context without pressing this relation into a deterministic model. Thus Adorno's theory stands in clear opposition to any form of orthodox Marxist criticism; it should be noted, however, that it is grounded in Marx's analysis of commodities. The concept of commodity fetishism became a fundamental element of Horkheimer's and Adorno's analysis of the cultural sphere. They unfolded this approach in the chapter on the culture industry of *Dialectic of Enlightenment,* by demonstrating the impact of monopoly capitalism on the production and dissemination of culture. This treatment became central to the New Left's understanding of commercial culture and their own political strategy. They demanded the practical application of Horkheimer's and Adorno's uncompromising critique. But Adorno, in his later years, shifted the emphasis of his critique to the resistance contained in the work of art; he refused to move from the aesthetic to the political sphere and openly advocated theoretical investigation as the only viable form of criticism in an age that had compromised any political mass movement. He specifically rejected any immediate political use of aesthetic theory and literary criticism. Since the proletarian masses had been successfully integrated into capitalist society in the West, according to

---

[24]For a more extensive discussion of Adorno's position see my essay "Autonomy of Art: Looking Back at Adorno's *Ästhetische Theorie,*" *German Quarterly,* 54 (1981), pp. 133–148.

Adorno, political resistance had to concentrate on theoretical reflection. This conclusion makes the aesthetic sphere even more important, because it is the only realm that offers freedom against the rigidity of the social system. Adorno therefore upheld the concept of aesthetic autonomy as the central category of his theory, and any attempt to employ literary criticism for political ends had to confront the idea of aesthetic autonomy in one way or another. The search for a materialist literary theory, in other words, had to come to terms with the Idealist tradition of German philosophy of art as it was preserved in Adorno's work.

Although the New Left in Germany had a general theme—the search for a materialist theory of criticism—it would be difficult to define the common denominator for the various trends within the movement. What we find are divergent, sometimes contradictory drafts of critical models. Any attempt to bring together and systematize the various positions developed in such radical magazines as *alternative, Kürbiskern, Das Argument, Kursbuch,* or *Ästhetik und Kommunikation* would be futile. Looking back at the turbulent discussion from a more distant point of view, we can differentiate three distinct approaches to the crisis in literary criticism: political aesthetics, aesthetics of commodity (*Warenästhetik*), and institution theory. We can view them as models privileging certain questions. For political aesthetics the crucial problem was the function of literature vis-à-vis the political system. Commodity aesthetics approached art from its economic aspect, asking to what extent literature is defined and determined by the fact that it is produced and distributed in a society for which the exchange of commodities is essential. Institution theory perceived literature as an institution which is related to other institutions. The question then arises: How does one define the correlation between institutions that belong to different spheres—for example, the cultural and the social?

Political aesthetics was largely indebted to the work of Herbert Marcuse and at least to some extent the later essays of Walter Benjamin which emphasize the need for writers to define their social stance. Commodity aesthetics was clearly rooted in Critical Theory. Its initial guidelines were the chapter on the culture industry in Horkheimer's and Adorno's *Dialectic of Enlightenment.* But soon critics like Wolfgang Haug and Hans Heinz

Holz,[25] who pursued this approach systematically, moved away from the position of the Frankfurt School and tried to ground their investigations more immediately in the work of Karl Marx. They returned to the opening chapter of *Das Kapital,* on the concept of commodity, which had been the point of departure for Horkheimer and Adorno a generation before. Institution theory can also be traced back to the Frankfurt School, yet it would be misleading to view this approach simply as a continuation of Critical Theory. The impact of Brecht and Benjamin was equally significant. Benjamin's critique of the academic criticism of the twenties and the thirties and Brecht's analysis of feuilleton criticism clearly helped institution theory to outline the social context of criticism in theoretical terms—that is, to go beyond conventional background studies. The discussion focused in particular on Benjamin's essay "The Work of Art in the Age of Mechanical Reproduction," which defined the production and reception of art in terms of its changing social function, using the decline of "aura" as the starting point for the examination of the impact of mass reproduction on the function of art.[26] Institution theory—the studies of Peter Bürger for instance—utilized Benjamin's interpretation of the avant-garde movements as a political critique of bourgeois aestheticism and contrasted this reading with Adorno's understanding of aesthetic autonomy as the ultimate defense of the avant-garde.

An important impetus to this approach was provided by Habermas' *Strukturwandel der Öffentlichkeit* (Structural Change of the Public Sphere) of 1962, which established a decisive category for the ensuing discussion. Habermas' historically grounded theory of the public sphere encouraged the development of a functional definition of literary criticism which captures its social dimension without the limitations of reflection theory. The concept of the public sphere, which mediates between the social and the cultural sphere without reducing the one to the other, became crucial for the sociology of criticism. The essays collected in this volume attempt to pursue the systematic and historical

---

[25]Wolfgang Fritz Haug, *Kritik der Warenästhetik* (Frankfurt, 1971). Hans Heinz Holz, *Vom Kunstwerk zur Ware* (Neuwied and Berlin, 1972).
[26]Benjamin, *Gesammelte Schriften,* 1/2:431–470.

dimension of this approach. In a similar way, Peter and Christa Bürger emphasized the social aspect of literature by using Benjamin's model for a definition of literature as an institution.[27] Peter Bürger argued that both Adorno and Lukács failed to develop a social theory of art because they defined the social element in terms of the individual work of art rather than of a general framework that controls the production of individual texts—("epochale Funktionsbestimmungen von Kunst in ihrer sozialen Bedingtheit").[28]

While Habermas in 1962 searched for conditions that would permit us to restore the authentic form of the public sphere, the suggestions in the final chapter of his study were limited by the relatively narrow range of the political debate of that time. Following the tradition of Horkheimer and Adorno, he was not inclined to view the proletariat as an essentially progressive factor within advanced capitalist societies. This assessment explains the ambivalence of his investigations; they simultaneously critiqued and idealized the liberal public sphere. Habermas' analysis of the decline of the classical public sphere (and with it the decline of literary criticism) was based on the conceptual framework he found in the liberal theory of the late eighteenth century, especially in Kant. By the same token, his concept of culture, like that of Marcuse and Adorno, was historically grounded in the liberal age, the period between 1770 and 1850. Its center was the autonomy of art. For the early Habermas this notion of culture had to be critically exposed, since it was determined by liberal capitalism; at the same time, however, the ideal had to be restored as the only viable cultural tradition which is at least partially preserved in late capitalism. This ambivalence, noticeable earlier in the work of Marcuse and Adorno, changed the direction of Critical Theory in the seventies. While during the thirties and forties Adorno and Marcuse had critiqued conventional notions of cultural tradition, Habermas' examination of culture, especially in *Legitimation Crisis* (1973), stressed the basic, categorical threat to the cultural tradition which an administered society represented.

---

[27]Peter Bürger, *Theorie der Avantgarde* (Frankfurt, 1974). Christa Bürger, *Der Ursprung der bürgerlichen Institution Kunst* (Frankfurt, 1977).

[28]Peter Bürger, *Vermittlung—Rezeption—Funktion* (Frankfurt, 1979), p. 174.

During the first phase of the movement, the New Left still used the classical distinction between high culture and mass culture—namely, authentic works of art and commercialized forms produced for mass consumption—but during the seventies this opposition was either abandoned or at least modified. The shift can be recognized in the work of Negt and Alexander Kluge, who, pursuing the approach of Habermas, examined the origin and fate of proletarian countercultures by contrasting them with the dominant public sphere of the bourgeoisie.[29] Habermas himself, confronted with Niklas Luhmann's systems theory, began to address the question of how genuine culture can be preserved more systematically in late capitalist societies. While Negt and Kluge dismissed the public sphere of the bourgeoisie and argued in favor of proletarian culture, Habermas, with a less orthodox understanding of the proletariat, found it difficult to determine the locus of oppositional cultural traditions which cannot be subsumed under the system. His return to Benjamin in his highly controversial essay "Consciousness-Raising or Redemptive Criticism: The Contemporaneity of Walter Benjamin" was clearly an attempt to redefine the problem by contrasting Benjamin's approach with that of Marcuse, whom he labeled a true Marxist.[30] According to Habermas, Benjamin's intention was not so much to critique ideology, as offered by Marcuse, as to rescue the tradition, which was always threatened by the forces of history. The question whether the opposition set forth by Habermas was historically and systematically correct is ultimately of secondary importance. The ensuing debate limited itself too much to the problem of whether Benjamin was a Marxist, thereby shunning the real issue that Habermas wanted in the forefront: that Benjamin's theory offered insights that transcended the scope of traditional Critical Theory. Habermas' own contribution in *Legitimation Crisis* systematized the historical situation of the early seventies by focusing attention on the con-

---

[29]Oskar Negt and Alexander Kluge, *Öffentlichkeit und Erfahrung: Zur Organisationsanalyse von bürgerlicher und proletarischer Öffentlichkeit* (Frankfurt am Main, 1972).

[30]The original German version appeared under the title "Bewusstmachende oder rettende Kritik—Die Aktualität Walter Benjamins," in *Zur Aktualität Walter Benjamins* (Frankfurt, 1972), pp. 175-223; the translation was published in *New German Critique*, no. 17 (Spring 1979), pp. 30-59.

cept of crisis, which was widely used to describe the predicament of those years. Habermas argued that during the liberal age the idea of aesthetic autonomy had a revolutionary component, precisely because art was not needed for the support of the economic or political system, but nurtured residual needs that are not fully integrated into the system of needs. In late capitalist societies, by contrast, this revolutionary component is fading away. Habermas' thesis was that "the socio-cultural system will not be able, in the long run, to reproduce the privatistic syndrome necessary for the existence of the system.[31] He speaks of prebourgeois traditions as nonrenewable and holds that "the structures of bourgeois culture, stripped of their traditionalist padding and deprived of their privatistic core"[32] are not necessarily relevant any longer for the formation of motives and could become just a façade. Using Benjamin's notion of "post-auratic" art,[33] Habermas proclaimed the denouement of the traditional cultural sphere; for him it was by no means clear that the social system still needs the values that had been preserved by established cultural institutions.

Habermas' highly abstract theoretical treatment of this question was paralleled by the debate over the relevance of literary history, and in particular the history of criticism. Can we still use the model of Enlightenment criticism? May we follow the examples of Weimar Classicism or Romanticism? In the late forties critics like Ernst Robert Curtius and Max Rychner suggested that the return to the great tradition was the only viable direction for German criticism. But as soon as the restoration of West Germany was completed—that is, as soon as her economic and social system had regained all the characteristics of advanced capitalism, it became obvious that this approach, which put its faith entirely in the strength of tradition, would not succeed. When the first major economic and political crisis of the Federal Republic—the economic recession of 1966–67 and the erosion of the Erhard cabinet—pointed to basic structural problems, it also became clear that the cultural sphere would be affected by these problems. The literary tradition, and with it, of course, the tradition of criticism, lost its unquestioned legitimacy. The literary

[31] Habermas, *Legitimation Crisis* (Boston, 1975), p. 78.
[32] Ibid., p. 79.
[33] See my note 68 to Chap. 1 here.

situation of West Germany in the late sixties was characterized by a fundamental crisis. The institution in its entirety was questioned to a degree for which there was no parallel in the United States. The radicals coined the slogan Literature Is Dead. Since neither the publishing houses nor the mass media were expropriated, the slogan had to be applied to the *function* of literature. Past and present literature, and in fact any conventional discussion of literary issues, had seemingly lost its meaning. Whatever individuals felt about the value of specific literary works, there was no consensus that could serve as a basis for the general discussion.

This crisis called for a thorough reassessment of the literary system; its essential parts and the way in which it was embedded in the larger social system. Since the legitimacy of the cultural sphere was no longer taken for granted, its conventional character became apparent, not least of all in the mechanisms of literary criticism. At this juncture the focus of attention shifted from the form and content of literary criticism to the institutional framework. And this change affected both the academic community and the mass media. One of the targets of student criticism was the literary canon, selection of major authors who were to be taught at the secondary schools and the universities. It was the first time since 1870 that the relevance of authors like Lessing, Schiller, Goethe, and Joseph von Eichendorff had been called in question. During the so-called Zurich literary controversy (*Züricher Literaturstreit*), when the spokesman of the older generation, Emil Staiger, once again defended the norms of the classical tradition, Holz suggested that this tradition was badly compromised by Germany's recent past:

> The Neoclassicism and Neohumanism of German *Geisteswissenschaften* [humanities] turned out to be the precursor and the façade of barbarism. It was left to the Classicist ideologues of the bourgeois world to define the task of art as a transfiguration of our existence. A dubious concept of tradition has to make a rough and ready repair of those elements which do not fit the sentimental need for harmony of these Neohumanists.[34]

---

[34]Hans Heinz Holz, "Grundsätzliche Aspekte einer Literaturfehde," *Basler National-Zeitung*, 15 January 1967; reprinted in "Der Zürcher Literaturstreit: Eine Dokumentation," *Sprache im technischen Zeitalter*, no. 22 (1967), pp. 146–150.

That the literary tradition, especially Weimar Classicism, helped to legitimize National Socialism is part of a problematic that goes back to the 1870s, when conservative literary historians appropriated this tradition for the Second Empire. During the latter part of the nineteenth century it became the accepted view among academic critics in Germany that Goethe and Schiller, and—although to a lesser extent—the Romantics prepared the way for the foundation of Bismarck's Empire. This theory was later extended to include the Third Reich. Although this highly compromising association of German Neohumanism with Fascism was rejected after 1945, only two decades later the conceptual framework of this mode of historiography came under criticism.[35] Then the New Left pleaded to restore to the canon of great writers such authors as Heine, Börne, and Johann Georg Forster, who had been expurgated by the conservatives and the radical nationalists. This measure, however, left unanswered the larger question of the legitimation of the literary heritage. Was the category of tradition to be thrown out, as the radicals suggested; was it to be redefined, as the more orthodox Marxists proposed; or were the concepts of literature and the work of art, both of which imply aesthetic values, to be replaced by the neutral notion of the text, as semiotic critics suggested?

The debate over the literary tradition had significant practical results when the curricula of the secondary schools and the universities were reorganized in the seventies. The critics of the educational system argued that the traditional form of literary studies had favored the upper social classes. Thus they proposed a substantial cut in the hours allotted to the study of the German classics and literary history. The time saved was to be used to analyze such nonliterary texts as newspaper articles, commercials, and posters. The rationale was that the students should familiarize themselves with the language of the modern mass media in order to deal with present-day society, and the literature of the past accordingly had to be sacrificed. Similar trends could be recognized at the universities. The traditional curricula had emphasized literary history, concentrating on the eighteenth and nineteenth centuries. The conventional definition of literature (*Dichtung*) was relatively restricted, leaving sub-

---

[35]See *Ansichten einer künftigen Germanistik*, ed. Jürgen Kolbe (Munich, 1969).

stantial parts of literary life virtually uncharted. Moreover, theoretical investigations were not particularly encouraged. The reform movement changed that: the new curricula stressed systematic problems at the expense of historical studies. The need for a theoretical basis was clearly recognized, but not so the need for a balanced program. While theoretical seminars were burgeoning, familiarity with the literary tradition was waning.

Since the mid-seventies, when the new generation of high school students had begun to populate the universities, academic critics have complained that these students do not know their own literature. Any work written before 1900 is being ignored as prehistoric. This unexpected result of the reform movement caused, to some extent at least, a shift in alliances. Radicals and conservatives would unite their forces to fight for the reinstitution of the literary tradition. The abolition of this tradition, ordered by state bureaucracies as a seemingly progressive measure, made it obvious that the legitimation crisis of the sociocultural system was much more serious than had previously been assumed.

Although the split between the ideological camps was fairly obvious during the decade between 1965 and 1975, in recent years the picture has become more diffuse. The restoration of the classical tradition, eagerly advocated by academic and journalistic critics alike, is only part of a larger change within the cultural sphere. By 1974 it was clear that the cultural revolution of the New Left had failed. That novels, poems, essays, and plays were well received by an audience that only a few years before had completely rejected the conventions of the literary institution signaled a considerable shift of the current. With unrestrained glee major feuilleton critics stressed that literature had returned to its normal function, implying that criticism would also resume its traditional role. Indeed, critics were again solicited to decide which novel deserved to be called the most important event of the literary season.

The conventions of the institution of criticism have now been reestablished to such a degree that an observer coming from the outside will find it difficult to detect traces of the crisis. It would seem that the majority of the critics have repressed the turmoil of the past decade, although the problems of criticism were not solved. It might be more appropriate to say *because* they were not solved. While literary production, including literary criticism, is supposedly in full bloom, one cannot overlook the fact that the legitimation crisis is still smoldering. In a recent essay Jörg Drews summarized the present situation as follows:

> The fruitful provocation for literary criticism which resulted from the cultural and political changes in the Federal Republic around 1970, a challenge which was accepted by the best critics at that time, is lacking today. The momentum is lost; the business of book reviewing is being carried on as usual and without fresh ideas (and still by the institutions that were hardly transformed after 1965), just as the state and society, supported by the present economic prosperity, carry on without new perspectives.[36]

Feuilleton criticism depends just as much on the publishing industry and the mass media now as it did twenty years ago.

Drews's evaluation suggests that the legitimation problems of criticism are long-term problems, ultimately rooted in the structure of the sociocultural system and its relation to the economic and social systems. Since these relations are anything but stable—and this also applies to countries other than West Germany—it may be realistic to assume that the institution of literary criticism may confront serious problems in the future as well. I would be skeptical at least of any attempt to solve this question by formulating a new approach, for instance by divorcing literary theory from practical criticism—that is, interpretation. If one maintains that the present crisis of criticism has to do with the difficulty of defending interpretation and therefore strives to overcome this situation by developing a theoretical model that defines conditions of meaning rather than the meaning of an individual text, one only displaces the legitimation crisis. This theoretical model, whatever its form and content may be, must respond to the questions of the cultural system. The requirement, in other words, would be that the model which allows the critic to understand the conventions that control literature can be legitimized in terms of the surrounding system. If, on the other hand, the relevance of these critical investigations cannot be proved, criticism may well lose its privileged position.

---

[36]Jörg Drews, "Die Entwicklung der westdeutschen Literaturkritik seit 1965," in *Deutsche Literatur in der Bundesrepublik seit 1965*, p. 258.

The seminal essay of this collection, to which the later ones are more or less indebted, is the first, "Literary Criticism and the Public Sphere." It was written for the first issue of *Literaturwissenschaft und Linguistik,* a journal designed by its editors to bridge a noticeable gap between the disciplines of literary criticism and linguistics. I was invited to address myself to the situation of criticism at that time. But when I took a closer look at the problems involved, I came to the conclusion that any fruitful analysis would have to begin with the eighteenth century. The second essay, "Art Evaluation and Reportage: The Aesthetic Theory of the Later Heine," might be considered an example of the kind of history of criticism I outlined in the essay "Prolegomena to a History of Literary Criticism." The Heine essay was written for a German anthology of scholarly contributions on Heine that came out in 1977. The essay entitled "The End of an Institution? The Debate over the Function of Literary Criticism in the 1960s," was first presented as a lecture in 1971. The occasion was a conference at the University of Massachusetts on the West German Literature of the 1960s. This lecture gave me the opportunity to deal more specifically with the crisis of the institution of criticism during the late sixties. "The Task of Contemporary Literary Criticism" can be seen as a continuation of the preceding essay. It is the revised form of a lecture I gave at the Free University of Berlin in the summer of 1974, when the first symptoms of the *Tendenzwende* became noticeable. The essay "Promoters, Consumers, and Critics: On the Reception of the Best-Seller" was originally written for the Fourth Wisconsin Workshop, held in October of 1972. The overriding theme of that conference was the problematic of popular and mass culture. "Prolegomena to a History of Literary Criticism," an essay that returns to the theme of the first article, but now from a more methodological point of view, was first presented as an address at the *Germanistentag* held at Düsseldorf in 1976. The concluding study, "Critical Theory, Public Sphere, and Culture: Jürgen Habermas and His Critics," which grew out of a paper presented at the Institute for Twentieth Century Studies (Milwaukee) in 1977, is an attempt to reflect on some of the central categories used in my studies, in particular the Habermasian concept of the public sphere.

1 *Literary Criticism and the Public Sphere*

As long as a cultural institution is sheltered from close public scrutiny, by and large its social foundations remain concealed. They are brought into view only when the meaning and the function of the institution are called into question. Such questioning uncovers the tacitly accepted social determinants which underlie the institution. The most recent attacks on literary criticism therefore do not represent just another typical generation conflict of youth versus Establishment.[1] Such conflicts belong to the internal history of literary criticism, a discipline which, with only slight exaggeration, could be described as being in a state of permanent crisis. The current conflict appears to involve not the formation of new blocs squaring off within the institutional framework, but rather an attack on the institution itself, an attack which, to be sure, incorporates the familiar structure of the struggle between young and old.

Any intellectual system permits certain questions to be raised while rejecting others as irrelevant. In this sense established literary criticism has always considered it self-evident that its role is necessary. When asked why, it could only answer that it was performing a function vital to the maintenance of the literary system of communication. Yet the latest attacks on this cultural institution have raised questions that must be heard, even

Translated by Ronald L. Smith and Henry J. Schmidt.
[1]The following remarks refer primarily to the critical essays collected by Peter Hamm in the volume *Kritik—von wem/für wen/wie: Eine Selbstdarstellung deutscher Kritiker* (Munich, 1968); cited as *Kritik*.

44

though from the viewpoint of institutionalized criticism they must be considered illegitimate. It is worth noting that the "outsiders" who are attacking do not direct their polemic merely against the conservative modes of West German literary criticism. They do not seek to replace certain outdated norms of taste with others. Rather, they are attacking the methodology of criticism in general, the creation and use of standards and norms of all types. They are irritated by the self-assurance of a critical establishment that considers itself perhaps not infallible but at least indispensable. Thus the liberal critic is spared no more than his conservative counterpart; indeed, in certain respects the former may be considered the more appropriate target, since his critical statements uphold as fundamental and irrefutable precisely that which the challengers wish to call into question.

Despite the differences of opinion among the various critics operating within the public literary industry, they are unanimous in their belief in the autonomy of literature, the objectivity of criticism, and the social independence of the critic. Literary life is considered a closed realm of communication, where in discussions among authors, critics, and readers only literary arguments are admissible. Extraliterary factors are essentially ignored; in cases where they are empirically verifiable, they are labeled mere evidence of decline. As a result, author and literary public appear only in their specific, abstract roles. The socioeconomic system surrounding the realm of literary communication is characterized quite neutrally as one of "material conditions"—necessary for the process of communication but nonetheless of no influence on the function of literary life or, especially, of literary criticism. This sense of self-assurance is now being vehemently attacked by the younger faction.[2] They insist that this is an illusion which leads the critic to self-deception about his actual role. First of all, he uses the illusion of autonomy to secure an inappropriate position of power for himself. He usurps from the author and the literary public the offices of both judge and lawgiver. An ideological concept of autonomy has led, perhaps unintentionally, to an authoritarian mode of criticism. As Peter Hamm notes, "For that reason, the

[2] Namely Peter Hamm, Yaak Karsunke, Wolf Rosenberg, Heinz Ohff, Bazon Brock, and Hans G. Helms.

major critic uses his evaluations to rescue precisely those 'values' which progressive art forms are seeking to liquidate. In more concrete terms, he is trying to rescue his own value, his own alleged individuality—that is, to maintain his own claim to domination."[3] Criticism becomes a rigid, dogmatic opinion which no longer allows the public to form its own differing judgment. The subjective taste of the critic remains obscured and is presented as objective.

If the complaint here involved only a misuse of the critic's legitimate function, the solution would be a simple reform. Martin Walser and Reinhard Baumgart, for example, suggest reducing the role of the critic to that of a private citizen stating his opinion, as anyone may do. The more radical dissidents reject such a reform, since it leaves untouched the illusion of an autonomous system of literary values. According to the radical argument, the elitist consciousness of the "star" critic is not to be identified as mere subjective arrogance, but represents the typical behavior of a social group which, under the guise of freedom, seeks to hide its own superfluity and its dependence on the apparatus of the culture industry. The specialized critic who lives by his pen is not independent. He does not review an occasional book which interests him—he reviews in order to make a living. To give just one quote: "Since critics have to live off their fees, they are forced to write prodigiously. After hasty reading comes a hastily written criticism. The system successfully prevents those serving it from engaging in more exact analyses that might ultimately turn back on the system itself."[4]

Employed by this apparatus and entrusted with a special assignment as a theater, film, or literary critic, one is no longer free to reflect on the system itself and its involvement in the commodity market. The functionary is denied any insight into the social process that serves the apparatus. Criticism thus contributes, voluntarily or not, to the preservation of the social status quo. The radicals judge a critic's position in terms that make an individual critic's progressive or conservative view of a work inconsequential. Instead, the conditions of production form the criterion of analysis, and these are, at present, beyond

---

[3]Peter Hamm, "Der Grosskritiker," in *Kritik,* p. 38.
[4]Yaak Karsunke, "Uralte Binsenwahrheiten," in *Kritik,* p. 46.

the influence of the critic. The self-understanding of the critic as someone who has a position allegedly granted by the public sphere ought to be destroyed, for this public sphere no longer exists; under the present conditions, the function of literary criticism becomes tantamount to public relations work.

All polemic aside, the question remains: Is the model of literary criticism under attack here false or is it merely inappropriate to the current situation? Does this attack on criticism wish to destroy something that was never of value, or does it seek to expose something that has become outdated by the socioeconomic process? The following analysis intends to show that the latter is the case. A critical discussion of established literary criticism becomes meaningful if it is consciously brought into the context of the history of that criticism and reconstructs its development. In this way, the crisis as it now exists can be seen not merely as a *factum brutum,* but as the result of a set of problems that have accumulated historically.

The concept of criticism under discussion has a two-hundred-year-long history. Prior to the eighteenth century it was unknown. Within that time span it has undergone changes that have brought it far from its origins, but the institutional framework that arose with the original idea has remained. This framework has managed to integrate its various diverging currents so that established criticism has been able, with some justification, to confront its opponents as a unified bloc. The assertion that the modern notion of criticism did not exist before the Enlightenment needs to be explained, for it is difficult to draw a sharp line between the seventeenth and eighteenth centuries in the history of literary theory.[5] Western European Classicism of the early eighteenth century is indebted to the previous epoch and sees no reason to deny this tradition. In terms of function, however, there is a demonstrable difference. Although the literary criticism of the Enlightenment based itself on the poetics of the seventeenth century and only gradually freed itself from the influence of the past, it should be emphasized that these traditional postulates were placed in a new context of legitimation. Rules of genre, aesthetic norms, and patterns of reception can

[5]The German conditions, which stress a distinct boundary between Baroque and Enlightenment, are not representative of European literature in general.

keep the same content but still gain a new meaning. The concept of "rule" in poetics is ambivalent; it can have an authoritarian as well as a rational basis. When René Wellek states that the Neo-classicists were not authoritarian but rationalist,[6] he assumes a functional restructuring of the inherited poetics. He is justified in doing so in the context of the history of modern literary criticism. But Wellek's analysis also obscures the qualitative change that took place, for Rationalism was the first system to view the traditional rules as laws, to be subjected to the same scrutiny as the laws of nature. This new approach encourages criticism of the traditional rules when they are not derived from evident principles. Two separate but related problems in the realm of poetics emerge from this—analysis of the aesthetic norms and their application to the literary work at hand. The result is a conceptual split between literary theory and practical criticism, although in the eighteenth century both were pursued by essentially the same group of writers. This separation makes it possible to redetermine the role of the critic. His role is that of mediator between the general law and the individual work of art. His critical judgment is based on a universally valid system of norms which claims to be evident as the laws of nature. So his judgment is objective, insofar as it appropriately describes the relationship between the norms and the work at hand. Its truth is apparent to any intelligent observer. Montesquieu's idea of the separation of powers can indeed, as Hans Mayer has suggested, be applied to the concept of Rationalist art criticism. Concerning the jurisdiction of art criticism, he writes: "Its job is to see that the artist observes the rules and, through its critical proclamations, to point out transgressions."[7] This role of the public judge seems less arrogant, however, when one realizes how it is rooted in the separation of powers—the power to make the rules has been taken away from the critic. He may formulate certain norms in his writings, but he is merely citing standards that were already independently established as valid. Rationalist criticism postulates its intersubjectivity on the basis of universal, timeless aesthetic norms.

[6]René Wellek, *The Later Eighteenth Century,* Vol. 1 of *A History of Modern Criti-cism: 1750-1950* (New Haven, 1955), p. 13.
[7]*Meisterwerke deutscher Literaturkritik,* ed. Hans Mayer (Berlin, 1954), 1:xxiv.

If the critics are restricted to the role of judges, who, then, are the legislators? Mayer's answer, that "the actual rulemakers were the ancients,"[8] is only partially satisfying, for it obscures the specifically rationalistic foundation of the system. The rules of antiquity can claim irrefutable validity only insofar as they are in agreement with the *ratio*. The authority of age alone would not protect them from critical doubt.[9] Rationalist criticism is based on the idea of restricting the power of authority through the concept of law. In the early bourgeois period the chief purpose of law, as the epitome of universal, abstract norms, was to combat the arbitrary use of authority. This was, of course, more clearly articulated in the sphere of politics than in that of aesthetics. Because of its autonomy, law serves a protective function—it is the wall erected by the bourgeoisie against absolutism.

Even in the eighteenth century, however, the situation grew more complex. As soon as people saw through the fiction of ahistorical aesthetic laws, they had to face again the problem of ensuring the possibility of critical judgment. The debate over taste, which extends throughout the century, is one of the focal points of this discussion. When taste becomes the criterion of aesthetic evaluation, reception and the role of the literary public become a part of the theoretical debate.

It must be noted that the concept of taste was not unique to the Enlightenment but had a long tradition behind it. In the seventeenth century it was closely linked to the culture of the social elite. Good taste, mediated by both heredity and environment, distinguished the life style of the aristocracy and the social groups attached to the aristocracy from the life style of other

---

[8]Ibid.

[9]This distinction was clearly drawn by John Dryden: The rules "are founded upon good sense, and sound reason, rather than on authority: for though Aristotle and Horace are produced, yet no man must argue, that what they write is true, because they write it" (*Essays*, ed. William P. Ker [Oxford, 1926], pp. 228–229). Murphy explicitly establishes that the only rules that can be considered lasting and immutable are those which rest on the general constitution of mankind; statements by poets and critics which are based on examples are, in the final analysis, arbitrary. Cf. Aisso Bosker, *Literary Criticism in the Age of Johnson* (Groningen, 1930), p. 64, n. 1. What Montesquieu formulated in regard to political laws is valid for aesthetic laws as well: "Les lois ... sont les rapports nécessaires qui dérivent de la nature des choses" (*Oeuvres complètes*, ed. André Masson [Paris, 1950], 1:1). For background information on the history of ideas, see Richard F. Jones, *Ancients and Moderns* (St. Louis, 1936).

levels of society; superior taste was the basis of their claim to cultural leadership. This concept was a powerful instrument in the hands of the ruling class—witness the servile dedications of the English professional writers of the Restoration era, in which they assure their aristocratic patrons of the importance of their critical approval.

In the eighteenth century there was a reevaluation. The concept of taste gradually dissociated itself from the courtly value system and became a purely aesthetic category, presumably freed from social prerequisites. The introduction of taste into the theory of art necessarily led to a contradiction with the Neoclassical concept of law in the eighteenth century, for a judgment of taste given by the reading public appears to be arbitrary when compared to a deductive criticism based on rules, since judgments of taste cannot be demonstrated in the work itself. When differing mediators of taste collided, as in the arguments between the aristocracy and the bourgeoisie, the reliability of taste was called into question. How could the judgment of a certain social class or of a certain individual be universally binding? This question could no longer be avoided. The psychological capacity of human beings to make an aesthetic judgment that was intersubjectively valid and independent of individual preconditions needed further investigation.

Johann Christoph Gottsched, the leading literary theorist of the early German Enlightenment, provided a possible solution. His Classical system absorbed the concept of taste by neutralizing it. The supremacy of the rules was never seriously called into question, since good taste was defined as agreement between the rules and one's individual preference. For Gottsched the sole value of taste was as a means to characterize a still rather vaguely conceived aesthetic judgment. He defined taste as follows: "It is, namely, the ability to judge correctly the beauty of a poem, a thought, or an expression, when one has perceived that beauty without directly consulting the rules themselves."[10] Gottsched leaves no doubt that taste alone is no adequate basis for aesthetic criticism. An evaluation based on taste is fallible, since it depends on external circumstances.

[10]Johann Christoph Gottsched, *Versuch einer kritischen Dichtkunst*, 4th ed. (Leipzig, 1751), p. 125.

The radical suggestion of Jean Baptiste Dubos to make taste the cornerstone of aesthetics was diffused by both Gottsched and his predecessor Johann Ulrich von König, who tried to integrate taste into the Rationalist position of deductive argumentation. When taste became an independent aesthetic category, however, a reconciliation with the Rationalist conception of criticism became far more difficult to achieve. We should particularly note the debate in the camp of English Empiricism, where the consequences of moving into such subjective areas were most clearly formulated and were recognized as a problem. David Hume, in his 1757 essay "Of the Standards of Taste," denies that beauty is an objective property of a work of art and asserts instead that it is a subjective quality in the beholder, a view that destroys the basis of Gottsched's integration of subjective criticism into Rational theory. Hume does not, however, consider taste to be merely arbitrary. In place of the Rationalist fiction of law he sets up a fiction of anthropological uniformity—although taste is subjective, it, like human nature itself, is in principle uniform and universal: "The general principles of taste are uniform in human nature."[11] The concept of taste is formulated so abstractly that the social background remains invisible. It refers not to specific social groups or classes but to "man in general," as Hume puts it. He notes explicitly that the critic must eliminate likes and dislikes when evaluating a work of art. This is of decisive importance for the concept of criticism in the eighteenth century: the judgment of the critic may be subjective, but it is nevertheless legitimized before the forum of readers who have constituted themselves the public sphere. Hume makes it clear, however, that this literary public sphere is restricted to educated circles only. Not everyone possesses good taste; one's natural potential must be developed through education and practice. The contradiction within the liberal public sphere becomes evident—it does not do justice to its own idea. Although in principle the capacity to form an accurate opinion is considered present in everyone, in practice it is limited to the educated.

[11]David Hume, *Philosophical Works*, ed. Thomas H. Green and Thomas H. Grose (London, 1882), 3:280. Hume treats deviations psychologically as an individual incapacity of the subject. The "delicacy of imagination" differs from person to person. Nonetheless, it can be developed—taste can be improved through practice. Cf. pp. 275-277.

The controversy about the role of taste was most precisely formulated in Kant's *Kritik der Urteilskraft* (Critique of Judgment). Kant's transcendental critique of jugments based on taste overcame the aporias of the taste controversy by developing and justifying the subjective principle of taste as an a priori principle of judgment, thus sweeping aside Empiricism and Rationalist objections. A judgment based on taste is not a cognitive judgment; rather, it results from the reflection of the judging subject on his own feelings of pleasure or displeasure. But since these subjective conditions by virtue of their very form can be present in every individual, a judgment of taste is a priori possible. In this way, subjectivity and universal validity can be reconciled. Thus Kant underscores once again, albeit on a reflective level, the Enlightenment's intention to institutionalize criticism as a formal principle that is self-supporting rather than rooted in tradition. In principle, everyone has a basic judgmental capacity, although individual circumstances may cause each person to develop that capacity to a different degree. This means that everyone is called upon to participate in criticism; it is not the privilege of a certain social class or professional clique. It follows that the critic, even a professional one, is merely a speaker from the general audience and formulates ideas that could be thought by anyone. His special task vis-à-vis the public is to conduct the general discussion.

In the Age of Enlightenment the concept of criticism cannot be separated from the institution of the public sphere. Every judgment is designed to be directed toward a public; communication with the reader is an integral part of the system. Through its relationship with the reading public, critical reflection loses its private character. Criticism opens itself to debate, it attempts to convince, it invites contradiction. It becomes a part of the public exchange of opinions. Seen historically, the modern concept of literary criticism is closely tied to the rise of the liberal, bourgeois public sphere in the early eighteenth century. Literature served the emancipation movement of the middle class as an instrument to gain self-esteem and to articulate its human demands against the absolutist state and a hierarchical society. Literary discussion, which had previously served as a form of legitimation of court society in the aristocratic salons, became an arena to pave the way for political discussion in the middle classes. This happened earliest in England, where those social institutions first arose which for decades comprised the basis of the literary-political public sphere—coffee houses and clubs, reading societies and lending libraries. We should note again, however, that this literary public sphere, which evolved into a basis for the political emancipation of the middle class, was not bourgeois in its origins. It was rooted in aristocratic court circles and only gradually freed itself from their domination. Once it became self-sufficient, this public sphere considered itself free of class structures and their particular interests. Though this was not actually the case (its "general public" consisted mainly of the bourgeois middle class and the titled gentry), the self-understanding of this public sphere presupposed general accessibility. In principle, social privileges were not acknowledged whenever private citizens gathered together as a public body. In the reading societies and clubs, status was suspended so that a discussion among equals could take place. This attempt to liberate critical discussion from social prestige was of central importance in the new concept of criticism. Authoritarian, aristocratic art judgments were replaced by a discourse among educated laymen. The role of the critic was derived from this discourse. A private individual among private individuals, the critic enjoyed no special privilege. He spoke for others because he was better informed; thus he claimed a right to be heard. His judicial and pedagogical powers were limited, however, by the general consensus that public opinion should be the ultimate judge.

The model of the liberal public sphere was an ideal that social reality never fully achieved. Nevertheless, its effect is evident even today. Journalistic literary criticism, as Peter Glotz has shown,[12] is still under its influence. The book reviews of the leading national newspapers are still directed toward "the reading public," in spite of the fact that the mass of uninformed readers cannot understand such demanding reviews. But by the end of the eighteenth century the assumption that the literary public consisted of a homogeneous circle of informed laymen was being exposed as fiction. This disintegration showed up more quickly in the literary public sphere than in the political one, which met its own crisis during the Industrial Revolution. The fragmentation of the public sphere was caused in part by

[12]Peter Glotz, *Buchkritik in deutschen Zeitungen* (Hamburg, 1968).

53

the realization of the educational program that had been postulated in the model. The bourgeoisie, in contrast to the aristocracy, promoted the spread of education, so that in the course of the eighteenth century, in England as well as on the Continent, there was a steady growth in the number of readers (that is to say, the potential audience for literature).[13] This expansion led to a loosening of the bond between the leading intelligentsia and the broad reading public. A cleft appeared between the artistic intentions of the productive intelligentsia and the taste of the general readership. "A new antagonism develops, a tension between the literature of the cultural élite and that of the general reading public, and lapses of good taste are to be observed, in which the weaknesses of the light fiction of a later age are already discernible."[14]

In a certain sense the fragmentation of the reading public represented a regression. When literature is used for entertainment, critical reflection is ignored; the public character of the discussion was partly discarded in the small intellectual circles where literary production and criticism could still interact directly.

These changes influenced both the concept of literary criticism and the role of the critic. Around 1770 the critic in Germany faced a new situation, brought about when the bourgeois avant-garde broke away from its class and divorced its artistic goals from the taste of the general reading public. Artistic duty toward the literary work seemed to conflict with the duty toward the literary public. The basis for mediation had become fragile.

In his discussion of Gottfried August Bürger's poems Schiller pointed out that the modern poet cannot depend on an agreement between the taste of the masses and that of the connoisseur: "There is now a great distance between the masses of a nation and its select elements. The reason for this lies partly in the fact that conceptual enlightenment and moral refinement make up a unified whole which is far more than the sum of its parts. Beyond this cultural difference, the element of convenience makes segments of the nation extremely dissimilar in

[13]Cf. Richard D. Altick, *The English Common Reader* (Chicago, 1957), pp. 30-77, and the literature listed there.
[14]Arnold Hauser, *The Social History of Art,* trans. Stanley Godman (New York, 1951), 2:542.

their manner of feeling and in their expression of that feeling."[15] The disintegration of the reading public into the broad masses and the "educated class," which Schiller considered a *fait accompli,* prevents the critic from identifying with any general consensus and defining his role and function in its context. In the same review Schiller points out the difficulties involved in creating a work that can please both the mass public and the small circle of literary connoisseurs.[16] This describes, too, the dilemma of a system of criticism that can no longer be sure of its partner in dialogue—its audience. Should the critic make his judgments on behalf of the broad public or of the minority? Schiller concluded from this dilemma that aesthetic judgment should be sharply separated from the question of reception. In contrast to Bürger, who had cited popularity (*Volkstümlichkeit*) as a measure of perfection, Schiller asserted that "the first indispensable requirement for the perfection of a poem is that it must possess an absolute inner value which is in no way dependent on the varying powers of comprehension of its readers."[17] The value of popularity is not totally denied, but it is placed on a lower level in the hierarchy of definitive values: popularity is an additional asset for a work of art that has already passed the test of autonomous aesthetic criticism. The Schillerean critic has the task of guarding the level of literary discussion, which has been endangered by new, less critical groups of readers. This function separates him from the general reading public. When the general public is considered to have an inadequate aesthetic sense and only the minority is viewed as a deserving partner for discourse, the general validity of literary criticism can no longer be legitimated by the literary public sphere. The recently institutionalized post of the critic is forced to seek support from a small literary elite,[18] and the critic begins to appeal to values that

[15]Schiller, *Sämtliche Werke,* ed. Otto Güntter and Georg Witkowski (Leipzig, 1925), 19:230–231.

[16]"What a task it is to satisfy the refined taste of the connoisseur without going over the heads of the great mass of people—without depriving art of some of its dignity by courting the childish level of comprehension of the general population" (Schiller, 19:231).

[17]Ibid., 19:232–233.

[18]In his essay "Über naive und sentimentalische Dichtung" (On Naive and Sentimental Poetry), Schiller compares the actual circumstances in a society based on division of labor to the ideal conditions of aesthetic receptivity. He

are to a great extent divorced from social connotations. The aesthetic canon of German Classicism can be compared to Neoclassical dogmas only in regard to external form, for the Neoclassical dogmas were held to be laws of a rational system of nature. The field of critical inquiry expanded when this idea of aesthetic "laws of nature" was seen to be a fiction. The separation between theory and criticism collapsed, as August Wilhelm Schlegel determined in the introduction to his lectures on literature and art, "for they simply cannot exist without each other, and each one can be developed and perfected only through the mediation of the other."[19] Schiller's critique of Bürger sounded harsh because it sought to do more than examine the individual weaknesses of the poems under discussion; it tried to attack a literary position that resolved the problematic relationship of production, reception, and criticism in a way that was unacceptable to Schiller in his Classical phase. Bürger embodied the position of the *Sturm und Drang*. The noticeable opposition between the intelligentsia and the middle class was to be overcome through an expansion of the reading public—the people as a whole, rather than the educated elite and their institutionalized spokesmen, were to become the decisive forum of reception. Bürger categorically denied those elite groups any ability to judge his poems: "For I live and die in the belief that no conceivable number of armchair judges, nay, not even judges on a throne, can touch a hair of any literary work into which Nature has blown the breath of life."[20]

In establishing popular acceptance as the seal of perfection, Bürger necessarily points toward abolishing judges of art al-

---

concludes that only a class of people freed from labor, who are "busy without working," can come to an adequate judgment of poetry. For "the after-effects of any lasting exertion ... hinder the aesthetic powers of judgment to such an extent that among the working classes there will be very few individuals who, in matters of taste, will be able to judge with certainty and, just as importantly, with uniformity" (Schiller, 17:558). Schiller seeks his ideal critic, whom he clearly distinguishes from the journalist, in such a class of individuals freed from labor: "Only such a class can maintain the beautiful entirety of human nature, which is momentarily destroyed by any bit of work and is thoroughly destroyed by a life of work; only such a class can, through its feelings, provide laws for the common judgment in all matters of pure humanity" (Schiller, 17:560).
[19]August W. Schlegel, *Kritische Schriften und Briefe*, ed. E. Lohner (Stuttgart, 1963), 2:9.
[20]From the foreword to Gottfried August Bürger's poems; quoted from *Meisterwerke*, 1:348.

together and replacing criticism with the presentation of the process of a work's effect (*Wirkungsprozess*). Johann Gottfried Herder's historical-genetic criticism ultimately moves in the same direction; there the interpretation of the art object is more important than an evaluation of it. The innate positivity of the Romantic conception of art criticism is evident in Herder, though the philosophical premises differ. Herder's criticism is rooted in a process of understanding which penetrates the conditions of origin of a work and from that point observes its development from germination to completed work. The concept of an aesthetic norm is extrinsic to this procedure. Such a norm never has more than a relative validity—it is valid within the context of a certain cultural time and place, and can be considered an expression of that epoch. Herder counts the norms among the conditions of origin; their historical claim to validity (*Verbindlichkeit*) presents a factor that the critic must take into consideration as an element of the cultural context. Herder negates, along with the rules and norms as aesthetic laws, the possibility of an abstract formal comparison as well. For him the individual structure of a work permits only a criticism based on its unique conditions of origin. One can only compare the effect on the beholder—as, for instance, with a comparison of Sophocles and Shakespeare. Yet Herder never introduces an empirical-psychological unit of measurement in the sense of the older aesthetics of impact.

The *Sturm und Drang* movement thus attempted to eliminate the concept of the judge of art because this concept represents an illegitimate authority intruding among the creator of the work, the work itself, and its readers. The increasing social distance between the writer and the society makes the critical discourse of the public sphere, whose exponent is the critic, appear to be an attack on art. The arbiter of art is interpreted as a representative of evaluations based on taste, behind which there are assumed to be particular social interests that seek to limit the author's power to express himself. The *Sturm und Drang* established an ideal in the concept of the genius, freed from all heteronomous norms, an ideal that affirmed the primacy of the creative capacity over the receptive-critical capacity. The correlative of the concept of the genius is the idea of a poetic criticism that empathizes with its object and adheres to it. This criticism is directed toward a like-minded reader; it is no accident that Herder in his Shakespeare essay calls on the "small circle" as the real targets of his enthusiastic tract. Nevertheless, Herder avoids a conclusion that was extensively developed in Romanticism—art and life are not yet strictly divided. This conclusion can be avoided because the creative accomplishment of the genius is seen in conjunction with the collective stream of folk poetry.

In rejecting the rational and dogmatic judgmental facets of art criticism, Romanticism could find a common ground with the *Sturm und Drang*. It was not, however, prepared to follow the subjectivism of the "Age of Genius." In an early essay Friedrich Schlegel described the situation of art theory in his era as an antinomy:

> Here it [the theory] presented works that were sanctioned by the stamp of its authority as eternal models for imitation. There it established absolute originality as the ultimate measure of every artistic value, while showering the faintest suspicion of imitation with unceasing scorn. In its scholastic garb it demanded unconditional acquiescence to even its most arbitrary, obviously idiotic laws. Or it idolized Genius with mystical, oracular dicta, made the artistic lawlessness of Genius its first principle, and with proud superstition paid tribute to revelations that were often quite ambiguous.[21]

To reestablish a sound basis, this troubled discipline needed an art theory which could overcome the dangers of dogmatism, skepticism, and subjectivism.

The derivation and development of that theory is not the task of this examination. Only conclusions that touch the relationship between criticism and the literary public are relevant here. In their theory of art the Romantics dealt with the incongruity between the artistic intentions of the literary and cultural elite and the taste of the broad middle-class readership. The public, which in the form of an aesthetic elite, had still played a part in Schiller's theorem, is eliminated as an immanent factor from the system of Romantic literary criticism. Though communication with the public sphere, in the form of public lectures and speeches, played an important role in the social activity of the

---

[21]Friedrich Schlegel, *Prosaische Jugendschriften*, ed. Jakob Minor (Vienna, 1882), 1:90.

Romantics, especially the Schlegels, nevertheless in the evolution of a theory of art, which led to a specifically Romantic concept of criticism, there was no longer any place for the public sphere as a legitimizing partner of discourse. Romantic criticism stands with its back to the literary public, whose preferences and opinions can exert no influence, whether positive or negative, on the evaluation of an art work. This negation of the public is directed primarily toward modern society. In antiquity, however, where a normatively binding taste still existed, the public sphere could serve as a judge, making the art critic dispensable.[22] In his review of *Wilhelm Meister* Friedrich Schlegel demonstrates the immanent (in the strict sense of the word) procedure, which neither calls on a judgment of taste nor depends on prescribed, heteronomous, aesthetic norms. He treats the novel as a work "which one can learn to understand only from itself,"[23] not from any conventional concept of genre. Criticism is derived entirely from the critic's reflection on the work—that is, from the potential for reflection which is inherent in the work itself and is completed by the critical cognitive subject. The goal of criticism is to unveil the immanent nature of the work. In his analysis of Lessing, Schlegel speaks of "a criticism that would be not just a commentary on an already completed, wilted literature, but rather the organon of a literature that has not yet been completed, structured, even begun."[24] This notion represents a decisive change in the function of art criticism. The Rationalistic aim of approval or disapproval is alien to this criticism. Its goal is the completion and perfection of a work of art that is necessarily imperfect in its individual finitude when compared to the idea of art itself. In the process of critical appropriation, the critic eliminates his own subjectivity, so that the result is an objective judgment based on empirical investigation. "The critic does not judge it [the art work]; art itself is the judge, in that it either accepts the work through the medium of criticism or it rejects it, deeming it beneath all criticism."[25] For the Romantic concept of criticism,

[22]Cf. A. W. Schlegel, *Kritische Schriften*, 2:37.
[23]Friedrich Schlegel, *Kritische Friedrich-Schlegel-Ausgabe*, ed. Ernst Behler (Munich, Paderborn, Vienna, 1958–80), 2:133.
[24]Friedrich Schlegel, *Schriften und Fragmente*, ed. E. Behler (Stuttgart, 1956), p. 55.
[25]Walter Benjamin, *Schriften* (Frankfurt, 1955), 2:486.

the characterization of a work implies its evaluation; analysis and evaluation are one and the same. Only in this way, since prescribed norms are unacceptable, can subjectivism be avoided. Romantic art theory establishes criticism as an absolute—self-sufficient, with no nonliterary purpose. Its function is to divine the development of literature and to influence it through guidance and stimulation. Its earlier function of mediating between literature and the reading public, which had been a source of its legitimation at the beginning of the eighteenth century, dissipated as art was freed from the control of specific social groups. The critical discourse that was initiated by the constitution of the public sphere diverged more and more from the needs of the public when those needs were considered inappropriate.

From this situation came a problem that is evident in literary criticism even today—the discrepancy between the social institution of criticism and its immanent concept. The organization of literary life through book markets, critical journals, clubs, salons, and reading societies corresponded to the model of the liberal public sphere. By excluding social privileges, the discussion was to serve as an instrument of self-understanding, working toward the common goal of "enlightenment." "Private citizens who gather into a public engage in an open discourse concerning what they have read, incorporating it into the commonly pursued process of enlightenment."[26] In addition, the discussion of art had not yet become dominated by specialists and experts; along with discussions of politics and morality, it served as a humanizing influence. It thus spoke to a universal public. The development of the capitalistic book market moved in the same direction by turning literature into a commodity and making it available to everyone. When attempts were made to slow the broad distribution of books through small printings and high prices, which ensured a profit, the pressure of competition caused them to fail. New forms of distribution, such as lending libraries, reading societies, and inexpensive editions, helped bring literature to levels of society which at the beginning of the century had been excluded. This institutionalized literary system, which had developed sharply defined social roles, followed

[26]Jürgen Habermas, *Strukturwandel der Öffentlichkeit* (Neuwied and Berlin, 1965), p. 63.

its own socially conditioned dynamic, one that did not run parallel to the changes in the concept of criticism. By the time of Romanticism this division of labor was already in existence. Romanticism could scorn the literary industry, it could seclude itself in esoteric circles from contact with the masses, but it was not in a position to alter the literary system as a whole. Thus Romanticism seemed to the liberalism of the Vormärz movement in literature (1840–1848) to be an era of exaggerated, unhealthy literary isolation, where exclusive cliques looked down their noses at the general public. Robert Prutz, in his *Vorlesungen über die deutsche Literatur* (Lectures on German Literature), states: "The Romantics separated themselves from the mass public by considering themselves better, wiser, more full of spirit than the rest. So it was inevitable that they should group together in cliques and coteries to avoid being lost in the masses they despised."[27]

Whenever Romantic criticism maintained its strict concept of literature, it ignored the trivial literature directed toward a broad readership. Such works were considered unworthy of criticism; any criticism dealing with them was labeled illegitimate, as Ludwig Tieck pointedly wrote in his *Dramaturgische Blätter* (Dramaturgical Pages): "The opinions of the rabble—its praise, its misguided criticism, its poetic drivel—all these outpourings of ignorance find their place today in our daily press.... It serves the majority of them right to be counted among the garbage of our literature."[28] The charge condemned a general public that delighted in tales of knights and damsels and had lagged far behind the development of authentic literature.

This disintegration of the literary public sphere resulted in the loss of its former political function; as Prutz wrote, it meant that literary discussion could no longer involve "the circumstances of history, the affairs of the nation, the community, or its citizens."[29] Together with the aesthetic cliques came a broad, depoliticized reading public oriented toward mere consumption.

The Young Germany movement in literature (1830–1840) saw

[27]Quoted from *Das Junge Deutschland*, ed. Jost Hermand (Stuttgart, 1966), p. 31.
[28]Quoted from *Meisterwerke*, 1:794.
[29]*Das Junge Deutschland*, p. 32.

in this cleft between the small circles of literary producers and the mass consuming public a severe blow to the efficacy of literature. The Young Germans dedicated themselves to the liquidation of a system that necessarily reproduced the separation between aristocratic and vulgar literature. To them it was a matter of restoring a literary public sphere that could serve as an instrument of political liberation. This is the basis of their vehement, undifferentiated attacks on Goethe and the Romantics, whom they blamed for the depoliticizing process. Their polemic was directed not so much toward Goethe's literary works (its value was disputed only by moralizing Teutomanes like Wolfgang Menzel) but toward his personal aristocratic attitude and his alleged indifference to the pressing issues of his time. Ludwig Börne could never forgive Goethe for remaining inactive as reactionary forces gained strength in Germany; Goethe had in fact gone so far as to make his own peace with them. The real argument centered on a demarcation of current ideological fronts; literary history provided the characters in the battle. Börne opposes Jean Paul to Goethe. Heine, in his *Romantische Schule* (The Romantic School), prefers Schiller to Goethe, not so much on the basis of aesthetic excellence as for his revolutionary themes, which Heine emphasizes in opposition to Goethe's indifference. Regardless of individual reactions to certain past authors, there was a general sense of standing at the threshold of a new era and a tendency to view the literature of the immediate past as the expression of a closed, irretrievable historical period. Heine's slogan of the "end of the age of art" was a clear expression of this consciousness.[30] In a similar way, Ludolf Wienbarg formulated the distinction between the past and his own present efforts:

> Those previous giants of our literature lived in a sphere closed off from the world, nestled soft and warm in an enchanted ideal world, looking down like mortal gods on the sorrows and joys of the real world, nourishing themselves from the sacrificial fires of the emotions and desires of the public. Today's writers have descended from those secure heights; they are part of the public, they mingle

[30]"Today's art must perish, because its principle is still rooted in a bygone regime, in the past era of the Holy Roman Empire." Cf. Heinrich Heine, *Sämtliche Werke*, ed. Ernst Elster (Leipzig, 1887–1890), 4:72.

with the masses, they love, they get excited, happy, and angry like all the rest.[31]

In this juxtaposition, the description of the past (which appears more polemically here than in Wienbarg's other judgments), serves as a foil for a new literary system in which the forgotten public resumes its rightful place. The literary republic does away with the privileges of the author. Wienbarg does grant the writer one advantage, however, calling him the pacesetter, the agent of public dialogue who influences the development of public opinion through his own production. In the same context the Romantic concept of the poet is rejected: "The poets and writers of aesthetic prose stand no longer in service to the Muses alone, but also in service to the Fatherland; they are the allies of all the mighty endeavors of the time."[32] The writer's task is thus above all the promotion of critical discourse.

It is no accident that the writers of Young Germany looked back proudly to Lessing, the representative of Rationalist criticism and uncompromising polemicist. "He was the living criticism of his times, and his entire life was polemic," wrote Heine. "This criticism had an impact on the farthest regions of intellect and emotion, on religion, science, and art."[33] Heinrich Laube adds: "It is an unceasing pleasure for me to observe this architect, Lessing. Here is criticism with vitality, one that needs no artificial phrases; here is truth, insight, stimulation."[34] All of this represents a renewal of Enlightenment values—the critical author is seen as spokesman of a public sphere defending itself against the power of the state. The position was historically justified in that the political situation in Germany lagged behind that of Western Europe, for the German bourgeoisie never got beyond a compromise with the absolutist state. Literature was seen once more as a training ground for political liberation; and the literary revolution was to serve as preparation for a political one.

---

[31]Ludolf Wienbarg, *Ästhetische Feldzüge*, ed. Walter Dietze (Berlin and Weimar, 1964), p. 188; in part a parody of Goethe's "Prometheus."
[32]Ibid.
[33]Heine, 4:240.
[34]Laube, from the introduction to "Rokoko" (1846); quoted from *Lessing: Ein unpoetischer Dichter*, ed. Horst Steinmetz (Frankfurt, 1969), p. 291.

That the Young German authors accepted the liberal model of a literary-political public sphere mediating between state and society, without questioning its socioeconomic basis, is apparent above all in their concept of the role of the public. The public is returned to its rightful place as an active participant in discourse; it is designated as arbiter of literary life. Laube postulated a "democratic plateau" of literature that would no longer have need of cultural heroes, since everyone would be educated and capable of writing. The tendency of the early Enlightenment toward popularization is repeated in the statement "Science and art emerged from closed rooms and entered the marketplace."[35] The movement of literature toward democracy (or toward a republic, if one wishes to distinguish the more radical aims of the Young Hegelians from those of the Young Germans) implied the creation of a public that would differ from both the mass of the lower middle class and the narrow educated elite. Only the widest general audience could be properly addressed. It appears from the confidential reports of the official censors of the time that the Young German authors met with a measure of success in this regard, that their works reached more than a cultural elite. The result was the parliamentary edict of 1835, banning the distribution of their literature precisely because it was available to all classes. The refashioning of literature into an instrument for the journalistic treatment of current political issues went straight to the core of the concept of criticism. The general animosity the Young Germany movement felt toward Romanticism, however, prevented a careful examination of the Romantic theory of art, and this in turn resulted in a lingering feeling of uneasiness in regard to aesthetic norms. In the tenth lecture of his *Ästhetische Feldzüge* (Aesthetic Campaigns), Wienbarg posed the rhetorical question "What distinguishes us and our time from other men and times who could boast of a shared, common attitude toward life?" His answer was "the lack of unity and thus the lack of strength and security, therefore the lack of truth. We are as unsure in our actions as in our enjoyments, as wavering in our creativity as in our judgment. Our heads collide, as do our feelings. It is a world of dissonances, which looks to the

[35]Laube, "Die neue Kritik," in *Das Junge Deutschland*, p. 104.

future for its sustaining continuity."[36] The insecurity, which Wienbarg conceded more honestly than did his fellow combatants, was rooted in the fact that all the various critical currents from the Enlightenment through Romanticism were still present and demanded a decision from the critic. At the same time, however, the mere continuation of these aesthetic and critical traditions proved impossible in view of the changed historical circumstances. Despite a great sympathy for the Enlightenment, it was impossible to return to a rationalistic poetics guided by a strict set of rules, or to the abstract aesthetic of Schiller, so indebted to Kant's *Critique of Judgment*. On the other hand, aesthetic evaluation could not be permitted to degenerate to the level of mere personal taste, as was so often the case with post-Romantic criticism. Wienbarg sought to lead aesthetics out of its isolation and to elucidate its relationship to the dominant *Weltanschauung* of the time, in terms of historical progress: "We thereby confirmed the idea that aesthetics, if anything at all, is a historically closed discipline; as such it adheres to a much higher yet more limited standpoint than most observers generally admit—namely, the standpoint of the prevailing *Weltanschauung* itself."[37]

One can conclude that an apparent change in taste is not coincidental but is rooted in a change in the general philosophical viewpoint. Consequently the critic must develop aesthetic guidelines within the context of the concrete historical situation. Wienbarg's emphasis lay, of course, not so much on a study of the past as on an analysis of current questions.

The self-limitation of the aesthetic realm became a problem of the first order. Ideological tendencies growing out of social conflicts negated the concept of the autonomous work of art. This movement toward ideologies manifested itself in a prose that Wienbarg found to be both more concise and more vulgar that the artistic language of previous epochs. The aim of this prose was to combine two linguistic aspects that had always been strictly separated—poetic expression and communication. Heine's prose, the recognized model for Young German writers,

---

[36]Wienbarg, p. 91.
[37]Ibid., p. 83.

is characterized by a highly subjective blending of "facts, phenomena, episodes, visions, and details of consciousness; it is a potpourri of realities taken from a variety of levels and dimensions which come into contact with one another through association, reflection, and the memory of the never entirely fictitious author."[38] In such a work one would search in vain for the integral unity of the work of art and its aesthetic semblance. The boundary between poetic and publicistic writing has been erased, not through arbitrary distortions by the author, one must immediately add, but rather through an insight into the factors which conditioned the modes of production in that era.

According to the theory of art criticism in the Age of Goethe, the work of art expresses something that can be presented only through the medium of the art work. Where this theory fully dominated, it enjoined the critic from any use of extraliterary categories. It proved untenable when confronted with a literature that no longer affirmed the concept of a closed work of art but opened itself up to external reality and consciously accepted ideological elements without integrating them in the traditional sense. Heine's *Romantische Schule* represents a new type of literary criticism, one that combines in a highly unorthodox manner personal characteristics, descriptions of works, satire, historical commentary, and critique of ideology. In contrast to Romantic criticism, which Heine praised for "a fine sensitivity to a work's particular characteristics,"[39] this criticism was subjective and polemical. It was polemical because of the conviction that literature could no longer exist beyond reality and therefore had to be tendentious, whether intentionally or unintentionally. It was subjective because of the realization that an objective canon of values would have to be related to sociopolitical reality, a reality in such a state of flux that it would soon contradict any dogmatic canon. It was no longer possible to mediate art and critical consciousness in a representation that uses abstract rules as measuring devices; nor was it possible to retain the Romantic procedure which completed the work of art in the critical process without the participation of the cognitive subject, as it were. "For the

---

[38]Wolfgang Preisendanz, "Der Funktionsübergang von Dichtung und Publizistik bei Heine," in *Die nicht mehr schönen Künste*, ed. Hans Robert Jauss, *Poetik und Hermeneutik*, 3 (Munich, 1968), 350.

[39]Heine, 5:232.

time being Heine felt that the only thing that could be 'represented,' in the actual sense of the word, was subjectivity as such, as the point of reference for all experience of reality."[40]

This statement could stand not only for Heine's prose but for his criticism as well. It casts off the illusion of critical objectivity. Heine finds fault with Lessing and even more with the Schlegels for lacking a solid theory, and he is not prepared to follow A. W. Schlegel, his academic mentor, by taking the route of an historical assessment of art. In Heine's work the critical subject makes its presence explicitly known. It describes its personal stand toward the work, the person, or the critical tendency being analyzed. It registers its reactions, clarifies its premises, and voices its individual perspective. The purpose of this is not to provide the reader with impressions but to hinder any dogmatic understanding of the statements. Heine was fully aware of this procedure, as shown in this remark from his work on Börne: "This constant assertion of my personality [is] the most suitable means of encouraging a self-evaluation from the reader."[41] His emphasis on subjectivity should not be viewed as a resumption of the old role of arbitration. The polemic, sharp as it may be, does not claim to have final answers. It seeks to provoke—it challenges the reader to pursue further the connection between literature and politics and to draw the broad extra-aesthetic context into literary criticism. Historical, political, social, and ideological matters are thus introduced into the realm of literary criticism. In place of Romantic criticism there emerged a journalistic criticism, which no longer insisted on the integral nature of a work of art. In Börne's case, literary criticism was avowedly a continuation of political discussion in a public sphere that had been depoliticized by state censorship.[42] The politicized criticism produced by the Young Germany movement was not, strictly speak-

[40]Preisendanz, p. 345.

[41]Heine, 7:132.

[42]Börne blamed the lack of a literary-political public sphere for the shortcomings of German criticism. The German critic, usually an educated intellectual, considered himself not a representative of the public sphere but an official of the state. German criticism "has no real sense of a public sphere; that sense died from lack of use. It also lacks good manners, skill, decency, courage, and presence of mind. In Germany everyone who cannot do anything else writes; those who cannot write become reviewers. That is quite pardonable in itself; everyone is entitled to speak his mind in matters of public interest. But what is missing is a

ing, socially engaged, as Marx and Engels later pointed out. Like literature, its criticism was directed toward the public as a whole, not yet toward the viewpoint of a single class—that is, the functioning of the autonomous public sphere was not called into question.

In politically backward Germany, the liberals viewed literature as the only available vehicle for political struggle. Since there was no self-sufficient political public sphere, the literary sphere had to step in (imitating the Enlightenment) as a stimulator and promulgator of action. "We Germans," wrote Johannes Scherr, "have no other public life than that of literature; our only deeds are literary ones."[43] Because of Germany's slowness in developing, the political consequences of the literary public sphere did not become evident until the 1830s and 1840s. Jost Hermand has rightly argued against the widespread denigration of the Young German movement, pointing out that despite the unclarity of its purely literary goals, it introduced a form of critical discourse in Germany which paved the way for the more politically conscious writers of the Vormärz.[44] In his essay "Die neue Literatur" (The New Literature), Georg Herwegh writes, "Our new literature is a daughter of criticism; our best authors brought their works to the public in journals; many a budding talent is taking that same route now."[45]

The Vormärz movement intensified the currents of the 1830s and accentuated the priorities of politics over literature. It judged an individual's talent according to its role in the overall movement: "In literature a writer's value does not depend on himself, but only on his position in relation to the whole."[46] Literary criticism assumed the function of a critique of ideology more precisely than in the generation of Young Germany. Young Friedrich Engels recognized only Börne as a precursor in

public opinion, an urn wherein all votes could be gathered for counting." "Einige Worte über die angekündigten Jahrbücher der wissenschaftlichen Kritik," *Kritische Schriften,* ed. Edgar Schumacher (Stuttgart and Zurich, 1964), p. 57.

[43] *Das Junge Deutschland*, p. 349.

[44] Hermand, "Nachwort," in *Das Junge Deutschland*, esp. pp. 389–391.

[45] Georg Herwegh, in *Der deutsche Vormärz*, ed. Jost Hermand (Stuttgart, 1967), p. 10.

[46] Friedrich Engels, "Alexander Jung, 'Lectures on Modern Literature,'" in Karl Marx and Friedrich Engels, *Collected Works*, trans. Richard Dixon et al. (New York, 1975), 2:288.

this regard. Engels at that time had of course no clearly developed background of social theory for the politicization of literary criticism as he postulated it. It arose from the conviction that ideological discussion, when carried out in the public sphere, could, as critical consciousness, effect political change. For the Left Hegelian Engels, the smooth functioning of the public sphere was still a given fact. Not until his analysis of Thomas Carlyle's *Past and Present* did Engels undertake an in-depth criticism of literary life. There he exposes the contradiction between the fashionable "literature industry" and the social reality of a class society. While the liberals placed faith in public opinion to act as a political regulatory factor, Engels characterized this as the "public prejudice" of high society[47]—that is, of the class which, through its control of industry, holds political power in its hands. What the liberals called "public opinion" and held to be independent of particular social interests was in Engels' eyes an attempt to stabilize economic and social inequity.

The liberal public sphere was subjected to a more basic and penetrating critique by Marx. We mention this critique here for two reasons. First, it dissolves in principle the institutional basis of previous literary criticism, which had not been questioned even by those groups such as the Romantics, who had distanced themselves to such an extent from the origins of literary criticism as public discourse. Second, the critique of the bourgeois public sphere established the necessity of rethinking the institutional foundation of criticism.

Marx's critique arose primarily from Hegel's philosophy of law. Hegel had smoothed over the contradictions arising from the conflict of individual and supposedly rational general interests by integrating them into a hierarchical theory of the state. Marx, on the other hand, accepted the development toward a bourgeois constitutional state—with the intention, to be sure, of proving the contradiction between its theory and its actual manifestation. The bourgeois public sphere assumed that the economic system was free from domination and could regulate itself, so that public and private interests would remain separated. But Marx showed that capitalism, in spite of its formal freedom

---

[47]Friedrich Engels, "The Condition of England: *Past and Present* by Carlyle," in Marx and Engels, 3:446.

of contract, leads to conditions of force and domination which contradict the idea of the public sphere. The literary audience forfeited its claim of representing the entire society, since the public sphere was not equally accessible to everyone. Furthermore, the separation of public from private interests proved to be a fiction from which only the bourgeoisie profited. Finally, public opinion, contrary to its own theory, is not identical to rationality so long as bourgeois society perpetuates conditions of force.

Marx encountered in class society a public sphere that had betrayed its own principles. He concluded that to realize the idea of the public sphere, it would be necessary to do away with its liberal form. As the public expands, as the lower classes participate more and more in the institutionalized media of communication, the principle of publicity must turn increasingly against the bourgeoisie. As the interests of these nonpropertied classes gain increasing attention, the idea of property itself began to be analyzed. The economic basis of the public sphere eventually becomes a subject for discussion. "When the mass of nonproperty owners begin to discuss publicly the general rules of social interaction, the reproduction of social life as such (rather than merely the amassing of private wealth) becomes a matter of public interest."[48]

New problems for the foundations of literary criticism emerge from this critique. If the rationality of public opinion is exposed as being based on a false self-understanding of the bourgeoisie, the public can no longer be a source of legitimation for criticism. For this public is not identical to the population as a whole—it represents only "good society," whose judgment (though it cannot admit this) is determined by its social position. Thus, in view of the obvious conflict of class interests, there arose a problem of method which had previously been dismissed as irrelevant, since it contradicted the idea of an autonomous public sphere: it is suspected that both literary production and critical reception are no longer directed toward or speak for the total society; they are suspected of expressing special class interests in their writings. Criticism, if it wishes to go beyond mere description, thus cannot be satisfied with confronting a work directly and evaluating it

[48]Habermas, *Strukturwandel,* p. 141.

according to its own intentions. Criticism must deal with the attitudes of both author and reader insofar as these comprise the context of the work. The object of criticism is thereby broadened to include the cultural system itself, a system based on division of labor, in which the intellectual products stand alienated from their producers. Culture is posited absolutely and is withdrawn from social praxis; it has become an ideology and has forced its producers into a situation of dependence. Thus the "task of philosophy, which is in the service of history, once the holy form of human self-alienation has been discovered, is to discover self-alienation in its unholy forms."[49] The ideological element in the literary system is its claim of being independent of man's social actions. Criticism has to destroy this illusion, for it merely obscures the actual dependence of the institution of literature on the established social order.[50] This suspicion of ideology differs from the immanent criticism of the Romantic era in two ways. First, it holds extraliterary factors to be relevant to the meaning of a work of art. Second, in a radical way it insists on its claim to criticize any work of art.

In his model of base and superstructure, Marx was able to formulate experimentally the possibility of a theory of culture which could provide literary criticism with a methodological access to the conditions of literary production, conditions which under the premises of the classical literary public sphere had to remain invisible. For this model of the public sphere, discourse was autonomous, with no connection to material activities of mankind or to the development of material forces of production. Marx, on the other hand, insisted on the dominance of the material forces of production over intellectual production, as manifested in religion, morality, and art: "The mode of produc-

---

[49]Karl Marx, "Contribution to the Critique of Hegel's Philosophy of Law: Introduction," in Marx, *Selected Writings*, ed. David McLellan (Oxford, 1977), p. 64.

[50]This dependence, however, should not be understood positivistically as a causal determination of the individual work of art through social determinants. It concerns rather the totality of the literary system as a part of the cultural system. In the introduction to his *Kritik der politischen Ökonomie* (Critique of Political Economy), Marx noted that the development of material conditions of production does not necessarily run parallel to the development of culture. Periods of great artistic achievement are not always related to progress in the relations of production. Cf. Marx and Engels, *On Literature and Art* (Moscow, 1976), pp. 82–84.

tion of material life conditions the social, political, and intellectual life process in general. It is not the consciousness of men that determines their being, but, on the contrary, their social being that determines their consciousness."[51] Therefore, the shifts in the intellectual production designated as the superstructure, shifts which the history of literature also pursues, can be comprehended only within the context of changes in the material base.

The model describes the relationships that can provide guidelines for literary criticism, although it does so schematically, without specifying particular conditions of mediation. Although it was not formulated to take account of the special aims of art criticism, it does offer some orientation. This model should not, however, be (as Engels saw it) a description of a situation governed by laws of nature. It derives its function far more from the theory of revolution, which converts reflection into practice. The superstructure cannot be understood as merely the sum total of all the elements of consciousness which can be derived from material conditions. Marx understood clearly that the model offered only a general framework that needed to be filled in, especially regarding the various stages of transmission from the economic base to the cultural phenomena which are as far removed from this foundation as literature is.

The current task of literary criticism is prefigured in Marx' revelation of the ideological character of the bourgeois public sphere. In the public sphere, the literary audience had insisted that aesthetics must be set apart from the problems of real life and that one's association with art is not at all related to one's role as a private property owner. This idea of the public sphere maintained that public discussion participated in a process of humanization, insofar as the reception of art could be converted into social praxis through the mediation of the political public sphere. Yet this essential connection was lost in the later stage of development of bourgeois society. The relationship between the literary and the political public sphere was severed by the middle-class public as it set itself apart more distinctly from the masses. The educated elite withdrew to a "sacral" reception of art which sought to shelter the work of art from a vulgarized

[51]Marx, *Selected Writings*, p. 389.

world of reality in order to preserve the human potentials which, though repressed by society, were preserved in the work. The lower classes, however, were soon caught in the jaws of the capitalist culture industry, which steadily eroded the concept of autonomous culture. Both of these courses led toward depoliticization: the social impotence of the elitists, who clutched tightly onto art, corresponds to the subjugation of the masses to the apparatus of the culture industry. In short, the cultural system, which traditional literary criticism had always considered naturally given, now had to be critically analyzed in its own right, for this system obscured its social underpinnings. When the critic, as the spokesman of an educated public, appeals to literary tradition, he refers to a property of the privileged group, which does not grant the masses any right of codetermination over the use of the cultural heritage.

The contradictory recent history of literary criticism took place before the background of a fragmented literary public sphere, largely robbed of its original function. The most obvious symptom of this crisis was the separation of elite and mass culture, a split that has had great consequences for the institution of literary criticism. Although there had existed a difference between the advanced consciousness of the minority and the more backward one of the broad public in the past, the situation that arose in the late nineteenth century was nevertheless a qualitatively new one, for this difference could now be institutionally anchored in the social system. By applying industrial production methods to literary creativity and by utilizing the market situation to produce a literary commodity designed for mass consumption, the literary industry was able to analyze and with increasing success to satisfy the needs of the middle and lower classes. The industry had previously considered this segment of the market to be marginal and thus left it to chance, but now it became increasingly scrutinized and controlled. The public's needs were not only satisfied but manufactured and manipulated as well. This was the beginning of what has since come to be known in critical sociology as "consumer culture."

To characterize this development merely as the commercialization of art is inadequate, for works of art made their appearance as commodities as early as the eighteenth century. The autonomous character of the commodity had in fact allowed art to gain a measure of autonomy, since it was removed from spheres of direct domination. This autonomy was then posited as absolute by the ensuing art theory. In consumer culture, in a logical extension of the capitalist system, the reception of art was drawn into the realm of marketing, with its system of controlled production and consumption. The form of literary discussion specifically related to the liberal public sphere was eliminated. The sophisticated adaptation of calculated and manufactured needs to mass production compromised the bourgeois concept of autonomous culture. The essential notion of autonomy is negated when art is turned into consumable "culture commodities," for bourgeois culture was based on the premise that the use value of literature should remain untouched by its exchange value as a commodity.

The structural transformation of the public sphere, which in the final analysis rests on the social frictions of advanced capitalist class society, did not leave untouched the position of institutionalized literary criticism. The literary intelligentsia, considering itself the bearer of advanced consciousness, held fast to the concept of the autonomous work of art, which follows only its own laws. This group drew back from all that it abhorred as the vulgarization and commercialization of culture. Placed on the defensive by the social system, it insisted on the principle of *l'art pour l'art,* which by then was recognized as elitist. The aesthetic discussion was conducted in informal groups and specialized literary journals, the general public being more or less excluded.[52] This meant the end of the model of the liberal public sphere. Only a minority of select initiates could take part in the deliberations. The idea of representing the public interest was discarded. In extreme cases the intelligentsia shunned all contact with the public, as it did, for example, in the early days of the intellectual circle around Stefan George.

[52]It is a moot point whether this social distancing represented a culpable self-exile or was forced by the society, for the question does not take into consideration the dialectical forces at work in the decay of the literary institutions. Psychologically it was certainly to a large extent a freely chosen inner exile. One must still consider, however, that this withdrawal was in one aspect legitimate: these exiles confronted society with an ideal it had sacrificed. This could only be achieved, however, at the price of social exclusiveness. One could claim with justification that this represented a misjudgment of the situation by the intelligentsia.

The social isolation of this avant-garde destroyed the liberal idea of literary criticism, and not merely through the esoteric attitudes of its adherents. Their changed self-image was more significant than the change in the mode of communication. The judicial role of art criticism became authoritarian once it divorced itself from its traditional function as mediator between the art work and the public and escaped the control of a public endowed with full and equal rights. Literary criticism assumed the form of a decree that allowed no opposition. Convinced of their exceptional talent, the elitists withdrew from discussion and became irrational. George and his circle are exemplars of this procedure. The alternative of subjective impressionism led to the same result. It suspended every claim to normative standards and substituted personal feelings as the sole judgmental criterion. In this irrational form the role of the literary critic could be fit neatly into the apparatus of the modern culture industry, thus losing its original element of protest against precisely that apparatus.

At the turn of the century this possibility was not yet available. When esoteric literary criticism encountered mass journalism, it drew back sharply and made no secret of its disdain: "The literary criticism practiced in German newspapers and magazines has not the slightest claim to respect, neither through its level of education nor through its insights," wrote Rudolf Borchardt in his *Rede über Hofmannsthal* (Speech on Hofmannsthal).[53] The elite felt alienated from the broad public and disavowed sharply the institutional basis of criticism—they attacked the professionalized mode of literary reviewing in the name of a sanctified art.

This confrontation reflects the advanced stage of a social process to which the protesting avant-garde and the incriminated journalism were equally exposed. With the onset of the phase of high capitalism, the system of literature was subjected to a more rigorous division of labor, in accordance with the laws of the marketplace. This situation dissolved the unity of poetic and critical production which had found its expression in the concept of "author." Within criticism itself, since the mid-nineteenth

[53]Rudolf Borchardt, *Reden*, ed. Marie L. Borchardt with Rudolf Schröder (Stuttgart, 1955), p. 47.

century there had been a split between the criticism of the daily press, found in the feuilletons, and literary history, which had taken refuge in the universities. Journalistic critics and academic literary historians increasingly occupied different social roles. The journalist had no secure social status; he belonged to none of the traditional social groups with respected role definitions. In a society as status-conscious as the German society, he seemed the most proletarian of the intellectuals. This profession was a gathering point for members of the intelligentsia who either could not or would not assume a place in the academic hierarchy. The expansion of the press in the latter half of the nineteenth century lowered the social prestige of the journalist even further.[54]

The transition from independent author to employed journalist reflects the broader transformation in the organization and function of the press. As soon as the consolidation of the political public sphere allowed newspapers to be run primarily as business ventures, the relationship between the publisher and the editor changed, to the detriment of the latter. The early liberal editor could consider himself an emissary of the public, whose general interests he guarded, independent of the private economic interests of the publisher. The restructuring of the newspaper into a business placed the publisher in a dominant position and reduced the editor to an employee who takes orders. In an expanded editorial staff, his assignment became specialized to that of coordinator and salesman of news reports. The great number of news items, including those in the cultural realm, demanded a tight organization in order to satisfy the public's demand for up-to-date information. Literary criticism was thereby reduced to book reviewing. The historical dimension was thereby diminished and handed over to the historians as an area of specialization. The daily reviews, which sought to give readers information about the most recent publications, gradually became an appendix of the book market, providing

[54]Because of the great need for workers, the educational standards had to be lowered. The journalist of the Vormärz period was usually an academic who had completed his studies; he considered himself a writer and in many cases was only temporarily engaged in journalism. But the educational level fell with the great influx of workers into this field. There were fewer academics, and many of those were former students who had failed at the university. Within the framework of a commercialized press they were used as intellectual skilled laborers. For most of them the ambition of becoming an author was beyond their reach.

immediate reactions to the constantly rising tide of books, dependent on the space at their disposal, calculated for fast reading and therefore hastily written. "The critiques have become short. . . . There are hardly any analyses and interpretations of works any more. . . . The critic no longer argues, he only dictates." This is Mayer's summary of the dominant tendency of the twentieth century.[55] The statement must be qualified, as he well knows. For the time period 1900–1933 Mayer himself points out countertendencies—there were critics who fought the commercialization of criticism. And after 1945 there were a number of newspapers and magazines with a broad geographical circulation which tried to restore the literary public sphere of the liberals. They encouraged argumentative criticism and debates among critics. One may doubt, however, that the autonomy of the public sphere was reconstructed by this method. It is revealing to hear the confession of the editors that they have no clear conception of their readership; apparently they are not terribly interested in establishing a close contact.[56] They view themselves less as agents of a deliberating public than as autonomous promoters of avant-garde literature. The opposition of elite and mass culture, a decisive factor in the modern situation, is still in evidence here and takes the form of a clearly defined division between areas of cultural communication; there is merely some shifting of borders. As the formerly isolated literary intelligentsia is reintegrated into society, the opposition can be absorbed into the system itself. A type of division of labor has taken place: The leading national periodicals direct their criticism toward an educationally privileged public, leaving the mass public to regional newspapers and boulevard press.

It was not merely the breaking up of cultural communication that turned the idea of the liberal public sphere into a fiction. The position and function assigned to the critic by the apparatus of the mass media set limits to the development of critical deliberation. These limits are for the most part invisible, since the interference is not in the form of open censorship; nevertheless, they can be discerned. Freedom of expression was granted to the literary segment of the journals only on condition that they maintain an immanent mode of criticism. Even when the subject

[55]Hans Mayer, ed., *Literaturkritik im zwanzigsten Jahrhundert* (Stuttgart, 1965), p. 38.
  [56]Cf. Glotz, *Buchkritik*, esp. pp. 104 ff.

matter encourages the use of political arguments to continue the discussion, journalistic criticism tends to avoid doing so.[57] The idea of immanent criticism, once a defense against the intrusion of private social interests, has changed its function. It makes taboo those zones of literary production and reception in which general social claims are expressed. The emancipatory element of literary criticism has narrowed itself to freedom of expression for the critics, who in the final analysis remain dependent on the apparatus of the consciousness industry and thus can make only limited use of the freedom of expression available to them.

It is important to note here the role of the literary intelligentsia in contemporary society. When the intellectuals broke free socially from the academic class, they were driven into the position of outsiders. Avant-garde criticism was at the same time a socially exiled criticism, looking down on the press industry. After 1945 the culture industry expanded into a system of interconnected large-scale organizations—a move that created a great number of positions which could be filled only by intellectuals and offered the economically insecure intelligentsia a chance for social reintegration. By accepting these positions, the socially "free-floating" intelligentsia became an established elite of cultural functionaries, though they were still without equal rights. The appartus of the media (radio, television) provides them with an unexpected potential for exerting influence, but it subordinates them as employees. This new group of critics retains, to be sure, its consciousness of avant-garde exclusivity, its social position in regard to the broad public that lies below the educational level of these critics' work. This consciousness does not hinder the working of the apparatus; rather, it helps indirectly to stabilize the system. After being assimilated by the culture industry, this group places itself socially on the side of the status quo. The aesthetic claim to dominance accepts the gap between the privileged minority and the uneducated masses as natural and unavoidable. Literary criticism thus lies in the hands of a group whose consciousness is far removed from the convictions of the nineteenth-century liberal journalist. The group, as an elite, stands isolated from the broad reading public and is linked to a communications apparatus over which it has no control.

[57]Ibid., pp. 83 and 195 ff.

It is a very difficult task to mediate between a complex literary work that is the product of an advanced consciousness and a fragmented, unevenly informed reading public. Within the West German literary system, the critics seldom take this task seriously, because they consider such mediation to be impossible from the start. The editors of the large newspapers realize that the attitude is questionable; yet they give in to the wishes of their prominent reviewers, who reject not only the literature of the masses but the mass audience as well.[58] In discussions of the state of criticism, the lack of a normative aesthetic code has often been made responsible for the crisis. Current criticism, as some observers have argued, displays a frightful mixture of standards and criteria as well as an unholy war among cliques and schools; in short, a situation that can be overcome only through a return to basic values. One questionable aspect of this critique of criticism is its unreflected trust in values. Neither the social position of the critic nor the actual structure of the public is considered a factor in the crisis, since the autonomy of the literary system is taken for granted. The dilemma of contemporary criticism does not lie in the fact that its guild is unable to agree on its purpose. The contradictions among the various conceptions provide only a distorted view of their causes. Theories of art are at everybody's disposal. Anyone is free to appeal to Lessing, Herder, Friedrich Schlegel, or Börne. Often the differences in historical situation and theory between these critics go unnoticed or are intentionally minimized in order to maintain an appearance of continuity.[59] The result is an eclectic criticism which at various times can call on either the Rationalist role of judge, the Romantic concept of productive criticism, or the publicistic function in the sense of the Young Germany movement. Walser described this contradictory self-image in deprecatory but appropriate terms: "a bit of doctor, a bit of Moses, a bit of traffic cop, a bit of world spirit, a bit of Aunt Lessing, a bit of Uncle Linnaeus."[60] The objection is not rigorous enough if it tries to make only stylistic

---

[58]Ibid., pp. 118 ff.

[59]Hans Egon Holthusen, for example, puts Rationalist, Classical, Romantic, and modern criticism together under one concept in order to demonstrate that the critical method has always been essentially the same. Cf. "Über den Kritiker und sein Amt," in *Ja und Nein: Neue kritische Versuche* (Munich, 1954), p. 9.

[60]Walser in *Kritik,* p. 13.

deficiencies responsible for the contradictions. The forms of expression under attack are characteristic of previously legitimate forms of style. Walser chastises the critics for reinstating old practices: "They function as public advisers; they seem to consider themselves evaluators and judges."[61] The rhetoric of criticism can no longer be believed; it has lost its function, which was tailored to the liberal public sphere of the nineteenth century. With the breakdown of that sphere, its institutional basis was lost.

What will be the probable results to literary criticism of the disintegration of the bourgeois public sphere? We should not be too hasty in filling out its death certificate. A subsystem can continue to function within any highly specialized modern social system, even when the conditions that led to its genesis are no longer operating. One could argue that the present crisis of literary criticism can be overcome only when the literary intelligentsia dares to step into modern industrial society and addresses the tasks of communication in mass society. Instead of cultured feuilletons, which because of their language and content can be understood by only an educated minority, there would be comprehensible information for the broad range of readers—information not just about advanced literature, but also about the popular literature that is actually read by the public. Peter Glotz is correct in making elitist cultural pessimism responsible for the almost exclusive orientation toward belles-lettres in West German newspaper criticism.[62] It is nourished by a belief in the priority of the educated bourgeois public. Glotz's call for a democratization of criticism is reminiscent of the demand for mass reception in the late essays of Walter Benjamin, but with one decisive difference: Glotz views the current social structure, determined by the concept of the industrial society, as naturally given and unchangeable. The relationship between work and freedom appears to be an unalterable constraint. In this context, entertainment is assigned the function of diversion, which is necessary to keep the masses ready to work. Adorno cited this as an argument against the democratization of art as long as the culture industry remains under the control of the ruling class: "The abolition of educational privilege by the device

[61]Ibid., p. 12.
[62]Glotz, *Buchkritik*, pp. 66 ff.

of clearance sales does not open for the masses the spheres from which they were formerly excluded, but, given existing social conditions, contributes directly to the decay of education and the progress of barbaric meaninglessness."[63] The positive attitude toward education indicates that this is spoken essentially from the perspective of the bourgeois public. Adorno was well aware of this public's diminishing ability to evaluate an art that is withdrawing so radically into its own material. Nevertheless, this public seemed to Adorno by virtue of its privileged position to be superior to the manipulated and illiterate masses, to whom literature was accessible only as a reified cultural commodity. According to Adorno the work of art, insofar as it contains the highest level of consciousness of its time, is excluded from mass communication. He therefore insists that criticism should ignore reception, that it should proceed as immanently as Romantic criticism had done.[64] With one difference, of course—it must perceive the dialectic between the autonomy of the work of art and its character as a commodity: "Pure works of art which deny the commodity society by the very fact that they obey their own law were nevertheless always wares. . . . The purposelessness of the great modern work of art depends on the anonymity of the market."[65]

"Democratization" of criticism, as urged by Glotz, is criticized by Adorno because it would result, under the existing social conditions, in a mere popularization. What remains for Adorno is the antinomy of aesthetic immanence and mass society. A reconciliation between them seems unthinkable, as is evidenced by Adorno's objections to the late writings of Walter Benjamin. By contrast, and despite the disapproval of his friend, Benjamin used the premises of Marxism, which was both materialistic and critical of ideology, in an attempt to overcome the aesthetic antinomy of the advanced bourgeois epoch. The essay on Eduard

[63]Max Horkheimer and Theodor W. Adorno, *Dialectic of Enlightenment*, trans. John Cumming (New York, 1972), p. 160.
[64]Adorno states in his essay on Valéry, "Great insights into art thrive either in absolute distance, out of the logic of the concept itself, undisturbed by any so-called understanding of art (as was the case with Kant or Hegel), or else in absolute nearness, to the attitude of one who stands in the wings, who is not the public, but who helps complete the work of art in the aspect of crafting, of technique" (*Noten zur Literatur* [Frankfurt, 1958], 1:177–178). The renunciation of a criticism based on the public and on taste is as harsh here as in the Romantic era.
[65]Horkheimer and Adorno, p. 157.

Fuchs quotes a letter from Engels: "It is above all this appearance (*Schein*) of an autonomous history of constitutions, of legal systems and of ideological conceptions in each specialized field of study, which deceives most people."[66] This critique of the seeming independence of the cultural superstructure from the material base of production also undermined the model of the liberal public sphere, which was thought to be shielded from private economic interests. The qualities of freedom, equality, and rationality, inherent in the concept of the public sphere, could only be saved if private property, as the social base, were socialized. Only through the exclusion of private interests could there be any hope of bringing about what the bourgeois public sphere had always called for—the emancipation of mankind.[67] As a result, literary criticism that remains true to its public mission cannot be separated from the idea of a critique of ideology and social criticism.[68]

---

[66]Engels, Letter to Franz Mehring, July 14, 1893; quoted from Walter Benjamin, "Eduard Fuchs: Collector and Historian," *New German Critique*, no. 5 (Spring 1975), p. 27.

[67]"The positive abolition of private property and the appropriation of human life is therefore the positive abolition of all alienation, thus the return of man out of religion, family, state, etc. into his human, i.e. social being" (Marx, *Selected Writings*, p. 89).

[68]The starting point of the mature Benjamin's materialistic theory of art is the point at which the condition of production forces in bourgeois society makes possible a qualitative change in the production and reception of art—in the proletarian masses and in technology. According to Benjamin, the potential for the technical reproducibility of a work of art leads to the possibility of a change in its function. Technical reproduction destroys the aura of the work of art, which was the sign of its genuineness, but was at the same time the sign of a late bourgeois concept of culture which had become ideological, presenting itself as a "secularized ritual" in the service of beauty. Cf. *Illuminations*, trans. Harry Zohn (New York, 1968), p. 226. For the art theory that is to be developed, there is an inseparable connection between technology as a means of production and the masses as a receiving public. "The capacity for technical reproduction of art alters the relationship of the masses to art" (*Illuminations*, p. 236; translation modified). The masses' need for diversion, which bourgeois art theory and Adorno as well considered to be a flaw of the masses, is transformed into a positive quality—the mass public is incapable of submerging itself in art as the intellectuals had done. "The masses in their diversion submerge the work of art into themselves" (*Illuminations*, p. 241; translation modified). Diversion contains within itself the possibility of setting aside the cult of beauty, so withdrawn from praxis, and of preparing a new, critical attitude toward art. Benjamin anticipated a critical rationalization of experience from the collective reception of art by a mass audience conscious of its interests. This would reconstruct the idea of the public sphere and dialectically overcome the separation between the intelligentsia and the public.

2 Art Evaluation and Reportage: The Aesthetic Theory of the Later Heine

On June 30, 1840, Heinrich Heine, then Paris correspondent for the *Augsburger Allgemeine Zeitung,* wrote an extensive report on the organization of the French press. The topic was of current interest for his German readers; they were well acquainted with the difficulties of writing and publishing political information. In Germany of the Vormärz period, freedom of the press was one of the unattained demands of the liberals. As Heine later wrote in his introduction to the French edition of *Lutetia,* one had to disguise the truth in order to speak it. The omnipresence of the censor necessitated a tactical use of language which at times made it difficult to understand the author's real intent. Heine explained to his French public, "I often had to adorn the ship of my thoughts with flags whose emblems were not the true expression of my mind. But the journalistic pirate cares little about the color of the banner on the mast, blown about so lustily by the wind—I thought only about the good cargo I had on board, to be smuggled into the harbor of public opinion."[1] Heine owed his French audience such an explanation; since the July Revolution it had grown accustomed to the free development of public opinion, even though attempts were not uncommon under Louis-Philippe to restrict freedom of expression and

Translated by Ronald L. Smith and Henry J. Schmidt.
[1]Unless otherwise indicated, quotations are cited from the following edition: Heinrich Heine, *Sämtliche Schriften,* ed. Klaus Briegleb, 6 vols. (Munich, 1968–75). Further references to this edition will be made in the text itself, as follows: 5:230.

to exert pressure on opposition newspapers. The constitutional system provided in principle for the complete freedom of the press (according to Article 7 of the Constitution),[2] so that the government could use only indirect weapons against oppositional forces on the Right and Left. This was vastly different from the conditions in Germany, where freedom of opinion was not really assured even in the liberal southwestern states.[3] The readers of Johann Friedrich Cotta's *Allgemeine Zeitung,* the liberal German bourgeoisie, could not but see in this description of the French press the weakness of their own position. The French conditions under the July Monarchy represented, from the German viewpoint, an advanced position toward which the Germans could orient their own political demands. But the goal of Heine's comparison of the press in France and Germany was not to point out once again this obvious dissimilarity. He was more interested in demonstrating that the opposition of freedom and restriction—that is, public expression in France and the restriction of public debate in Germany—was valid "only in external appearance" (5:280). A closer examination reveals, according to Heine, that the French press "suffers from a particular type of restriction which is completely alien to the German press and is perhaps even more debilitating than our censorship across the Rhine" (5:281). The irony of this statement cannot be overlooked; the praise of Germany's lack of freedom from the mouth of Heine can hardly be taken literally. The unusual twist signaled a necessary change of perspective. The historically asynchronous nature of German and French conditions (the basic theme of Heine's reports from Paris) is not ignored, but to the critical observer it does assume an altered shape in the 1840s. The practical solution to the liberal demands of 1830 was not in accord with the theory behind them. There was a great difference between the human emancipation on which the young Heine had counted and the political system of Louis-Philippe. Astonished and disappointed, Heine recounted this disparity in his *Französische Zustände* (The French Situation). But not until his essays of the late 1830s and early 1840s did he systematically

---

[2] Irene Collins, *The Government and the Newspaper Press in France, 1814–1881* (London, 1959), p. 62.

[3] Franz Schneider, *Pressefreiheit und politische Öffentlichkeit* (Neuwied and Berlin, 1966).

analyze this contradiction. The economic and social dominance of the bourgeoisie and the political system derived from it (that is, the constitutional monarchy) stood increasingly in opposition, in Heine's view, to the general liberation of mankind promised by liberal theory. The critical observer had to learn to distinguish between postulates and material actualization; the ideological character of legitimation had to be exposed. In *Französische Zustände*, Heine, because of his still limited knowledge of the French situation and its background, at first could not fully come to terms with this task. His judgment of people and institutions vacillated; he sought to stay out of the quarrels of the political parties. In *Lutetia* as well, as Heine conceded in the introduction, contradictions can be found. They rest, however, no longer on a lack of orientation but on the difficulty of formulating a critique of the French situation from a revolutionary perspective and in such a way that it did not play into the hands of the conservative forces (Heine had observed repeatedly in France the appropriation of Leftist criticism by the reactionary elements). France's problem—the tension between the idea of freedom and its realization in society—needed to be treated in a manner that would not lead to a suppression of the progress made by the French bourgeoisie when it overcame the Bourbon restoration. However, neither could it be denied that this victory had led to problematic social consequences.

Heine's remarks on the French press must be read in this context. The constitutionally ensured freedom of the press, in contrast to what might theoretically have been expected, created not a system of free reporting but forms of restriction unknown in Germany. Heine described with great precision the transition from a press based on politically motivated publication of ideas to commercial exploitation of the free-press system. Until 1848 the German press was considered essentially a forum for deliberation, utilizing capitalistic modes of production and distribution only insofar as needed to fulfill its purpose of shaping public opinion; in France, however, Heine was confronted with a newspaper system that had been dominated since the mid-1830s by capitalistic profit concerns. As a result, freedom of opinion became linked to the profit interests of entrepreneurs who invested their money in a newspaper. Heine notes: "The French daily press is to a certain extent an oligarchy rather than a democracy, for the founding of a French journal involves so many expenses and difficulties that only persons in a position to wager the largest sums are capable of establishing a journal" (5:281). This circumstance was brought about largely by two interlocking factors: the bourgeois form of political domination and the economic laws of the literary market.

Politically the structure of the French press was determined by the efforts of the government to control or suppress the publications of both the extreme Right and Left. To avoid a conflict with the Constitution, the authorities used the strategy of imposing such prohibitive fines for alleged misuse of the freedom of the press that the economically weak newspapers of the Republicans or extreme Monarchists were often driven out of business. Only publishers with solid capital resources could afford to pay the fines levied. But these publishers, as a result of their economic interests, were generally friendlier toward the political system than toward the Legitimists or radical Democrats. Another effective means of controlling the establishment of oppositional newspapers was the institution of a security deposit: the editor had to register his newspaper with the authorities and at the same time, to guarantee his political loyalty, had to deposit a considerable sum as security.[4] The system exploited the weakness of its enemies. Their inability to amass sufficient capital is characteristic of the way the middle class dominates. Freedom of opinion remains a privilege of the capitalist bourgeoisie. Heine describes the results: "In this way, forced to acquiesce to the existing parties or the government, the journals fall into a restrictive dependence, and ... into an exclusivity in their communications which makes the strictures of German censorship seem like a rose garland" (5:281).

Heine had good reason, especially after 1835, to fear the intrusion of German censorship, which was anything but harmless. The "friendliness" of German censorship, in comparison to the immanent restrictions of the French press, lay in its directness and obviousness—the journalist submits to political pressure but does not have to accommodate the profit interests of a publisher who, in order to stay in business, must increase his circle of subscribers. He can do this only, as Heine notes, by placing

[4]Cf. Collins, *The Government,* pp. 73 ff.

himself at the disposal of a political interest group, or (which Heine does not mention) by printing popular literature in the feuilleton. In 1836 the introduction of the serialized feuilleton novel raised the number of readers dramatically, and the papers that resisted this trend were soon relegated to insignificance.[5] Heine had to explain to his German readers that the long-demanded freedom of the press in France was being threatened by the very social class that had institutionalized it. And he rightly underscored the idea that the new restrictions were manifested not so much through external force as through economic pressures.

Using the press as an example, Heine described a fundamental alteration of the public sphere in France. He noted the transition from its early liberal self-image as *opinion publique,* politically legitimated by its dispute with absolutism, to a peak bourgeois phase in which the previously eliminated private economic interests intrude into the public sphere, shaping it to the benefit of these interests. He hinted at, but did not elaborate on, the utilization of the public sphere as an instrument of class domination. Heine left no doubt that the French bourgeoisie had cleared away the last remnants of the *ancien régime* and had seized control for itself. In *Lutetia* there are frequent allusions to this dominance in the references to François Guizot, the minister and parliamentarian: "Guizot never wanted anything but the rule of the middle classes, which he believed to be suited, by virtue of their education and wealth, to represent and guide

[5]The "littérature industrielle," as Charles Sainte-Beuve called it, first arose from the needs of the newspaper publishers who sought to widen the circulation of their publications. Emile de Girardin led the way with his newspaper *La Presse* (which was friendly to the government) by printing a serialization of Balzac's novel *La Vieille Fille* in 1836. The expansion of the market through the acquisition of new readers permitted a new calculation—in place of the usual yearly subscription rate of eighty francs, Girardin charged only forty. At the same time he caught the attention of the business world, which naturally preferred to advertise in newspapers with a large readership. *Le Siècle* immediately followed suit, as did the *Journal des Débats,* and, later, *Le Constitutionnel,* which had resisted the commercial trend until 1844 and thus had fallen to 3600 subscribers. Under its new editor, Louis Véron, circulation quickly rose to 25,000 upon the publication of Eugène Sue's novel *Le Juif errant.* See Albert J. George, *The Development of French Romanticism* (Syracuse, 1955), pp. 59–66, as well as Arnold Hauser, *The Social History of Art,* trans. Stanley Godman (London, 1951), 2:725ff. On the altered situation of the writer, see Nora Atkinson, *Eugène Sue et le roman-feuilleton* (Paris, 1929).

the business of state" (5:336). Heine concludes: "His real business is the maintenance of that regiment of the bourgeoisie that is equally threatened by the marauding stragglers of the past and by the plundering avant-garde of the future" (5:367). Heine thus assumed as part of his task in Paris the description of the forms and consequences of this domination.

If one compares Heine's later pronouncements on France's political and social system to his articles as a correspondent in the early 1830s (*Französische Zustände*), particularly those which were not incorporated into the book version (5:128 ff.), one notices how much more cautious, moderate, even positive his comments of the 1840s were. This could leave the impression (and indeed has done so) that Heine recanted his advanced position, that he avoided polemical invectives, perhaps because of his financial dependence on the French government or because of the editorial policies of the *Allgemeine Zeitung*. This comes close to a charge of depoliticization. Such a charge is unfounded. Moderation of form should be regarded rather as an indication of an increased politicization. In the 1840s Heine could for the most part shed his polemical tone; he was able to formulate his criticism in a manner that was to some extent conciliatory, because he had learned in the meantime to distinguish between foreground events and structurally significant processes. Although in 1832 Guizot and Casimir Périer, as ministers of Louis-Philippe, were still objects of Heine's ridicule, in the 1840s he treated ministers, as well as the king, more leniently. The earlier reports contained direct statements of Heine's disappointment with the representatives of the new class; for the most part his criticism was directed toward specific individuals. As a result, his assessments tended to waver.[6] These swings of the pendulum ceased when Heine recognized the structure of the system, its possibilities and its limitations, and began to judge its representatives from that viewpoint. Part of this recognition was the essential insight that the French bourgeoisie, which had assumed

---

[6]Whereas Heine reported, for example, on February 12, 1832 (5:134–136), that Périer revealed his worst side in the Parliament—that is, as a petty and narrow-minded politician, he treated him on February 24 (5:137) as a dignified representative of bourgeois rule. On his evaluation of Louis-Philippe, cf. Jeffrey L. Sammons, *Heinrich Heine: The Elusive Poet* (New Haven and London, 1969), pp. 220–247.

dominance in 1830, represented not merely an extension of the Third Estate from the *ancien régime* but something qualitatively new. The form of social criticism developed in Heine's early work, emphasizing the philistine elements of the German middle class,[7] was no longer applicable to the circumstances in France. Although occasional observations can be found which point to the tradition of criticism of philistinism (merchant and shopkeeper stereotypes, for example), the reports for the *Allgemeine Zeitung* (1840-1843) indicate that Heine was fully conscious of the distinction. The critique of philistinism was based on the difference between the educated elite and the lower middle class. Yet it was not the petite bourgeoisie which took hold in France, but the financier bourgeoisie (represented in Heine's reports by James Rothschild) and to a lesser degree the industrial bourgeoisie.[8] It would no doubt be a mistake to attribute to Heine intimate knowledge of French economic history, but he was able to find the important points at which the juncture of infrastructure and superstructure was visible. Heine's principal insight was that the political form of the constitutional monarchy, in the final analysis, served to ensure the private property of the ruling levels of society, and that the radicalization of the Revolution thus could not be welcomed by the leading figures of the business world. He notes: "And they truly do not want a republic, these noble knights of wealth, these barons of industry, these chosen ones of property, these enthusiasts for peaceful ownership who comprise the majority in the French Parliament. Even the King does not harbor such a deep fear of the Republic as they" (5:248).

Heine's articles did not, however, develop such a critique in a systematic fashion. To accommodate the form of the feuilleton—which was further restricted by the editors of the *Allgemeine Zeitung* with an eye on the political censor—[9]Heine had to blend his analysis of the essential social and political con-

---

[7]Günter Oesterle, *Integration und Konflikt: Die Prosa Heinrich Heines im Kontext oppositioneller Literatur der Restaurationsepoche* (Stuttgart, 1972), pp. 18-22.

[8]Cf. Hauser, *The Social History of Art*, 2:720-725.

[9]It is interesting to note the letter of February 27, 1840, from the editor Gustav Kolb to Heine, urging him to suppress the political aspects and concentrate on art and literature; cf. Michael Mann, *Heinrich Heines Musikkritiken* (Hamburg, 1971), p. 29.

texts into reports on the cultural scene, with a sprinkling of anecdotes, personal portraits, society notes, and so on. The political commentary is kept unobtrusive by making it practically invisible. The elegant and witty presentation served to divert attention from the seriousness of the material discussed in order to assure circulation. Judgmental statements about the French bourgeoisie are found as scattered remarks which the reader must then piece together into a composite picture. Heine depicted the new system as the reign of money. This implies a deep-seated change in cultural and moral values. Whereas feudalism assessed the status of a person according to his or her birth and the Napoleonic Empire placed primary emphasis on military glory, the July Monarchy was the first to legitimate money (capital) in its pure form: "The citizen-king Louis-Philippe ascended, he, the representative of the money which now rules but is at the same time attacked in public opinion by the vanquished party of the past and the deluded party of the future" (5:505–6).

Such sentences function as signals; they contain, in condensed form, Heine's political position. That Legitimists and Republicans come to identical conclusions in their critique of the capitalist bourgeoisie indicates for Heine that neither party has correctly perceived the historical significance of the reign of money and that both parties have remained locked into an abstract negation which keeps them from achieving fundamental revisions of society. When the middle-class Republicans criticized the connection between economic power and political domination from a moral perspective, they removed the issue to an abstract level, away from their own underlying material interests. They thereby lost sight of the background of their own political goals. Heine predicted, with good reason, that in their seizure of power (bourgeois revolution), radical middle-class Republicans would become dependent on that same dominance of money which they so bitterly reviled in the representatives of the system (5:460). Heine's realistic view of the material basis of the new class, his recognition of guiding economic forces (to the extent that they were visible to him), prevented a lapse into abstract moralistic criticism which, as he correctly perceived, would have to remain politically ambivalent. Compared to the *ancien régime,* and to the Empire as well, the rule of the upper bourgeoisie represented an important step forward—as Heine repeatedly emphasized.[10] When he occasionally ridiculed the penurious bourgeois and his potential for resistance (5:333), his remarks were grounded in a Romantic critique of philistinism. More important, however, are the passages in which Heine attempts to explain to his German readers the dynamics of middle-class society. He illustrates these changes by emphasizing innovative technology as the most visible expression of the new forces of production:

> The opening of the two new railroads, one leading to Orleans, the other to Rouen, is causing a sensation felt here by anyone not confined to a socially isolated closet. The entire population of Paris is forming at this moment a chain, as it were, in which the people are transmitting an electrical shock to one another. While the great masses stand staring, numbed and awed, at the external appearance of the great forces of motion, the thinking person is seized by a frightful shudder of the kind we always feel when the most monstrous, most unheard-of things happen, whose results cannot be calculated or predicted. [5:448–49]

It is worth noting that Heine did not reduce this restructuring of conditions of production to the technological realm, but related it to the capitalistic mode of economics. The revised essay in *Lutetia* is clearer in this respect than the original newspaper article.[11] Whereas the latter centered on the negotiations between Rothschild and the French Parliament, thus using once again the device of personalizing abstract relations, in *Lutetia* Heine supplements his report with a general consideration of the operating methods of the stock corporations formed for the purpose of constructing the railroads. He draws attention to the relationship between the financier bourgeoisie and representatives of the old elite—members of the nobility and high government officials—who joined the boards of directors of these corporations. The culmination of this witty analysis points to the altered power relationships: "The rudder that will one day fall into [the hands of the money aristocracy], or in part has already done so,

---

[10]Very pronounced in the first book of the memorial to Börne (4:29).

[11]Reprinted in Heine, *Zeitungsberichte über Musik und Malerei,* ed. Michael Mann (Frankfurt am Main, 1964), pp. 150–159.

belongs to a completely different vehicle—it is the rudder of state, which the ruling aristocracy of wealth is controlling more and more each day. Those people will soon comprise the *comité de surveillance* not only of the railroad industry but also of our entire bourgeois society" (5:450). The new class made use of the old elite; in the final analysis it even restructured the political institution of its foes—the monarchy served to protect the interests of the bourgeoisie.

To make this change more comprehensible, Heine chose, in contrast to the Republicans, the position of the cynic. By maintaining a foundation of factuality, his reports, which seem to be exclusively factual, underscore the enormity of the events taking place behind the scenes. The purely political reportage, of which Karl Gutzkow, for example, was also a master,[12] does not do justice to this dimension. Heine's publicistic and literary achievement consists of restructuring the function of aspects of the feuilleton—the portrait, the anecdote, the description of milieu—so that the structural processes shine through. Rothschild became his model of bourgeois domination. Unlike Börne,[13] Heine did not pursue the path of moralistic accusations; his portrait of the banker is rather amicable, though richly laced with ironic overtones: "Herr von Rothschild is therefore the hero of the day, and he plays such a large role in our current *misère* that I shall have to speak of him often, and as seriously as possible" (5:451).

The accompanying description is anything but serious, although the theme is serious indeed. In characterizing Rothschild as a man who knows the top people in every profession and every field and befriends them all, Heine points to the venality of all the skills offered on the market. Artists are no exception. The power of capitalist financiers stretches even further (as Heine illustrates through Rothschild's collection of busts) to the highest levels of political life. The crowned heads are his debtors. Austria is not alone in becoming dependent on Rothschild to supply its monetary needs. Heine shocked his German readers, who were still accustomed to sacral and monarchical authority,

---

[12]Karl Gutzkow, *Briefe aus Paris* (Leipzig, 1842).
[13]See Heine's critique of Börne (4:28).

by comparing the Rothschild banking agency to the royal court and the holy of holies in the temple:

> I am most fond of visiting him in the offices of his agency, where I can observe as a philosopher how not only God's chosen people but all other peoples as well bow and scrape before him. . . . Even before entering his chamber, many are seized by a shudder of reverence like that felt by Moses on the Horeb when he realized he was standing on holy ground. . . . That private chamber is indeed a remarkable place, one which arouses sublime thoughts like those we feel when we gaze on the mighty ocean or the starry heavens—we see there how small is man, how great is God! For money is the god of our time and Rothschild is its prophet. [5:355]

This blasphemous commentary, which must have shocked the audience of that age far more than the readers of today, is directed not so much against Rothschild personally or even against the diminution of traditional religious values; it criticizes more the attempt to impart a ritual dignity to the abstract workings of capitalism. Heine is well aware that his protest must not fail to address the current stage of social conditions. A personal attack on Rothschild would be senseless, since he represents only the power of a financier's capital. Heine's critique of the July Monarchy begins at the point where the social contradictions can no longer be explained through bourgeois-liberal theory; in other words, where the real antagonisms can no longer be overcome through the ideas of 1789.

Critical observers agreed that the July Monarchy in France was a labile system. The feeling was widespread that the revolutionary epoch had not ended, that the process begun in 1830 would have more radical results. In the *Briefe über die französische Bühne* (Letters on the French Stage), 1837, Heine, too, articulated this mood of foreboding: "Perhaps France is nearing a horrible catastrophe. Those who begin a revolution usually become its victims" (3:306). Later, in his introduction to *Lutetia*, he claimed to have predicted the end of the July Monarchy. He was able to refer to statements like the following:

> I repeat, I am filled with an unspeakable sadness when I see the people dancing during Carnival, where the wild *Mummenschanz*

excites demonic passions to a monstrous level. I felt a kind of horror when I visited one of those colorful night festivals now presented in the Opéra Comique, where, by the way, the revelry is far more lavish than at the balls at the Grand Opera. Here Beelzebub plays with full orchestra, and the daring hellfire of the gas lamps tears one's eyes out. [5:395]

The dance on the volcano evokes with sufficient clarity the social and political unrest seething beneath the surface of a glittering cultural life. These are antagonisms which no longer fit into the familiar scheme of the political struggle between feudalism and bourgeois control. Not long afterward, Heine spoke of the actual conflicts, which were not solely political but also social, in contrast to the oppositions within the bourgeois sphere which are resolved *in camera* and essentially merely stabilize the system: "Communism is the secret name of the fearsome antagonist who pits the rule of the proletariat in all its consequences against the current reign of the bourgeoisie. It will be a frightful duel" (5:405). In place of parliamentary debate comes class struggle. For Heine in the 1840s, however, this also marked the point of orientation from which the rise and rule of the bourgeoisie could be evaluated.

Heine's writings in *Lutetia* concerning Communism usually refer not to Marxism but to Babouvism, the early French socialism that was very active in the early 1840s as a secret movement.[14] Lorenz von Stein reported at nearly the same time on these first attempts by the proletariat to establish an alternative public sphere.[15] Whether Heine was thinking only of Philippe Buonarrotti and the group of Babouvists is of secondary importance in this context. More significant is his reference to the rising dynamism of the masses, to the formation of a politically conscious proletariat prepared to challenge the rule of the bourgeoisie. This altered Heine's perspective. In retrospect the liberal revolution of 1830 proved to be the emancipation of the upper bourgeoisie: "The bourgeoisie, not the people in general, began the revolution in 1789 and completed it in 1830. They are

[14]Leo Kreutzer, *Heine und der Kommunismus* (Göttingen, 1970), esp. p. 19.
[15]Lorenz von Stein, *Der Socialismus und Communismus des heutigen Frankreichs* (Leipzig, 1842); also his *Geschichte der sozialen Bewegung in Frankreich von 1789 bis auf unsere Tage* (reprint, Hildesheim, 1959).

the ones . . . who until now have held in check the insistent masses who demand not only equality of laws but equality of pleasures as well" (5:324). In the event of an invasion by a conservative foreign power, Heine feared (justifiedly so) the collapse of the labile system and predicted a social revolution. At another point Heine argued that a bourgeois republic could not survive in France because it was doomed to defeat in any struggle with its conservative neighbors (5:252). That explained the Legitimist position of the financial oligarchy, which felt protected by the monarchy.

Heine's reservations toward the Republicans, so evident in his memorial to Börne, among other places, were based on the insight that a mere change of political organization, given the persisting social conflicts, had lost its progressive character (5:251).

The differentiation between the bourgeoisie and the masses, which was steadily more apparent in France following the uprising in Lyon (1831), signified for Heine the transition to a new phase in which the fate of mankind is no longer identical to that of the victorious class. This does not mean that the positions reached by the bourgeoisie can be abandoned. Heine drew a clear line here between his view and that of the early socialists. They interpreted equality in a restrictive and mechanical way and their criticism of culture and society therefore failed to grasp the current state of forces of production. Marx and Engels, like Heine, rejected Babouvism as a movement that was, in effect, reactionary.[16]

Heine was appalled by the animosity toward art found in radical French early socialism. The reservations expressed in his introduction to *Lutetia* are well known: "In fact, I think only with fear and shuddering of the time when those dark iconoclasts will come to power—with their rough fists they will smash all the marble images of my beloved world of art, destroying all those fantasy-laden knickknacks so dear to the poet; they will chop down my laurel groves and plant potatoes there" (5:232).[17]

[16]Cf. Nigel Reeves, "Heine and the Young Marx," *Oxford German Studies*, 7 (1972-73), 44-97, esp. 83 ff.; also Kreutzer, *Heine und der Kommunismus*, pp. 28 ff. For Engels' critical position see "Fortschritte der Sozialreform auf dem Kontinent," in Marx and Engels, *Werke* (Berlin, 1958), 1:485.

[17]See also Heine's "Geständnisse" in Heine, *Sämtliche Werke*, ed. E. Elster (Leipzig, 1887-1890), 6:42.

The tone is ironic yet apologetic at the same time. In opposition to strict demands of utilitarianism, Heine offered an alternative in which art was not only without a purpose, but simultaneously (and this is not the same thing) was fruitless. Heine's literary work belied these false opposites, for its social function cannot be reduced to an affirmative utilitarianism. His defense overlooked precisely the critical value of the aesthetic object, which cannot be fitted seamlessly into society. The partial truth of these alleged opposites lies perhaps on the level of middle-class society, which developed from within itself the contradiction of the autonomy of art and the necessity of purpose—that is, marketability. Insofar as Heine, as a professional writer, was dependent on the literary market (and was also aware of this constraint), his work did take part in the contradiction between art's autonomy and its commodity form, and Heine placed himself on the side of autonomy in order to fend off the idea of marketability as an intrusion into his intentions. Seeing in the program of the French communists a continuation of these opposites, Heine reacted negatively to the restriction of artistic freedom and aligned himself with the idea of *l'art pour l'art*. Those who would conclude from quotations such as the one cited above that Heine ultimately sought a purely aesthetic mode of criticism[18] are ignoring the context in which Heine made such statements. They were balanced by others in which he stressed the critical and political function of art.[19] Such a documentation would supposedly reveal an inconsistency in Heine—he seems unable to decide whether he wants to be an artist or an agitator. The disadvantage of this procedure is that it generalizes Heine's own self-reflections as an artist and critic, formulated in concrete situations. When we use his remarks as abstract statements, we can indeed ascertain deviations and inconsistencies. He was not always successful in mediating contradictions grounded in objective circumstances. Historical evaluation of him must therefore

[18]Michael Mann reflects this tendency in the introduction to his valuable edition of the *Zeitungsberichte,* esp. pp. 17-18. This position is fully developed in Horst Krüger, "Die freie Kunst als ästhetisches Prinzip bei Heinrich Heine," dissertation, Würzburg, 1949.
[19]Cf. "Geschichte und Modernität: Heines Kritik an der Romantik," in my *Literaturkritik und Öffentlichkeit* (Munich, 1974), pp. 50-101; also Arnold Betz, *Ästhetik und Politik: Heinrich Heines Prosa* (Munich, 1971), pp. 68-81.

proceed beyond his own judgments and reconstruct the conditions from which they arose.

In situations where Heine was not personally involved, he was able to see much more clearly how an individual's freedom of expression is restricted in bourgeois society. This restriction is no longer accomplished merely through censorship, but also through the organization of the public sphere itself. Freedom of the press has a purely formal character: "Yes, as soon as one steps away from discussions of items of day-to-day interest, of 'relevant' concerns, as soon as one tries to develop ideas that are alien to the banal questions of political parties, as soon as one attempts to discuss merely the cause of humanity, the editors of today's journals reject such an article with ironic politeness" (5:282). Heine records here (without, to be sure, reducing it to its basic concept) a fundamental change in the structure of public opinion. The bourgeois public sphere took shape in the eighteenth century as the forum in which precisely these questions of humanity were to be discussed, questions about which the editors in Paris only smiled. Whereas the early liberal deliberation process presumed that a consensus could eventually be reached through the use of reason, Heine skeptically contended that such a consensus was, for the public sphere of the July Monarchy, not only unachievable but no longer even predicated as a goal of the debate. Public opinion had dissolved into fragmented cells, each of which claimed to represent truth and denied the opinions of others.

Heine was not alone in his complaint. Around the middle of the century, particularly in Western Europe, objections were frequently heard against that institution with which the bourgeoisie prepared and achieved its political emancipation. Alexis de Tocqueville tried to show, using the United States as an example, the potential dangers contained within a radical democracy controlled by public opinion. For Tocqueville as well as English liberals like John Stuart Mill and Matthew Arnold, the rule of public opinion came to represent a threat, since it allegedly restricted the freedom of the individual.[20] What was

[20]Jürgen Habermas, *Strukturwandel der Öffentlichkeit,* 2d ed. (Neuwied and Berlin, 1965), p. 148.

institutionalized as a means of liberation and self-assertion was characterized by Tocqueville as an instrument of mass rule which locks the·bourgeois individual into an abstract, ominous equality. The public opinion of the July Monarchy represented a threat because it no longer emanated exclusively from the educated public. The unspoken requirement for participation in public deliberation (which was not expressed in the model, of course) was the ownership of property; this was, after all, the element that first led private individuals to oppose the power of the state. When in the nineteenth century the unpropertied classes strove to enter the public sphere and gained a voice through the formation of political parties, their material interests forced their way into public discussion as definite social demands.[21] With the increasing possibility that universal accessibility to the public sphere, as provided in the model, might become a reality, the educated middle class (to which Heine belonged) felt its way of life threatened. Heine was honest enough to admit this fear without making concessions to a reactionary interpretation of the principle of the public sphere. "The conflicts which until now have been relegated to the private sphere are now forcing their way into the public sphere. Some groups have needs that cannot expect to be satisfied by a self-regulating market system; for these needs they tend to look toward regulation by the state. The public sphere, which must now mediate these demands, is becoming an arena of competition among interests using crude forms of forceful confrontation."[22] We need to emphasize here the connection, outlined by Habermas, between conflicts of interest and force. The classical public sphere sought to eliminate this confrontation by weakening the absolutist state from the inside, as it were, through the application of rationalist morality, in the hope of making this force eventually superfluous. The relationship between theory and praxis as envisioned in the classical model, wherein praxis is formulated through the consensus of the partners in discussion,

[21]Oskar Negt and Alexander Kluge, *Öffentlichkeit und Erfahrung: Zur Organisationsanalyse von bürgerlicher und proletarischer Öffentlichkeit* (Frankfurt am Main, 1972), pp. 106 ff.
[22]Habermas, *Strukturwandel*, p. 145.

is broken asunder. Art, too, was affected by this structural transformation, affected in its production as well as its reception,[23] for literature's anticipation of political discourse was restricted in the eighteenth century essentially to the educated public—that is, to the middle classes and the progressive elements of the nobility. This debate was carried on in the name of mankind but without the participation of the majority of the population, which could not meet even the basic requirement of literacy. The debate took place, apart from certain exceptions, under the banner of moral criticism, not practical politics.[24] The material interests of individual social groups could therefore not be voiced directly. Disregarding political and social praxis, the public discussion surrounding this literature considered itself to be free of interest and purpose.

Heine had already divorced himself from this model in his review of Menzel's literary history (1828) and did so again in the *Französische Maler* (French Painters, 1831) (3:72). Heine spoke of the end of the Classical-Romantic period of art and thereby the end of aesthetic autonomy. In place of the aesthetic foundation comes a political one. Heine's argument was historical but not yet sociohistorical; the change in the function of art in the early 1830s was derived in his view from the altered sociophilosophical constellation: "A new belief imbues them [the young writers] with a passion of which the writers of earlier periods had no idea. It is the belief in progress, a belief that sprang from knowledge" (3:468).[25] Later on, Heine occasionally distanced himself from this direct literary activism; he was enraged by the rhetorical, tendentious poetry of the 1840s.[26] There is no reason to view this skepticism as a form of backsliding. In view of the Parisian art trade as Heine observed it, the radical form of activist literature as proposed by the Young Germans proved to be a self-

---

[23]Cf. my essay "Literary Criticism and the Public Sphere," in this volume; also my essay "Literaturkritik im Zeitalter der Massenkommunikation," in *Literaturkritik*, pp. 128–150.

[24]For a recent examination, see Jochen Schulte-Sasse, *Literarische Struktur und historisch-sozialer Kontext* (Paderborn, 1975).

[25]Cf. A. Betz, *Ästhetik und Politik*, pp. 50 ff., and Wolfgang Kuttenkeuler, *Heinrich Heine: Theorie und Kritik der Literatur* (Stuttgart, 1972), pp. 79 ff.

[26]For example, Caput III of "Atta Troll" (4:501–502).

deception which Heine could no longer share. The literary activism of the Young Germans overlooked the social institutionalization of art; it was founded on the principle of the public sphere, but it failed to take into consideration the alteration of this public sphere.[27] The Revolution of 1789, to be sure, continued to be, for Heine as well, a historical turning point wherein the "happiness of nations" (3:570) became the order of the day. But its continuation in the Revolution of 1830 was revealed as an occupation by a class that was no longer willing to support the emancipatory function of art. In Paris, Heine underwent a learning process, visible in his articles as a correspondent. In the July Monarchy, under the conditions of a fragmented and defensive bourgeois public sphere, the connection between art and politics became one of art and industry.

In the *Salon* of 1840 Heine withdrew his earlier prognosis that a new age of art would begin with and through revolution. "One might almost conclude," he observed, "that the renewed flowering of the visual arts has ended; it was no new springtime [as Heine had hoped], but merely an Indian summer. Soon after the July Revolution came a joyous surge in painting, sculpture, even architecture; but the upswing originated only from the outside, and after the forced flight there followed a most lamentable crash" (5:356).

He had a ready explanation for this failure of the visual arts, an explanation obviously indebted to Hegel's aesthetics. The slide was related to the spiritualization of mankind, which in the final result could benefit only music. Once more Heine followed a concept from the history of ideas, namely that historical progress had forced art into a marginal position: "Music is perhaps the final word of art, just as death is the final word of life" (5:357). This explanation remains unsatisfactory, since music is no less vulnerable to commercialization than the other arts. And Heine's sarcastic remarks on the Parisian concert business of the 1840s leave no doubt that he is aware of these negative changes in music. In *Lutetia*, Article 33, he writes, "The number of concert performers this season was legion, with no lack of mediocre pianists to be praised as miracles in public leaflets. Most of them

[27]Concerning the situation in Germany, see Oesterle, *Integration und Konflikt*, pp. 47–53.

are young people who themselves promote these laudatory remarks in the press. Such self-deifications, these so-called advertisements, provide most delightful reading" (5:359).

In his attempt to establish the critical function of art, Heine was unable to avoid the conclusion that conditions for knowledgeable audience reception had not become more favorable. The triumph of bourgeois society had manifested itself in art as industry, to which both aesthetic and political demands must succumb. The harmony between author, publisher, and public, which was still possible under early bourgeois conditions of production because all three "needed the market to pursue or articulate their social interests and goals in the face of feudalism,"[28] had already been shattered in the July Monarchy. Heine did not express the moralistic outrage so common among contemporary critics (Alphonse Du Valconseil, Gustave Planche, Alfred-François Nettement, and Charles Sainte-Beuve).[29] He reacted with irony or cynicism. His criticism simulated an agreement with the "accomplishments" of bourgeois art. Using Grand Opera as an example, he noted as early as 1837 the transformation from a public that understood art to one that merely consumed it. As director, Louis Véron made visiting the opera attractive by negating the aesthetic demands of the music. Heine writes: "He convinced himself that most people . . . attend the opera out of convenience and only enjoy themselves when lovely decorations, costumes, and dances hold their attention to such an extent that they completely ignore the damned music." As Michael Mann points out, the public switched from serious to comic opera: "The glutted public sought light entertainment in rapid sequences; and what went in one ear went out the other."[30]

The historical background of this remark involves a change in the composition of the public, a change difficult to reconstruct in detail. In Paris the disintegration of the educated public was

[28]Lutz Winckler, *Kulturwarenproduktion: Aufsätze zur Literatur- und Sprachsoziologie* (Frankfurt am Main, 1973), p. 52.
[29]For the reaction of French criticism, see George, *French Romanticism,* pp. 153–164. In an 1837 article in the journal *Artiste,* Gustave Planche polemicized vehemently against the state of literary criticism. He saw only narrow-minded or indifferent critics, no aesthetic impartiality. Cf. George, p. 156.
[30]Heine, *Zeitungsberichte,* pp. 95, 234; also Mann's *Musikkritiken,* p. 58, which points out that criticism of grand opera was widespread (Gutzkow, Liszt, Wagner).

already taking place, whereas in Germany this did not occur until after the founding of the Reich in 1871.[31] The quantitative difference can be grasped by examining the feuilleton novel. Sales were suddenly achieved which could come about only by reaching groups of new, inexperienced readers.[32] "Analysis of these groups clearly revealed to watchful authors that the literary level of their audience had declined tremendously, principally because it had expanded so greatly. More people could read than ever, but they lacked the habit of literature."[33]

Heine's observations reflected this change. His mockery of the new public presumed an educated audience that went to the opera not for mere diversion, but for aesthetic edification. This was the public to which Heine turned, provoking it with the report that the closed, educated world in which it lived in Germany, secured by a still predominately class-oriented society, was coming to an ignominious end under the reign of the new bourgeoisie. On the other side, the emigration of the artistic elite was becoming evident: "The fine aristocracy, this elite characterized by rank, education, birth, fashion, and leisure, fled to the Italian opera, this musical oasis where the great nightingales of art still warble and the springs of melody still ripple magically...."[34] Heine sympathized with this aesthetic elite but nonetheless emphasized the ultimately anachronistic nature of the separation by aligning it with the nobility as a dying class. The July Revolution had caused him to wonder whether political events had made the pure enjoyment of art impossible: "There is almost a Goethean egotism involved in achieving an untroubled enjoyment of art here, and I feel at this moment how difficult it is to engage in art criticism" (3:71). The balance shifted after the consolidation of the constitutional monarchy; compared to the bourgeois public's search for diversion, the posture of aesthetic reception seemed once more the superior one.

Art criticism under the conditions of the bourgeois art market

[31]Levin L. Schücking, *Soziologie der literarischen Geschmacksbildung,* 3d ed. (Bern and Munich, 1961), pp. 40 ff.

[32]The number of newspaper subscribers in France rose from ca. 70,000 in 1836 to ca. 200,000 in 1846. Cf. Hauser, *The Social History of Art,* 2:725.

[33]George, *French Romanticism,* p. 38.

[34]Heine, *Zeitungsberichte,* p. 98.

posed new tasks that were difficult even for Heine. The degree of difficulty is reflected in his inability to develop a consistent position which could overcome the various oppositions. His diverging positions refer again and again to the objective causes; his vacillations reflect the fundamental social origins of the crisis within art criticism. But unlike most of the critics of his day, he saw where the causes were to be found. He described cultural life as a market where creative talents had to sell themselves. He used the Opéra Comique to illuminate the connection between public taste, literary form, and marketing. Scribe appears as the man who, through his librettos, gives public taste its due: "I do not wish to suggest here a base greed, but only a realism that never loses itself in the romanticism of an infertile phantasmagoria, holding tight rather to the earthly reality of the rational marriage, the industrial bourgeoisie, and the *tantième.*"[35] Scribe produced for the market, adjusting form and content as needed. Actual consumption was the determining factor of the mode of production and thus of the product itself, which in its own right conditioned the attitude of its audience. Heine clarified certain aspects of this dialectical relationship. On the occasion of the art exhibit of 1843, for example, he sought to establish a relationship between the style of the pictures exhibited and the epoch. In order to determine the "temporal signature" (3:480), he attempted to find in the theme or in the manner of presentation the characteristics of the era. According to Heine, the bucolic motifs of a Watteau or a Boucher reflect the *ancien régime,* while the paintings of David and his school embody the spirit of the First Republic and the Empire. In the same sense, Heine argues that the "spirit of the bourgeoisie, of industrialism, which now permeates the entire social life of France" (5:481), would be similarly reflected in painting. This direct linkage works best where it attempts to capture in its style an essential characteristic of the era, as for instance the Revolution in the paintings of David: "We see here a forced enthusiasm for the marble model, an abstract, chilly cult of reason, the drawing correct, strict, harsh, the colors drab, hard, indigestible— Spartan soup" (5:480).

Heine's intention of reading the social traits of the 1840s into

[35]Ibid., p. 174.

the subjects of contemporary paintings shows a biting wit, but it was short-sighted: "The faces in the historical paintings, supposedly portraying heathen and medieval figures, are likewise reminiscent of pawn shops, stock market speculations, mercantilism, philistinism" (5:481). Such a statement can still be appreciated as an *aperçu* insofar as it points out a real discrepancy, but it is inadequate in terms of critical method, for the coordination of artistic style with economic base remains unmediated. This was Heine's difficulty—the general insight into the social conditioning of art production and reception did not yield specific criteria for an appropriate depiction of their relationship.

The change in reception, conditioned by the transformation of the public sphere, had become apparent; equally evident was a change in the position of the artist. The freedom won in the eighteenth century was precarious. Working for an anonymous market disrupted relationships with patrons and made writers more dependent on their publishers, who had to adapt their own economic calculations to the market situation: "During the Restoration and the July Monarchy the *littérateurs* lose the unique position they had occupied in the eighteenth century; they are no longer either the protectors or the teachers of their readers; they are, on the contrary, their unwilling, constantly revolting, but nonetheless very useful servants."[36] Even Heine could not easily escape this dichotomy of rebellion and subservience. For the writer—the German writer, that is—there was still no other audience than the bourgeois audience.[37] Heine discovered the lower levels of society as an important historical factor, but as readers they could as yet play no role for him.[38] His writing presumed a literary fluency that was not yet achievable by the broad public. Furthermore, Heine was, as a writer, dependent upon his publisher, who turned the manuscript into a book, thus creating an exchange value in the marketplace. The publisher might wish to stand up for his own author personally,

[36]Hauser, *The Social History of Art*, 2:718.
[37]For the French situation see Jean-Paul Sartre, *What Is Literature?* trans. Bernard Frechtman (New York, 1965), pp. 103–121. Cf. George, *French Romanticism*, pp. 38–45, who already presumes a proletarian public.
[38]Oesterle, *Integration und Konflikt*, pp. 62–63. For a more positive view, see Kuttenkeuler, *Heinrich Heine*, p. 131, n. 92.

but being subject to the general capitalistic conditions of production, he could not objectively divorce himself from the needs of the public as they are articulated through the market. The author's interest in his work's use-value cannot alter his primary dependence on its exchange value. "The twofold function of the market—as a field of cultural force and a place of commodity exchange where the surplus value achieved in production is realized—creates a decidedly contradictory dynamic."[39]

Heine also experienced this contradiction in his dealings with his publisher, Julius Campe. Their friendly association was unable to prevent deep-seated conflicts of interest, which for their own part may have had a negative effect on the personal relationship. Between Heine's concept of a politically critical literature and the ideas of the liberal publisher there could only be a compromise, no longer a complete agreement.[40] Campe realized that since Heine's polemic against the poet August von Platen, whom he had denounced as a homosexual, Heine had alienated himself from his German audience and had miscalculated the market conditions for his books: "Heine's circulation in the book market, however, shrank precisely in proportion to the way he articulated or disregarded the transitory character of the liberal-bourgeois social constitution, as well as the way he described an educational upheaval of material and moral aspects of life as a necessary precondition for a social revolution."[41] Heine had to learn that direct rebellion, verbal protest against the conditions imposed by German censorship and the literary market, was not conducive to establishing his own program,[42] that only a tactical adaptation to current conditions and a subversive utilization of them could overcome these difficulties. In 1836–37, as Briegleb notes, he began "to recognize how the consciousness

[39]Winckler, *Kulturwarenproduktion*, p. 45.

[40]See, for example, Heine's open letter to Julius Campe of 3 April 1839 (5:71–83), in which Heine attacks the mutilation of his texts by the publisher and his advisers. Campe pursued a conciliatory policy toward the government censors, one which protected the interests of his firm. Cf. the extensive commentary in Heine, *Sämtliche Schriften*, 5:688 ff.

[41]Klaus Briegleb, "Schriftstellernöte und literarische Produktivität," in *Neue Ansichten einer künftigen Germanistik*, ed. Jürgen Kolbe (Munich, 1973), p. 139.

[42]For example, Heine's letter of 28 January 1836 to the *Hohe Bundesversammlung* (5:20–21).

industry determines the form of entertainment, and utilized this insight in a dialectical learning situation."[43] To put it differently: the critical message is to be communicated through a manner of presentation which does not allow its basic intention of education and criticism to be openly recognized, but preserves instead the appearance of pure entertainment.

This strategy, forced on Heine by the prevailing circumstances, must, of course, be taken into account in an analysis of his own art criticism. He, too, had to use tactics of concealment when attacking censorship and commercialization. In order to reach the reader at all, the real meaning could be uttered only as a witty aside.[44] As a result, it is difficult to draw the line between tactical adaptation to the categories familiar to the public and the limitations of Heine's conceptual self-elucidation. Since Heine had to take into consideration the censor as well as the receptivity of his audience, the text in its final, published form risked the appearance of affirmation. Not coincidentally, his acknowledgment of the autonomy of art and his renunciation of literary-political activism are found in the *Briefe über die französische Bühne* of 1837, in which he repeatedly intimated that he dared not express his political thoughts freely without conflicting with German censorship, thus jeopardizing his economic existence: "Yes, dearest friend, I harbor a true timidity in regard to politics, and I skirt every political thought like a rabid dog" (3:291). This statement and similar signals, which always appear whenever Heine approaches a political theme, cast a revealing light on his affirmation of aesthetic autonomy. One can hardly accept this open statement unproblematically as the message of the author. We should examine very closely the context in which this oft-quoted statement appears.

"As you know," explained Heine, "I am for the autonomy of art; it should not serve as a handmaiden either for religion or for politics—it contains its own final purpose, like the world itself"

---

[43]Ibid., p. 146.

[44]"A writer who is political in every regard must make many bitter concessions to raw necessity, because of the cause for which he is fighting. . . . It is far more intelligent for us to control our enthusiasm and to speak in a sober if not a veiled fashion in a newspaper that might well be called a 'Newspaper of the World,' instructing hundreds of thousands of readers in all nations" (5:289).

(3:317). The presumed consensus ("As you know") implies at first glance tactical considerations, since Heine in his *Romantische Schule* (Romantic School) (3:468) and in *Zur Geschichte der Religion und Philosophie in Deutschland* (On the History of Religion and Philosophy in Germany) (3:639) had called for a political basis for literature, which included the political commitment of writers. However, two factors indicate that Heine's affirmation of aesthetic autonomy was more than just a tactical measure designed to mollify the censor. In the sixth letter, from which the quotation is taken, Heine wrote among other things about the controversial position of Victor Hugo in French literature. On this occasion Heine defended the Frenchman against the charge of being politically and socially indifferent. "Victor Hugo [must] hear the improper complaint that he feels no enthusiasm for ideals, that he has no moral base, that he is a cold-hearted egotist, and so on" (3:317).[45] Like Hugo, Heine himself encountered such reproach when Ludwig Börne and the German republicans labeled him indifferent and immoral. His defense of Hugo is therefore a self-defense as well. Significantly, the name of Goethe surfaces in this context—Heine regularly mentioned him when discussing aesthetic autonomy. Here Goethe is called on as the principal witness for the defense of pure art, a role that had already been assigned to him in the *Romantische Schule*. In the introduction to that work, Goethe had been linked to the abdicating "aristocratic literature," which was to be followed by a democratic one. The positive recourse to Goethe in the *Briefe* indicates that Heine's hopes for a politically based aesthetics, which he still supported as late as 1835, had been shaken. Neither can it be overlooked that in this context Heine distanced himself from Saint-Simonism, speaking conspicuously of the "erroneous demands of the new church" (3:317). This might suggest that Heine's earlier program was being, if not recanted, at least modified considerably.

We shall have to assume that Heine altered his aesthetic posi-

---

[45]Later, Heine severely criticized Hugo's *Les Burgraves*. In his article of 20 March 1840 he called it "versified sauerkraut" and an "indigestible concoction" (Heine, *Zeitungsberichte*, p. 141).

tion[46] and regrouped his previous theorems.[47] The change was not so much in Heine's concepts as in their evaluation and their use within the context of his argumentation. Whereas he had previously equated aesthetic autonomy with political conservatism, a new polarity was established in the *Briefe über die französische Bühne*—an autonomous art, responsible for itself, was set up against a functional art appropriated by certain groups or institutions. The democratization of art, postulated under the influence of the July Revolution, now took on a different appearance. For Heine the realization of a populist art took the form of a shallow popularity. Hugo's competitor is Dumas, of whom Heine wrote: "He speaks to the heart from the heart, and is understood and applauded. His head is an inn where good thoughts sometimes enter but never stay longer than a night; very often it is vacant" (3:319).

Heine demonstrated in Dumas' populism the transition to a clever but unscrupulous manipulation of the literary heritage, culminating not in enlightenment but in cheap effects. Still more important in this regard is the case of Meyerbeer. In the *Briefe*, Meyerbeer still represented the synthesis of democratic artistic intentions and aesthetic autonomy. The ninth letter insisted,

> Meyerbeer, whom the princes of this earth have showered with every possible honor, and who is so captivated by these distinctions, nevertheless had a heart in his breast which glows for the most sacred interests of humanity, and he openly confesses his adoration of the heroes of the Revolution. . . . His convictions, however, are not actually political and even less religious. Meyerbeer's real religion is the religion of Mozart, Gluck, Beethoven—it is music. He believes only in this, only in this belief does he find bliss, living with a conviction that is similar to the convictions of earlier centuries in depth, passion, and endurance. [3:341]

These emphatic statements, which again contain a personal ele-

---

[46]In this sense see also Kuttenkeuler, *Heine*, pp. 103 ff. Willfried Maier, in his *Leben, Tat und Reflexion: Untersuchungen zu Heinrich Heines Ästhetik* (Bonn, 1969), considers this change to be a transition from a politically engaged aesthetics to the principle of the autonomy of art. Cf. Heine, *Briefe*, ed. Friedrich Hirth (Mainz, 1950-51), 2:278.

[47]One should read in this sense also the defense of art against politics in the memorial to Börne (4:66-67); also Betz, *Ästhetik und Politik*, pp. 139-140.

ment, claim simultaneously for the composer both aesthetic autonomy and political engagement. Heine's formulation can only be understood as saying that a political function is incorporated into the religion of art attributed to Meyerbeer. The belief in art is manifested in works that have political implications. "It is fortunate for [Meyerbeer] that most Nordic authorities have no understanding of music, else they would see in the *Hugenotten* more than merely a struggle between Protestants and Catholics" (3:341).

Heine perceived this hidden political stance in more than the text; he went a step further and read Meyerbeer's music, especially its style of composition, as a political provocation. The comparison of Meyerbeer and Gioacchino Rossini in the ninth letter underscored the difference between melody and harmony:

> Rossini's music is characterized . . . by the preeminence of melody, which is always the immediate expression of an isolated sensibility. With Meyerbeer, on the other hand, we find the dominance of harmony. In the stream of harmonic masses, melodies fade away, even drown, just as the particular sensations of the individual human being are submerged in the collective feelings of an entire race; our soul gladly plunges into these harmonic streams when it is seized by the miseries and joys of all of mankind and takes sides in the great questions of society. [3:335]

This is obviously a description of democratic art; more precisely, Meyerbeer's operas are interpreted as democratic art: "He is the man of his time, and time, which always knows how to choose its people, has tumultuously lifted him onto its shield, proclaiming his leadership and making a triumphant entry with him" (3:336). But even this resonant praise is not without its irony, for even then, in 1837, doubts had begun to arise, as Heine's next sentences reveal: "It is not, however, a comfortable position to be carried in triumph in such a fashion—the misfortune or clumsiness of a single shield-bearer can lead to a serious wobbling, if not to outright harm . . . and the heavy burden of a laurel wreath can certainly cause one to break out in a fearful sweat" (3:336).

This raised doubts about Meyerbeer's reception, though not yet about his intentions. Later, however, Heine showed stronger reservations in regard to those intentions and thus also in regard to his music. Among the notes left behind by Heine after his death is this remark from 1847: "Meyerbeer is the musical *maître de plaisir* of the aristocracy." Another one reads: "Eclecticism in music was introduced by Meyerbeer."[48] Between these two dates lies Heine's politically motivated defection from Meyerbeer. In April of 1841 Heine still addressed the composer as the regent of German music and imputed to him a cosmopolitan mission,[49] but in 1843 undertones of animosity are evident.[50] By 1847 he no longer kept his disappointment secret. Meyerbeer's concern for his own fame turned into a manipulation of his success, thus proving him to be in another sense a "child of his time": "No matter how much we would prefer to keep silent, we must nevertheless confess at last that Meyerbeer's fame, this both artificial and costly machine, has come somewhat to a standstill. Has some pin or screw come loose in its complex working? A true, unselfish enthusiasm never reigned here for the great maestro, who knew nothing more than to entertain his public" (5:166). The popular composer was exposed as an entertainer who knew precisely how to calculate his effects. In the *Musikalische Saison von 1844* (Musical Season of 1844), written in 1847, Heine clearly ranks Meyerbeer below the "aristocratic" artist Rossini, whom he had labeled ten years earlier a representative of the Restoration.[51]

One result of Heine's turnabout in the 1840s was that he reex-

[48]Elster, ed., *Sämtliche Werke*, 7:428. According to Michael Mann these statements date from 1847 (*Musikkritiken*, p. 63, n. 83).

[49]"There is a deep significance in this utterance [the affinity between Meyerbeer and Goethe], and it leads me to think that German music may have been assigned a mission here in France, to act as a prelude or overture in preparing an understanding of our German literature" (Mann, *Musikkritiken*, p. 122). These statements are deleted in *Lutetia* and replaced by the satiric paragraphs on Meyerbeer's manipulation of his own fame (5:363–364).

[50]Mann, *Muskkritiken*, pp. 149–150.

[51]Rossini's bust in the *académie royale* was as revolting to Meyerbeer as the triumphal arch of Titus was to the Jews in ancient Rome—a mark of defeat (5:545). Heine had, it is true, withdrawn more and more from Romantic music since 1840. But his rejection of Meyerbeer, along with his critique of Liszt and Berlioz, do not derive simply from that, as indicated by his very critical discussion of Mendelssohn-Bartholdy, whom Heine considered to be more of a Classicist. Regarding his symphonic music, Heine wrote, "It is genuinely beautiful," and deserved therefore "the recognition of all persons who truly understand art" (5:529). Nevertheless, Heine unmistakably distanced himself from Mendelssohn, stating that he lacked not form and style but passion and truthfulness.

amined central concepts of Classical-Romantic aesthetics and applied them differently.[52] However, strange as it may first appear, this did not represent a break with the intent of the *Romantische Schule* and *Zur Geschichte der Religion und Philosophie in Deutschland;* his views reemerge in an even more sharpened form in the fragmentary *Briefe über Deutschland* (Letters on Germany) of 1844. Although Heine since 1837 had emphasized more strongly the autonomy of art, he did not mean to support an immanent aesthetics in the sense of Romantic art criticism. He used autonomy as part of an altered strategy that had its own social and historical basis. The self-satisfaction of art became the wall Heine erected against the cultural enterprise of bourgeois society. Thus in his later reviews and commentaries he came closer to a moral line of argument which resurrected the Classical-Romantic approach to criticism of trivial literature. As early as 1831, in a review of Ferdinand von Hiller's compositions, Heine differentiated between artistic truthfulness and an ingenious lie: "Such an attribute [manly truthfulness] is becoming rare nowadays, and even the product of genius is spoiled for us by the damned nuisance of the lie" (*Zeitungsberichte*, p. 77). This concept of untruthfulness, later employed primarily against the new forms of the culture industry, was conveyed aesthetically through the idea of an organic development of the work of art, which is clearly indebted to the Age of Goethe (and could hardly be applied to Heine's own work). In this sense Heine criticized in the eighth letter of his *Briefe über die französische Bühne* Joseph Bouchardy's *Gaspardo,* accusing it of lacking a natural development and progression of action (3:328). And he referred sarcastically to Michel-Nikolas Rougemont's *La Duchesse de la Vaubalière* as "a weak concoction, full of action, which is, however, not developed in a surprisingly bold or natural way, but is brought about laboriously, as the result of fussy calculations, just as passion too must feign its glow, being lethargic and cold inside" (3:327). He applied the same principles in his final judgment of Meyerbeer, whose "operas [are] not

---

[52]At the same time a change can be discerned in French literary criticism. Romanticism took on Classicistic features. The aesthetics of German Classicism was introduced to France by Jean Cousin. Cf. Hauser, *The Social History of Art,* 2:731–732. In the 1840s Heine took a more favorable view of Cousin than in the preceding decades.

so much organically composed as atomistically combined" (5:166–67). Heine's objection to the false synthesis of art and entertainment was formulated with the aid of an aesthetic theory that had originated in a different historical context and which could not possibly be applied to Heine's own production. Heine's works did not by any means grow organically—they were carefully composed, as their author repeatedly emphasized.[53] The aesthetics modeled on organic growth in Heine's late art criticism functioned primarily as social criticism.[54] It permitted Heine to articulate his misgivings toward the art market. What was expressed abstractly through such concepts as "truthfulness" and "lies" could be made more tangible in the particular work of art through the concept of the organism, although this theory was still incapable of explaining the historical reasons for the change.

Heine did not conclude from his emphatic affirmation of artistic autonomy that art criticism should therefore take an intrinsic approach. To that extent a gap existed between the postulate and the methodology. Yet this seeming lack of methodological consistency allowed Heine to pursue questions that organic aesthetics left unanswered. Heine's methodology examined, whether explicitly or implicitly, various economic, social, and political factors. It was historical, but it did not try to establish a historiography of literature, which would have isolated its subject from contemporary circumstances. Heine's goal was the dialectic of present and past, which holds that on the one hand, the past actively affects the present, while, on the other hand, our understanding of the past is determined by the present. Heine did not deny his subjectivity, but neither was it absorbed by the expression of his personal taste. The distinction becomes evident when individual taste conflicts with historical evaluation, as is sometimes the case with his music criticism. Unlike Sainte-Beuve or Matthew Arnold, Heine was not a professional critic who dealt exclusively with literature. He did not share the deep concern for literary tradition which so distressed Sainte-Beuve and Arnold in the face of social and cultural upheavals. He did

[53]See Heine's letter to Campe, 12 August 1852 (*Briefe,* 3:398–406).
[54]In contrast to Maier, *Leben, Tat und Reflexion,* pp. 221–226, who attributes to Heine an aesthetic theology of art.

not call for the preservation of values and standards; his procedure is critical in the sense that Hegel's philosophy of history is. The work and the artist are ultimately accountable to the forum of history—not to the past (tradition), but to a less repressive future. Heine did not abandon this position even when anticipation of the future seemed to cast art in general into doubt. He refused to rescue art by reconciling the conflict between his political ideas and his artistic anxieties (as a bourgeois writer). The subjectivity emphasized by him, the "constant assertion of my personality" (4:128), hinders in criticism the harmonious symmetry that historicism loves so well. To that extent, composition and style are not merely incidental in Heine's art criticism; the actual message is first manifested in the manner of writing. Any removal of individual excerpts (as "key statements," so to speak) from the context of an article or essay creates the danger of misunderstanding them, since Heine's use of language is strongly related to the semantic context.

Just as Heine's narrative prose cannot be grasped through the categories of Classical aesthetics (symmetry of the art work)[55]—as his contemporaries fully realized—neither can the intent of his criticism be derived from the Classical-Romantic theory of art, although he did utilize its theories. If one views the theory of art developed under Romanticism as the sole standard, one can see Heine's work only as a decline: the dominance of the feuilleton, which blurs the distinction between the realm of art and that of mundane reality. Not only does such a position fail to do justice to Heine's own ambitions; more importantly, it deals inadequately with the historical situation of art criticism. The insight that the reality of art may be unique but is not isolated was manifested in Heine's work in the very composition of his art critiques. Along with the new concept of literature came a new foundation of criticism. Its procedure can best be demonstrated through the use of examples. Heine's manner of working can be analyzed through a comparison to Sainte-Beuve, who exemplifies the professional critic.

---

[55]Wolfgang Preisendanz, "Der Funktionsübergang von Dichtung und Publizistik," in his *Heinrich Heine: Werkstrukturen und Epochenbezüge* (Munich, 1973), pp. 21–68; also in *Die nicht mehr schönen Künste*, ed. Hans Robert Jauss, *Poetik und Hermeneutik*, 3 (Munich, 1968), pp. 343–74.

Sainte-Beuve contributed regularly to newspapers. From 1849 to 1869 he chronicled French literary life. His *Causerie du lundi,* in which he discussed current and past literature, appeared weekly. The concept of literature should be understood here in its broadest sense. As René Wellek emphasized with mild reproach,[56] Sainte-Beuve by no means restricted himself to *belles lettres;* he was equally interested in philosophical and religious tracts, in literary academies, and in biographical and social circumstances. Sainte-Beuve's knowledge of Greek and Roman as well as French literature was extensive. This familiarity with tradition was incorporated into his evaluation of contemporary literature. He embodied par excellence the liberal critic, steeped in historical knowledge, who attempts to understand both author and work from the context of their own era. Though he never developed his own theory of art, his individual writings of the later, post-Romantic phase exhibit, despite their individualities, a high degree of consistency of methodology and manner of presentation. Whether dealing with an author or a single work, he attempted to construct a finished literary portrait. His *Causeries* of January 2 and 9, 1854, for instance, deal with Stendhal. It is of only secondary importance that these articles belong to the notorious misjudgments that have lowered his status as a critic in French literary history. His lack of understanding of Stendhal's novels demonstrates rather the limitations of a critical procedure in which tradition is more important than literary innovation.

In Stendhal's case, Sainte-Beuve distinguished immediately between the critic (including *causeur* and socialite) and the novelist. Although he could appreciate the former, he had serious reservations about the latter. His presentation followed the customary pattern—Henri Beyle's concept of art traced from biographical and historical background material. The stations of his life were cited, their relationship to the history of the Empire examined. Stendhal's point of view appeared as the result of a sensibility conditioned by his generation, a sensibility that developed under the Empire and found its application in the Restoration era. According to Sainte-Beuve, Stendhal was distin-

[56]Wellek, *The Age of Transition,* Vol. 3 of *A History of Modern Criticism: 1750– 1950* (New Haven, 1965), p. 37.

guished by the breadth of his vision and the richness of his historical experience, in contrast to the ideological narrowness of the Restoration years. The value of his oppositional standpoint was conceded by Sainte-Beuve. Nevertheless, the distance of the critic from his subject cannot be overlooked. Sainte-Beuve was well aware that he was writing in a different era, namely that of the Second Empire. The distinction entered dogmatically into his criticism: "Ce rôle [Stendhal's] a perdu beaucoup de son prix aujourd'hui. En littérature comme en politique, on est généralement redevenu prudent et sage; c'est qu'on a eu beaucoup de mécomptes."[57] Precisely this political conservatism was then reflected in his literary evaluation of Stendhal's novels; he denied them his approval (as was also the case with the novels of Henri Balzac) because they did not conform to the literary canon which for Sainte-Beuve still prevailed in 1854. Stendhal's main fault was that he disturbed one's sense of order and moderation. Sainte-Beuve expected a closed world of art with rationally oriented characters; he found instead a loosely constructed plot, unlifelike characters, and falsely drawn social circumstances. The critic's judgment was apodictic in this case; the tolerant historical methodology disagreed with its subject, for this subject did not support the concept of literary history which lay at the base of Sainte-Beuve's viewpoint. Sainte-Beuve achieved results (though not necessarily insights) when he could empathize with the author and the work, when a harmony existed between his own sensibility and that of the author. This historical tolerance was converted into rejection when he failed to find the presupposed concept of literature in the work. In such instances Sainte-Beuve's methodology is exposed as an impressionistic dogmatism. In his 1850 essay "Qu'est-ce qu'un classique?" Sainte-Beuve attempted to justify his historical method aesthetically by establishing a canon of exemplary authors.[58] This canon is broad, not classicistic in the French sense; it includes Dante, Ariosto, Shakespeare, and Milton, but these authors are removed from the historical process through the classicism attributed to them. The great authors of the past serve the critic as authorities by which to view and judge newer works.

---

[57] *Causeries du lundi*, 3d ed. (Paris, 1869), 9:315.
[58] *Causeries*, 21 October 1850, 3:38–57.

The concept of literature presumed here is, in the final analysis, conservative, since it insists on an immutable structure of the literary work. This attitude is reflected in the presentation. It conforms to the same laws Sainte-Beuve expected in a work of art—order, moderation, common sense, symmetry. Sainte-Beuve was striving toward a closed concept into which the critic is fully integrated. This position remained an unreflected one; he may have thought about this relationship between the critic and the object of criticism, but the process was not incorporated into the methodology. To be sure, Sainte-Beuve's goal as a critic was not scientific objectivity in the sense of the emerging positivism of Hippolyte Taine, but the self-sufficiency of the material presented. He assumed that literature could not be separated from other human actions and forms of expression; accordingly, he demanded that it be embedded in biographical, cultural, and social conditions. Nevertheless, this methodology should not be equated with a positivistic analysis of factors. Sainte-Beuve's attempt at an integration of cultural history stands nearer to Leopold von Ranke than to Taine. Empathy was still the most important hermeneutic instrument. Analysis "a son genre d'émotion aussi,"[59] demanding eloquence and poetic quality. The Romantic background of such statements is unmistakable.

Heine and Sainte-Beuve were very close in their literary origins. Using the ideal of truthfulness, both made the author responsible for the work. From this stemmed their common interest in biography and history. In its theoretical self-examination this interest pointed, however, in opposite directions. Heine's historical position becomes apparent when seen before the background of Sainte-Beuve's concept of criticism. The common prejudices against Heine's art criticism were based on the model represented by Sainte-Beuve. Heine and Sainte-Beuve wrote quite consciously for contemporary newspaper audiences; both authors understood the special demands of the feuilleton and avoided scholarly treatises. Sainte-Beuve adapted to these expectations by converting scholarly language to small talk. The result

[59] *Nouveaux lundis,* 22 July 1862 (Paris, 1892), 3:24.

was a successful compromise. Heine recognized the contradiction between the form of the feuilleton and his own intentions. He could not remove the contradiction, but he managed to profit from it—he enlisted the feuilleton form to serve the interests of enlightenment. This can be demonstrated in a concrete example.

Article 37 of *Lutetia* (11 December 1841) is one of Heine's best-known essays and is often cited by Heine scholars.[60] Most frequently quoted are his remarks on the rising influence of the Communists, thus purporting to document his attitude toward Marxism. But the reference to the menacing power of the proletariat is merely one element, albeit a significant one, in the context of the essay. We also find there talk of Christmas shopping, of the labile political situation under Guizot's administration, of exhibitions that reflected an increased interest in the Renaissance, and finally an extensive report on the painting "The Fishermen" by the French artist Louis-Léopold Robert, whose death was being mourned by the Parisian public. Such a number of topics in a single essay which in a modern book edition fills no more than seven pages (5:373–380) leads one to expect a potpourri. A theme is touched upon and immediately dropped. Yet this appearance of superficiality is deceptive. One would of course look in vain for a completed presentation in the style of Sainte-Beuve's *Causeries;* the careful composition, which is never conspicuous, first becomes visible in an analysis of details. A depiction of loitering in the French capital provides the initial perspective. The reporter takes on the role of a loiterer—interested in the action, but distanced from it. His leisure distinguishes him from the masses. Meanwhile, the heterogeneous themes are bound together not only through the role of the observer but also through the technique of composition. Heine begins with the displays of Christmas wares in order to move to the tense social situation, which could spawn political unrest. The third paragraph contains a sketch of the French workers' movement and its propaganda. The fourth paragraph returns, then, with a rather forced leap, to the theme of the exhibits:

[60]For a recent study see Preisendanz, *Heine,* p. 86, with reference to the structural aspect.

"But let us leave this dismal theme and return to the cheerful objects displayed behind the shop windows along the Rue Vivienne or the boulevards" (5:375).

The previously established contrast between joy and misery is immediately reasserted. The fifth paragraph pursues indirectly the theme of product displays by describing Paris' fashionable interest in the Renaissance—a renaissance of the Renaissance, whose character Heine portrays very ambivalently. In these fashionable handicrafts "lies such a sweet, melancholy wit, such an ironic kiss of reconciliation . . . an elegant shudder that overcomes us so strangely, we know not how" (5:376). The implied opposition of the wealth of the few and the poverty of the masses, of pleasure and destruction, is expressed in fashion, which is no more trustworthy than the society from which it emerged.

The subject of discussion changes in the next paragraphs, but the basic theme is merely modified. The contrast between wealth and misery, or life and death, is manifested both in the paintings and in the life of the artist Robert. Again Heine defines the contrast as a "signature of the time": "Yes, just as the reapers of this master are a work of joy . . . his fishermen reflect all the suicidal thoughts encamped in his soul" (5:377). The description of this picture, like most of Heine's pictorial descriptions, seems unsatisfying to a contemporary art historian, accustomed to working with good reproductions. Here, as in other instances, Heine invents a plot in order to illuminate the content for the reader. Yet he is also well aware of the mode of presentation. The formal aspect is brought indirectly into the discussion. In paragraphs six and seven the discussion of why Robert took his life seems to hover near the level of social gossip. Heine is obviously not interested in empirical truth; his answer is speculative. It relates the suicide to Robert's insufficient talent: "No matter how respectable, how splendid Robert's achievements were, they were still no doubt only pale shadows of the flowering beauties of nature which floated before his soul, and a trained eye would easily discern a tedious struggle with the material, which he controlled only through the most desperate effort. These paintings by Robert are all beautiful and solid, but most of them are not free, there is no immediacy of spirit in them—they are composed" (5:378). The closing paragraph continues the thought: "The fishermen . . . are too composed, the figures are tediously constructed and juxtaposed; they inconvenience one another more than they complement one another, and only the color balances the varying elements of the original portrait and lends the painting an appearance of unity" (5:379).

The apparent fragmentation, the leap from one topic to another, disguises the consistency with which Heine pursues his theme. He achieved a totality not through philosophical argument but through careful composition—by means of series, contrasts, mirroring, associative linking. There are no smooth transitions; heterogeneous elements are juxtaposed in such a way that the reader must discover the connections. In Article 37 of *Lutetia* he signaled a potentially threatening situation in France. The illusion of prosperity concealed economic and social contradictions that could no longer be overcome by parliamentary maneuvers. The bourgeoisie, he insisted, was lulling itself with false security from which it would be aroused by the proletarian revolution. This assertion, presented not as a result but as a process, was doubly related to art criticism—the description of Robert's painting underscored the social criticism of the message, and its theme was poverty. Such a parallel structuring may seem crude, but it was not Heine's final word. He presented a more extensive context by describing Robert's death as the result of artistic inadequacy. The forced composition of Robert's paintings points to social contradictions. The connecting elements— the tension of the composition, the lack of organic unity, the culture industry, capitalist society—are not mentioned; it is left to the reader to make this connection. In other words, Heine's politically engaged aesthetics of the 1840s cannot be documented by individual formulations, which would not even yield a consistent pattern; it is evidenced rather by the web of references and cross-connections within the text. "The totality lies not in the quantitative factor but in the significance of everything being discussed . . . in and through the context of the political and social circumstances."[61]

The theory of art developed by Heine from 1837 onward might well be called "satiric aesthetics." This term is not based solely upon its eminently polemical character, a conspicuous aspect in Heine's dealings with artists and virtuosi. "Satiric" in a

---

[61]Ibid., p. 88.

broader sense is the manner in which he used negation to withdraw from the cultural acquiescence represented most elegantly by critics like Sainte-Beuve. Heine was no confident and reliable reporter whose judgments could be accepted uncritically by the reader. One should proceed with caution when Heine ascribes positive aesthetic value to a work, for the textual context tends to relativize such pronouncements. By working contrapuntally (opposing one formulation with another), Heine was able to avoid being bound dogmatically to a fixed theory, and ultimately avoided the affirmative stance that a critic like Sainte-Beuve, despite all his reservations toward his own era, could not elude. This avoidance of affirmation is the basis of the critical value of Heine's satiric aesthetics. Its negative aspect points to the circumstances under which it was formulated—the Industrial Revolution. Though Hegel's aesthetics could count on a contemplative observer of art (the educated upper middle-class), Heine, like Charles Baudelaire shortly thereafter, saw himself confronted by a situation in which the contemplative observer either had embraced entertainment or had withdrawn into an esoteric enjoyment of art. As Adorno noted on the historical situation of aesthetics: "After these two [Kant and Hegel] came the sensitive literati, lodged uncomfortably between the objects as postulated by Hegel and abstract concepts. They combined a culinary understanding of art with an inability to conceptualize."[62]

Heine renounced the practice of positive conceptualization, from which norms and criteria are ultimately derived. This should be viewed not as uncertainty but as recognition of an historical impossibility. The truth content of works of art could no longer be derived from the kind of positive principles which ultimately are revealed in the historical relativism of a Sainte-Beuve. Heine witnessed the destruction of the aura of the work of art. Works that appeared at first genuine even to him, such as Meyerbeer's operas, were exposed as fabrications. In the words of Adorno, Heine had to "convert . . . the declining categories into transitional ones, through a determinate negation."[63] On August 24, 1852, Heine wrote to Julius Campe concerning the

---

[62]Theodor W. Adorno, *Ästhetische Theorie*, Vol. 7 of *Gesammelte Schriften* (Frankfurt am Main, 1970), p. 497.

[63]Ibid., p. 507.

newspaper articles he later published as *Lutetia:* "The hero of my book, the true hero of it, is the social movement . . . and I could probably with some justification call my book a primer [for revolution]."[64] This remark encompasses art criticism as well; it, too, plays a role in an analysis of an era, because it recognizes social conflicts through aesthetic phenomena.

Wolfgang Preisendanz has pointed out Heine's proximity to Robert Prutz,[65] who in his *Geschichte des deutschen Journalismus* (History of German Journalism, 1845) clarified the publicistic tasks of his time. This parallel is worth pursuing further, for Prutz is one of the few critical observers of German literature who have dealt with the division between serious literature and popular literature. Prutz's historical merit is that he freed himself to a great extent from the moralistic prejudices of Classical-Romantic aesthetics, so that the real connection between the audience, market, and production of literature became visible. What is overlooked by the aesthetic-moralistic condemnation of popular literature, as Prutz rightly pointed out, is that the appropriation of high literature is bound to presumptions of education and social circumstances which eliminate the majority of the public from reception. Neither the illiterate masses nor the middle classes locked into professions have the leisure time necessary to become extensively acquainted with literary tradition. The reception of art, Prutz concluded, has become a speciality for which society engages critics and scholars. Closer examination indicates, to be sure, that Prutz was not really questioning the value of classical literature, but that he was attempting to assign a new value to the "entertainment literature" enjoyed by the mass public. His defense of trivial literature is ultimately more of an apology for it, using the concept of "modern education" as the central argument. This approach is partly critical and partly affirmational. Its critical value lies in its reservation concerning the moralistic condemnation of entertainment literature, which attributes to the general public responsibility for the inferiority of the product. The affirmational element (though not intentionally so) is the concept of entertainment, the negation of which still preserves the disparaged elitist values. In

---

[64]*Briefe,* 3:410.
[65]Preisendanz, *Heine,* pp. 92–93, 96–97.

an extension of Hegelian thinking, Prutz confirms in the modern age the split between "reflective" literature for the educated audience and "folk" literature, concluding that the "literature of the educated"[66] has subjugated popular literature. This occurs, as Prutz does not fail to note, at the cost of the masses: "Real education, like real property, is real ability restricted to the very few; in a world where everything is a matter of privilege, taste and sensitivity for beauty have become a privilege as well."[67]

The reigning aesthetic principles are designed for the literature of the educated. Modern literature is not so much the result of an organic development as the result of criticism. It is ultimately a literature "from literary people for literary people." To that Prutz adds the comment, "We have abandoned the masses; is it any wonder that they seek their entertainment elsewhere?"[68] This statement, though it accurately describes the situation, turns the causes upside down. The term "abandoned" suggests a lost former participation, while in fact it was not until the nineteenth century that the masses, as a result of expanding formal education, insisted on participation in the literary public sphere. The prognosis is no less idealistic than the attempted explanation, which explicitly suppresses material factors.[69] Prutz hoped for the rise of a new populist literature, read by the educated as well as the mass audience, combining both taste and entertainment. He called for the "artistically beautiful book." This reconciliation of polarities presumes of course, according to Prutz, that a new national and sociopolitical situation can be achieved ("The praxis of the life of all peoples is the state").[70] Since Prutz was nonetheless unable to provide any indication as to when and how such a reconciliation could take place, his

---

[66]Robert Prutz, "Über die Unterhaltungsliteratur, insbesondere der Deutschen," in his *Schriften zur Literatur und Politik*, ed. Bernd Hüppauf (Tübingen, 1973), p. 19.
[67]Ibid.
[68]Ibid., p. 22.
[69]Ibid., p. 20: "But it seems to be the more fitting and only truly historical view to assume that the spirit creates its external form from within itself, and that factual details enter in as demanded by the idea, rather than the reverse view, which attempts to derive the grandest turning points of history from a petty pragmatism of external circumstances."
[70]Ibid., p. 23.

demands remained unachievable, as he himself realized.[71] Some examples could be given for a future populist literature (Karl Leberecht Immermann, Willibald Alexis, Berthold Auerbach), but as soon as Prutz examined the relationship between literary theory and political praxis the results seemed hardly encouraging: "We have no public sphere, except for a literary one; we meet no great talents, except for poets who are scorned or critics who are out-critiqued by other critics; we have no parties except for journalistic ones, no literary innovations except for curios in book-fair catalogs.[72] Since Prutz's projection of a populist literature could not be realized without a political restructuring, one can assume, if one extrapolates from the quotations cited, that only a political revolution could create the new literature.

The revolution anticipated by Prutz and other German liberals was the revolt of the middle class. Heine had observed the results of such a revolution in Paris. Initial hopes for a rejuvenation of art proved illusory. Prutz continued to view the bourgeois public sphere as an instrument of emancipation even after Heine had recognized its disintegration. While Prutz was urging the dissolution of "educated" literature, Heine was harking back to the principle of autonomy as a defense against commercialization. From his advance observation post in Paris, Heine was no longer able to disregard "material factors" as secondary, as Prutz did. The art criticism of the late Heine included reflection on the conditions emerging with a fully developed bourgeois-capitalistic society. This distinguished it from its liberal and Young German counterparts, which were trying to divorce themselves from the educated elite of the Age of Goethe.[73] The segregation of this elite from the general public ultimately stemmed from the literary market as it was institutionalized in the late eighteenth century. But its ramifications were qualitatively different, for the upheavals of the market in Germany occurred in a society that was still essentially prebourgeois. Under increased pressure from the 1770s onward, this Neohumanistic elite merely withdrew to a greater degree and

[71]Cf. ibid., p. 33.
[72]Ibid., p. 23.
[73]Cf. my essay "Literarische und politische Öffentlichkeit: Die neue Kritik des Jungen Deutschland," in *Literaturkritik,* pp. 102–127.

battled "trivial" literature with moral weapons.[74] Heine moved closer to this kind of criticism in the late 1830s when it became apparent that the literary radicalism propagated by the Young Germans had lost its emancipatory function in a fully developed, capitalist-market system. Heine's praise of Chopin, inserted into the tenth letter of the *Briefe über die französische Bühne* as a counterbalance to Liszt's popularity as a virtuoso, illuminates this concept: "His fame is of an artistocratic sort, perfumed by the praise of good society; it is as elegant as his own person" (3:353). Heine relates this elegance (which is not feudalistic but rather a negation of bourgeois standards) to pure art: Chopin "is not merely a virtuoso [like Liszt] but a poet as well; he can make us see the poetry that lives in his soul . . . his true fatherland is the dream world of poetry" (3:353). Significantly, however, Heine associates this dream world with the past; it reminds him of the fairy-tale world of German Romanticism. When listening to Chopin's music (he claims), he envisions mermaids, sea gods, and moonlight. This, however, treats the purity and beauty of Chopin's music, no matter how highly celebrated, as belonging essentially to the past—it has nothing to do with the prose of everyday reality. This melancholy is strengthened later on by the animosity toward art shown by French communism, from which Heine expected nothing less than the abolition of art. In *Lutetia* there is no talk of the aesthetic renewal which Heine, under the influence of Saint-Simonism, had anticipated in the aftermath of the July Revolution. Since the 1840s he had expected a revolution that would reach far beyond a reorganization of the political system. Article 46 of *Lutetia* proclaims global revolution: "the great duel between the unpropertied masses and the aristocracy of wealth" (5:407). But he expected no solution to the question of art from this necessary social upheaval, for he defined the material interests of the new class so narrowly—in conjunction with early French socialist theory—that he saw no room for human emancipation. By linking the regeneration of art to the abolition of the represssive Christian-stoic morality, he (faced with the animosity toward art of early socialist theory) could conceive of a nonbourgeois, proletarian art only in negative

[74]Jochen Schulte-Sasse, *Die Kritik an der Trivialliteratur seit der Aufklärung* (Munich, 1971), pp. 63–129.

terms. His satiric theory of art demonstrates what is *no longer* possible because of the development of the social conditions of production.

In his evaluation of the historical development of society, Heine was guided by the idea of universal revolution, but art was excluded from this perspective. It was still inconceivable to him that the masses could be receptive to art, although since the 1830s there had been indications in France of an independent proletarian literature.[75] To that extent the art theory of the later Heine, as a critical one, remained dependent on the liberal public sphere which it was fighting. This boundary did not, however, limit Heine in his literary praxis, which was more advanced than his theory of art.[76] That is to say, the sociocritical accomplishment incorporated in *Lutetia* transcended the critical negativity of his later view of art. Heine was aware of that—his introduction reflects the contradiction between his status as a bourgeois intellectual and the interests of society as a whole.

[75]George, *French Romanticism,* pp. 95 ff.
[76]This tension between art and politics is smoothed over by Betz, *Ästhetik und Politik,* p. 154. Kuttenkeuler (*Heine,* pp. 104-105) emphasizes resignation and considers Heine's attempt to develop a historical poetics to be, in the final analysis, a failure. On the critical achievement of Heine and its limitation, see Oesterle, *Integration und Konflikt,* pp. 125 ff.

3 *The End of an Institution? The Debate over the Function of Literary Criticism in the 1960s*

Looking back at postwar German literature from the perspective of the 1970s, we begin to realize that the earlier years of this period have become historical. The literature of the late forties and the fifties appears to be somewhat remote, separated from us by the new tendencies of the following decade. Would this observation suggest that the 1960s were qualitatively different from the postwar era, that they perhaps comprised an epoch of their own? I believe that there is much to be said for this hypothesis in the field of literary criticism. To demonstrate this, I must include an analysis of the 1950s as a background, for the problems of literary criticism in the 1960's were largely determined by the answers held over from the previous decade. I want to clarify the immanent logic of this process, and to do so in connection with the extraliterary circumstances that contributed decisively to its direction and tempo. Of course, this can be done only in the form of short theses that circumscribe the important turning points. It is thus not my intention to unfold a historical panorama. This essay restricts itself further to the branch of literary criticism which in Germany is called, in a rather pejorative sense, *Tageskritik* (everyday criticism). The central issue, then, is the function assigned to contemporary book reviewing

Translated by Ronald L. Smith and Henry J. Schmidt.

in the sociocultural system. Extraliterary factors—the reading public, the communications system, the book market—must unavoidably come into play. We are inclined all too easily to underestimate the significance of these elements, since they do not appear in the theory of criticism. Hugh D. Duncan has explored this point very well: "In the kind of analysis undertaken here, it is very important to discover who is assigned the right to criticize; what institutions assume the guardianship of criticism; how these institutions defend their guardianship in competition with other institutions; how those who are to criticize are selected, trained, and supported; to whom the criticism may be communicated; and on what occasions criticism is required."[1]

This perspective draws our attention to certain aspects of literary criticism which usually go unnoticed because they appear self-evident. The specific quality of the literary debate in the 1960's was that these self-evident notions were called into question. Literary criticism entered a fundamental crisis that could no longer be solved by theoretical self-reflection. My first two theses will attempt to illuminate the background of this crisis. After that I will examine the attitude of the 1950s (thesis 3) and the methodological crisis that emerged from it in the early sixties (thesis 4). The fifth thesis investigates the causes of this crisis, and the sixth and final thesis deals with the New Left's critique of established literary criticism.

1. There is a broad gulf between the aesthetic views of the reading public and those of professional book reviewers. If one compares the selection of works discussed in the leading newspapers and magazines with the reading matter of the average citizen, one cannot avoid the conclusion that literary criticism writes past the general (and by no means merely the uneducated) public. These positions are so far apart that the concept of literature has a different meaning for each. Of the 31 million readers in West Germany, only a fraction is seen as a potential audience for literary reviews. Literary criticism lacks the support of a broad literary public. Technically, to be sure, the expansion of the mass media to a communications network that reaches

[1]Hugh D. Duncan, "Literature as a Social Institution," in his *Language and Literature in Society* (Chicago, 1953), p. 60.

nearly the entire population has afforded the critic a greater opportunity to be heard; nevertheless, as a result of the increased distance between them, the position of the critic vis-à-vis the public seems, in fact, to be weakened.

To examine this imbalance, we need at least a sketchy overview of the breadth and composition of the West German reading public.[2] The German book trade can count on a purchasing public of around ten million people, approximately 25 percent of the adult population, as regular customers. To a progressive expert on education, this figure might seem discouragingly low, but in the social history of reading it represents an explosive expansion of the public in comparison to the eighteenth and nineteenth centuries. The literary critic, as the ideal mediator between book production and the public, was supposed to perform an important social role as expert, adviser, and literary educator, with the aid of the modern media. Such statistics as those above, however, provide no clue to the specific reading interests of the broad public. Surveys of the kinds of books purchased and read reveal an essentially unfavorable picture of literary criticism's potential for influence, at least in regard to the present goals of criticism. For the majority of readers, their association with literature is just one leisure activity among others and, if the demographic information can be trusted, not a very important one at that. Of the readers questioned, 78 percent responded that within the

[2]Twenty-eight percent of the West German adult population own no books at all. This does not mean that the remaining 72 percent can be characterized as avid readers. The number sinks rapidly when one subtracts those who have no desire to purchase further books (5.6 million = 18 percent and those who read so rarely that they could no longer remember their last book (6.3 million). Among the remaining nineteen million book owners are 8.7 million who bought their last book more than three months before the poll. One cannot include these among the intensive readers of literature. Cf. *Buch und Leser in Deutschland: Eine Untersuchung des DIVO-Instituts,* ed. Maria-Rita Girardi, Lothar Karl Neffe, and Herbert Steiner (Gütersloh, 1965), p. 81. Similar results were found by Gerhard Schmidtchen, who distinguishes three groups of readers on the basis of their frequency of acquiring and reading books: 29 percent of the adult population read regularly; 39 percent read more seldom; 32 percent read very sporadically or not at all. Altogether, 47 percent of the population buy at least one book per year. Cf. Schmidtchen, "Strukturpolitik: Eine neue Strategie auf dem Buchmarkt," in *Das Buch zwischen Gestern und Morgen: Zeichen und Aspekte,* ed. Georg Ramseger and Werner Schoenicke (Stuttgart, 1969), pp. 198-218, esp. p. 204.

past four weeks they had read entertainment literature; on the other hand, only 6 percent had read works of classical literature in that time.[3] There are, to be sure, significant differences among various professions and social levels, but overall the interest in entertainment literature is far greater than the interest in artistic or "high" literature. If we take this 6 percent figure as an index of a genuine interest in literature, we can assume for ten million regular readers a half million readers of artistic literature. But in view of the small printings of even the most significant literary and cultural journals, this figure seems to exaggerate the size of the literary critic's audience. Using the printing figures for the leading West German cultural magazines, which altogether amount to no more than 50,000 copies, we can calculate (using a figure of 3.5)[4] approximately 150,000—170,000 people who read book reviews regularly. This represents still only a fourth of the people interested in literature. The form of presentation of literary criticism is tailored to this small circle, even when the reviews appear in media with a larger circulation. The investigations of Peter Glotz[5] have shown empirically that the review editors of the leading newspapers and magazines intuitively focus on this literarily informed circle of readers—if, that is, the editors pay any attention at all to what appeals to a readership. Here the intellectuals are among themselves—certainly not as a social caste but nevertheless as a relatively closed group with common interests that are reflected in their language, their mode of thinking, and their literary preferences.

Statements about the composition of the general reading public are extremely difficult to verify. Anyone dealing with this problem encounters two obstacles: the lack of reliable data and the tangle of contradictory interpretations. The literary public can certainly no longer be equated with the bourgeois public of the nineteenth century. In the first place, new groups of readers have emerged from the social substrata. Moreover, the structure

---

[3] *Buch und Leser in Deutschland,* p. 197. According to Rolf Fröner, *Das Buch in der Gegenwart* (Gütersloh, 1961), pp. 124-126, contemporary "high" literature can count on a readership of only 1 to 2 percent.

[4] Cf. Robert Escarpit, *Das Buch und der Leser* (Cologne, 1968), p. 101, n. 67.

[5] Peter Glotz, *Buchkritik in deutschen Zeitungen* (Hamburg, 1968), pp. 104 ff.

of the middle class itself has changed.[6] A further question: Has the "educated" public in fact disappeared, as has often been asserted, or has it continued to exist in an altered form, having lost its previous "representative" status? Emil Staiger, at least, seems to have reckoned with its existence when in a lecture of 1966[7] he provoked the literary intelligentsia with arguments reminiscent of the Wilhelmine bourgeois critique of Expressionism. The positive echo unleashed in certain circles by this moralizing phillipic[8] indicates that Staiger had made himself spokesman of a group of readers who no longer found themselves represented in institutionalized literary criticism. Appeal-

[6]In the nineteenth century the German literary public was composed of the elite, the service class, and the middle class. The lowest level played only a minor role, as Rudolf Schenda has recently demonstrated; cf. *Volk ohne Buch. Studien zur Sozialgeschichte der populären Lesestoffe 1770 bis 1910* (Frankfurt am Main, 1970), pp. 441 ff. This composition has undoubtedly changed. Though still underprivileged, the working class today represents a considerable segment of the readership, especially in book clubs. The proportion of the service class has probably remained relatively steady, while that of the old middle class has presumably dwindled somewhat. This social group has never fully recovered from the economic crisis of the 1920s and 1930s. The defensive mentality observed by Theodor Geiger, *Die soziale Schichtung des deutschen Volkes* (Stuttgart, 1932), may have lessened somewhat as a result of the socioeconomic restoration after 1945, without disappearing entirely. Ralf Dahrendorf noted that the old middle class "is not daring but fearful, not expansive but defensive, not freedom-loving but protectionistic, not an element of progress but a retarding force": *Gesellschaft und Demokratie in Deutschland* (Munich, 1965), p. 109. This mentality does not encourage an interest in experimental or controversial literature. Such a defensive attitude demands a security of ideology and taste which is best guaranteed by old and pseudo-old principles. The new middle class, however, is of great importance for the expansion of book consumption. This group demonstrates a middle-class mentality but does not assume the corresponding economic and social position. Empirical evidence concerning the reading habits of this class is unfortunately sparse, since the statistics of publishing research are ordered according to conventional professional groupings, thus blurring the socially relevant distinctions. The pretension of belonging to the middle class could cause the orientation toward bourgeois ideology of education to be more pronounced here than in the working class. Owning books and being knowledgeable about literature are viewed as symbols of social prestige.

[7]Emil Staiger, "Literatur und Öffentlichkeit," *Neue Zürcher Zeitung*, 20 December 1966; reprinted in *Sprache im technischen Zeitalter*, no. 22 (1967), pp. 90–97.

[8]See H.R.S., "Ein Wort zur Zeit," *TIP*, Basel, 10 January 1967; "Der Nihilismus ein Luxusartikel," *Genossenschaft*, 4 February 1967; Hans Habe, "Sturm im Wasserglas," *Schweizer Illustrierte*, 6 February 1967; Hans Einbichler, "Zu einer Rede Emil Staigers," *Dolomiten*, 26 January 1967. All are reprinted in the special edition: "Der Zürcher Literaturstreit: Eine Dokumentation," *Sprache im technischen Zeitalter*, no. 22 (1967).

ing specifically to the classical literary heritage of Germany, Staiger articulated the resentment of a group that had lost contact with the process of formal and thematic innovation. It thus could no longer take part in discussions of advanced literature, but nevertheless considered itself the guardian of true aesthetic and moral values. Staiger's plea for a "pure" literature was directed not toward the masses but toward the educated group that was familiar with the canonized authors of German literature. The controversy that arose from Staiger's lecture made the cleft between the broad reading public and the literary intelligentsia more visible. But the line of division runs differently than the critics of mass culture ordinarily assume. This public is well aware of its separation from the semiliterate masses who read *Bild-Zeitung* or the *National Enquirer*. It presumable agrees with the complaints about the corrupting effect of mass culture, for it believes itself to be a protector of the literary tradition.

The controversy was historically outdated, but it was characteristic of the position of the West German and Swiss reading public. The educated public, with its ideology, seems to have maintained itself here more strongly than the theory of mass culture would indicate. The institutional weakness of German literary criticism is based in part on the loss of its mandate from this category of readers, which by no means can be dismissed simply as a "mass."

The membership of book clubs (around five million persons altogether) provides an approximation of the social structure of the current reading public and its tastes, since around 80 percent of the fiction produced reaches its readers through these book clubs.[9] Maria-Rita Girardi, Lothar Karl Neffe, and Herbert Steiner summarize the findings of the DIVO Institute as follows: "The chances of finding book club members are greatest among white collar workers who are not in top management, as well as lower and middle officials and skilled laborers."[10] Members with a ninth-grade education are most common (60 percent). This discovery seems to confirm the theory of those who see in these

---

[9]Cf. Arno Hochhuth, "Mobilisierung der Geistes," in *Wohin? Fragen, Widersprüche, Wege: Gedanken über eine Demokratische Zukunft der Bundesrepublik* (Berlin, 1966), p. 291.

[10]*Buch und Leser in Deutschland*, p.100.

book-club readers a new audience that had previously been unable to obtain books, which would suggest that one is dealing here with a separate group of readers, clearly distinct from the educated bourgeoisie. I believe, however, that this assumption is incorrect, for it fails to consider that in the book clubs the upper levels of income and education are overrepresented. At least 30 percent of their members have a high school certificate (*Mittlere Reife*) and more than 10 percent have completed college preparatory school or attended an institute of higher learning.[11] On the basis of these data, one could hypothesize that the book clubs represent a substantial part of the educated public. Thus their offerings can be seen to a certain degree as an index to the interests of their readers. The catalogues of the book clubs offer by no means only ephemeral works, as their critics have rather hastily claimed, but rather a characteristic blend of entertaining and educational selections. Alongside entertainment literature one finds titles of canonized "high" literature, even individual works of modern literature.[12]

The public's access to literature is not exclusively facilitated psychologically by the offering of inferior works, as Habermas assumes;[13] rather, the difficulty posed by any outstanding literary text is also avoided through a reliance on familiar works. These have become so entrenched by previous assimilation that the original difficulty of the innovative structure is less strongly felt. During the 1960s the literary intelligentsia made artistic innovation their decisive criterion of excellence, but this aspect plays only a minor role in the selections of the book clubs. Their promotional magazines emphasize the entertainment or instructional value of the works offered in their "reviews." Habermas is

---

[11]Cf. Wolfgang Langenbucher, *Der aktuelle Unterhaltungsroman* (Bonn, 1964), p. 273. The following statistics are given for the "Deutsche Buchgemeinschaft" for 1960: *Volksschule* (elementary school), 39 percent; *Mittlere Reife* (high school), 33 percent; *Abitur* (college preparatory program), 17 percent; university education, 11 percent.

[12]These titles were included in the offerings of the "Bertelsmann Lesering" in 1966: Grass, *Die Blechtrommel (The Tin Drum)* (1959); Andersch, *Die Rote (The Redhead)* (1960); Böll, *Ansichten eines Clowns (The Clown)* (1963). Other approved authors of "high" literature are Werner Bergengruen, Ina Seidel, and Manfred Hausmann.

[13]Habermas, *Strukturwandel der Öffentlichkeit* (Neuwied and Berlin, 1965), p. 182.

therefore correct in asserting: "The book clubs remove the bulk of artistic literature from classification and criticism."[14] To put it another way: The literature that is actually read is not the literature that is discussed, and the demands of criticism stand unrelated to the reading needs of the public. The public's interests are left to fend for themselves and are thus surrendered to the manipulations of the book industry.

2. The methods and economy of modern book production have forced the institution of literary criticism into a marginal position. The publishing business, concerned with rapid sales and a high return on investment, no longer relies on the impact of literary reviews and discussions. The publishers' planning must center on making their product marketable, regardless of the literary quality of the text. In the prearranged distribution process, reviews are of merely secondary concern. As a result of the immanent laws of the book market, literary production withdraws farther and farther from the influence of criticism.

In the West German book market, the 1960s revealed an acceleration of a process that had begun in the fifties and continued in the seventies—the transition from a multitude of small and medium-sized publishing houses to only a few dominant publishing giants. This process of consolidation featured publishing mergers, the sale of smaller enterprises to larger publishing concerns, and the intertwining of the book industry with other branches of the media industry. This process brings about a concentration of mass production in the hands of a small number of large businesses. [15] As a result of this shift to forms of operation that had long since been established in other branches

---

[14]Ibid., p. 184.

[15]As early as 1967, 5.2 percent of the publishing firms had market control of 53 percent of the total book production. Sixteen firms (one percent) had sales of over 25 million German marks (DM) each; 50 percent on the other hand had sales of under DM 250,000 each. Cf. Heidi Dürr, "Der Verlag auf dem Weg zum Grossunternehmen?" in *Das Buch zwischen Gestern und Morgen,* pp. 181–197. The author shows that in 1967 the majority of publishing houses were small businesses with a yearly production of only a few titles and sales of less than DM 250,000. The figures provided speak more for the tendency toward market domination by major publishers than against it, since these small firms will as a rule be unable, because of lack of capital, to risk large printings and thus can contribute only a small percentage to the mass of book production. Dürr also forecasts that in accordance with the immanent pressures of the book market, the best chances for survival will rest with the large publishers, which have a

of industry, production methods and printing quantities lost their connection to the particular quality of the product. Maximum return on capital could be achieved only through rationally planned and closely calculated mass production. This meant that publishers' offerings, production procedures, and determination of sizes of printings had to be divorced from traditional conceptions of the special status of the book as a unique commodity. This tendency was recognizable even at the end of the fifties. Hans Magnus Enzensberger wrote then: "The typical large publishing house is a thoroughly rational enterprise of the industrial type. Its goal is a very large, constant volume of production that utilizes the full capacity of the plant. The invested capital must be rapidly amortized."[16]

In 1958 that was perhaps still atypical of the West German publishing industry. In the meantime, however, developments have fully realized, if not surpassed, this prognosis.[17] Literature no longer has an apparatus of production and distribution at its disposal; rather, literature now stands at the disposal of this apparatus. It is selected, revised, manufactured, and distributed in accordance with considerations based on business economy, not on the literature itself.[18]

---

great deal of capital and a wide range of production, and also with the small, specialized publishing houses that have an established clientele. The medium-sized firms with sales of under three million DM are in danger, however, if they take on a cost-intensive mixed production arrangement. Cf. the prognosis of R. E. M. Van den Brinks: "We can assume that in countries with a relatively large number of publishing houses the expansion of the market and rising wages will lead to futher mergers and thus to a decrease in publishing firms, in an absolute as well as a relative sense. This will result in a movement toward an optimal capacity structure, which will then make possible a more intensive marketing procedure and a more effective distribution of books" (quoted from Hans Altheim, "Die Zukunft der Lesens," in *Das Buch zwischen Gestern und Morgen*, pp. 221–222).

[16]Hans Enzensberger, *Einzelheiten* (Frankfurt am Main, 1962), p. 116.

[17]Cf. Klaus Ziermann, *Romane vom Fliessband: Die imperialistische Massenliteratur in Westdeutschland* (Berlin-GDR, 1969), pp. 56 ff.

[18]Dieter Wellershoff summarized the situation in 1967 in this way: "The publishing houses, or shall we say the enterprises of the book industry, are under constant pressure to operate in a rational manner and to increase production as rapidly as possible. They must therefore take pains to ensure that the apparatus is kept busy. It is not possible to wait and see whether something grows literarily or not, to follow the flow of an unorganized natural growth, for the expenses cannot be increased and decreased at will" ("Literatur, Markt, Kulturindustrie," *Merkur*, 21 [1967], 1017).

As a result, literary production revolves around systematic searches for talent (in which, by the way, the critics operate as advisers), extended dealings in manuscripts, and reproductions of older texts in anthologies and series. From the perspective of the thoroughly rationalized publishing world, the task of criticism is that of public relations work. Literary critics occasionally took note of these changes, but they did not clearly realize that the structural transformation of the book market eventually had to influence the function of criticism. This indifference becomes comprehensible when we note that outsiders appeared unaware of the restructuring of the book market until a few well-known medium and large-sized publishers could no longer remain in operation and fell into the hands of big business concerns.

The modern book industry's drive for increased mass production can be seen in the continuous growth in the number of new titles each year. Between 1951 and 1960 their numbers rose from 14,094 to 22,524, a rate of more than 50 percent for the decade. This growth continued in the following years: in 1968, 32,352 new titles appeared, 4993 of them in the field of belles lettres.[19] These figures provide, nonetheless, only a vague picture of the volume of production, since they do not take into consideration the number of copies printed,[20] a total of approximately 75–80 million copies per year.[21] The institution of book criticism was not prepared for this explosive growth in the book market. Even today it has made practically no effort to deal with the imbalance between the reading capacity of the individual critic and the vast number of new works (not to mention new editions) each year. Disorganized and disoriented, it has looked on helplessly as the book industry has taken over mediation between literature and the public. Not understanding the guiding mechanisms of the book market, the critical establishment could merely confirm the growing gap between literature that is "worthy of discussion" and that which is actually read.

[19]Figures taken from the *Statistisches Jahrbuch für die Bundesrepublik Deutschland (1970)*, ed. Statistisches Bundesamt Wiesbaden.
[20]Up to 1961, for example, 6400 titles appeared as paperbacks, with a total of 256 million copies printed; see Langenbucher, *Unterhaltungsroman*, p. 113. Fifty percent of these are detective and adventure stories; see Ziermann, *Romane vom Fliessband*, pp. 98 ff.
[21]Ziermann, p. 57.

3. While the book market, the reading public, and the mass media were changing slowly but significantly in the years between 1949 and 1970, the climate of theoretical discussion in this time span was shifting radically. The difference between two typical statements concerning the function of literary criticism from the fifties and the sixties seems greater than the chronological distance would indicate. Compared to the decade that followed the founding of the Federal Republic, the 1960s seem more divided, more full of conflict. The difference can be shown by various aspects. We will examine three of these—the norms, the historical self-understanding, and the determination of the function of literary criticism in regard to literature and society.

After World War II, the younger critics (those born between 1910 and 1920) considered their most urgent assignment to be the restoration of the independence of literary criticism, which National Socialism had perverted into an ideologically channeled, affirmative view of art. These critics wanted to prove that criticism represented a self-sufficient institution of literary life, on an equal footing with literary production. Two writers pointed the way: Max Rychner and Ernst Curtius, both of whom had already taken part in the literary discussions of the 1920s. Their statements on the purpose, goal, and tradition of literary criticism influenced the attitudes of the younger critics in the 1950s and to some extent in the early 1960s.[22] In particular, Curtius' essay "Goethe als Kritiker" (Goethe as Critic), which first appeared in 1948 in the influential journal *Merkur*,[23] shaped the perspective of the younger critics. This essay referred explicitly to the literary theory and criticism of German Classicism and Romanticism. By stressing the paradigmatic significance of the Age of Goethe and, conversely, characterizing the history of German literary criticism after 1830 as a history of decay, Curtius constructed a value system that promoted a one-sided discussion of the history of literary criticism. In the 1950s

---

[22]For example, Walter Boehlich wrote, "Rychner is today our only significant critic who has made a profession of criticism": "Kritik als Beruf," *Merkur*, 4 (1950), pp. 348–349. The connection was affirmed by Rychner's praise of the younger critics (Holthusen, Hohoff, Boehlich, Horst, Fabri). See Rychner, "Junge deutsche Literaturkritik," in his *Arachne: Aufsätze zur Literatur* (Zurich, 1957), pp. 297–310.
[23]Reprinted in Ernst R. Curtius, *Kritische Essays zur europäischen Literatur* (Bern, 1954), pp. 31–56.

interest was focused on the Romantics and their predecessors.[24] Defining the tasks of literary criticism, Curtius coined this concise, oft-quoted formulation: "Criticism is the literature of literature. Or, more precisely, criticism is the form of literature whose topic is literature itself."[25] Fully in keeping with Curtius' intentions, this definition was taken to be a defense of an autonomous critical authority. A critic could justify his profession, or rather his "calling," as it might be more appropriately termed here, primarily as a service to literature and literary language. "Criticism," wrote Curt Hohoff, "is occasioned by literature. Along with poetry itself, it stands in the service of language."[26] Günter Blöcker took a similar position. In summarizing the standpoint of his generation in 1959,[27] he asserted that criticism, when it reaches its goal, is autonomous and an end in itself. As a part of literature its function is consumed by literature, insofar as it analyzes new works through comparison to older ones, points out potentials and limitations of innovation, and sets up literary hierarchies. The goal of literary criticism is thus "the understanding of the literary work, the most adequate grasp of it possible, the public determination of its worth and its Gestalt. Everything else is secondary."[28] Such factors as impact and communication to the reading public are included among these secondary considerations. Blöcker does not ignore the importance of the formation of public opinion; in fact, he sees its

---

[24]Difficulties had to arise with the use of theories that were formulated under quite different historical conditions and in relation to a different sort of literature. The typical escape from this problem was to subjectivize and modernize the theorems. Holthusen, for instance, defined the relationship of the contemporary critic to the critical heritage as a personal encounter and stimulus: "The characteristic of a great critic which is worthy of being canonized and passed on is chiefly his power to order and to judge—more precisely, his passion for forming ideas appealing to our critical consciousness" (*Ja und Nein: Neue kritische Versuche* [Munich, 1954], p. 10). The critic is indeed compelled to look back and follow the call of his predecessor, since literature represents a stored-up tradition, which can be cited at any time, in which greatness is always present and timelessly valid. In this context Holthusen poses the rhetorical question, "But under certain conditions are not also the ideas themselves binding over the centuries, perhaps even, in human terms, forever?" (*Ja und Nein*, p.10).

[25]Curtius, *Kritische Essays*, pp. 32-33.

[26]Curt Hohoff, "Aufgabe und Ziel der literarischen Kritik," in *Schnittpunkte* (Stuttgart, 1963), p. 100.

[27]Günter Blöcker, "Literaturkritik," in *Kritik in unserer Zeit*, ed. Karl Otto (Göttingen, 1962), pp. 5-27.

[28]Ibid., p. 15.

contours more sharply than most of his contemporaries. Nevertheless he does not admit it as an element of theory. The content and form of criticism are determined solely by the claim to adequate interpretation of the work of art and by the capability of the critic, in accordance with the rules of hermeneutics. Like Hohoff and Hans Egon Holthusen, Blöcker draws his mandate for criticism from literature itself, not from the readers for whom he writes. Even the supposition of a social purpose in the act of criticism is thrown into question.[29]

The postulate that criticism is a substantial part of literature itself was originally devised as an argument against the Fascist liquidation of literary criticism. It implies, however, not only the independence of critical authority from specific state and social agencies, but also, in principle, the self-sufficiency of criticism with respect to social processes in general. The critic and his work are responsible not to the public but to the work of art as a unique phenomenon. This led to an exaggeration and idealization of the critic's social role and a conspicuous blindness toward the discrepancy between his self-image and his real social function. The drab reality of the reviewing business is mentioned in passing, but these critical observations, as made by Blöcker or Karl Korn,[30] are not integrated into theoretical reflection. Critics complain about the commercialized business of literature, but they are resigned to it as a *fait accompli*. Demands are made for a socially respectable literary criticism, but no one seems to give much thought to its place in modern society. Curtius hoped that criticism would develop into an institution based on the Western European model, but this presupposes a clearly defined relationship to the public sphere, and this is precisely what was missing. The critics searched for social recognition, yet they increased the distance from their public. The critical establishment emphasized the *public* nature of critical deliberation while at the same time eliminating the criteria of judgment from public discussion. The critic is declared to possess a special, not rationally explicable talent that enables him, in contrast to the average

---

[29]"Literary criticism serves social purposes only to the extent that all speaking and writing about art and literature arises from a social need—the need to answer the work of art" (ibid., p. 10).

[30]Karl Korn, "Buchkritik in der Tageszeitung," *Akzente*, 2 (1955), 15-22.

reader, to interpret the text fully. "We must make it clear," writes Blöcker, in the tradition of Curtius, "that critical appraisal is, in the final analysis, not a scientific act. Truth can be illuminated only in personal engagement, in the shower of sparks that arises from the collision between a work of art and its evaluator."[31] Thus criticism, like literary creativity, can be neither taught nor learned, and is more a calling than a profession.

Obviously this concept of criticism was not favorably disposed toward the egalitarian tendencies of modern society and not even interested in the liberal mode of public deliberation. Only in a formal sense did the critical establishment adapt to the newly constituted democratic state, whose structure it viewed as a "protective power," as Holthusen wrote in his polemic against Enzensberger.[32] As long as West German society in its reconstruction phase seemed harmonious and unproblematic, there was no need to probe into the function of the postulated autonomy of literary criticism. The theorems and questions that had been formulated in the later years of the Weimar Republic as a response to a fundamental social and political crisis were therefore of no interest. The critics of the nineteenth century and the Weimar Republic were resurrected only when the domestic political climate changed and a political opposition movement arose which consciously overstepped the narrow bounds of parliamentary opposition.

4. The critics of the 1950s suffered under the inadequacies of the book-reviewing mechanisms. Nevertheless, they felt that the possibility of adequate literary criticism was in principle well established. In the 1960s the methods and criteria of evaluation, the role of the critic, and ultimately the function of the institution of literary criticism all became less certain. What seemed at first to be a dilemma of method turned out, in the process of self-reflection, to be a fundamental crisis. The younger generation of critics (in this case, those born between 1920 and 1930) reopened questions of theory and tried to adjust literary criticism to the needs of a democratic society. In so doing, they unintentionally clashed with the limitations of immanent literary

---

[31]Blöcker, p. 23.
[32]Hans Egon Holthusen, *Plädoyer für den Einzelnen* (Munich, 1967), p. 78.

discussion. The model of the autonomous literary public sphere, taken literally, proved to be no longer a valid premise. Consequently, the polemic directed at the literary establishment by the critics born after 1930 should not be seen as the sudden intrusion of inexplicable forces but rather as a logical continuation of thought processes that had been initiated by the liberal critics.

At first the crisis was held to be a linguistic and methodological problem. Curtius had pointed out earlier the social basis of criticism as a public institution, and his formulations had been utilized repeatedly. Nevertheless, the critics in the 1950s had drawn no conclusions from them for their own methods of communication. The grounding of book reviewing in society seemed to be an obvious fact; the specific nature of their relationship, however, remained unexamined. Even in 1963 at the Berlin colloquium of critics, there was no appreciable reaction to Harry Pross's remarks about the idealistic complacency of critics and their inadequate understanding of their own social conditioning.[33] The failure of criticism was described, by Walter Höllerer for example, as being rooted in the shortcomings of individual critics or types of critics. Because of their attitude and their method of procedure, they either forced literature into an arbitrary system or turned it into a plaything of subjective judgments. When Höllerer, in a provocative and well-known speech at the 1961 critics' colloquium, divided the critical profession into five negative ideal types,[34] he formulated a de facto description of the methodological pluralism of those years—reduced, to be sure, to witty psychological portraits. This satiric attitude foreshadows the polemics of the late 1960s. Höllerer's critical profiles can compare with Hamm's description of the "grand critic" and Walser's picture of the magisterial "universal critic." Still, this similarity of presentation should not obscure the

---

[33]"Today and for the immediate future it is no longer sufficient to defend the individual right of criticism. Neither is it a matter of mere freedom of criticism. It is a matter of equality, the equality of criticism with other forces of this society, for this society is built on literature as well. . . . Future critics will have to learn to comprehend their social scope" (Harry Pross, "Vom sozialen Umfang der Kritik," *Sprache im technischen Zeitalter,* nos. 9–10 [1964], p. 801).

[34]Walter Höllerer, "Zur literarischen Kritik in Deutschland," *Sprache im technischen Zeitalter,* no. 2 (1962), pp. 153–164.

distance that separates Höllerer's 1961 arguments from the attacks of the Neomarxists. Höllerer would never have characterized the crisis of literary criticism as a crisis of the institution. He saw it as a problem of theory, insisting that it could be solved by criticism itself. His goal was a method that does not objectify itself by uncritically appropriating the work of art. Rather, it should approach art critically, by reflecting on its own standpoint as well. This was a significant first step toward overcoming historical objectivism and its complement, impressionism. Nevertheless, the examples used by Höllerer show how greatly he was bound to the models and categories of the preceding decade. He even used Curtius to illustrate how his method should be applied, thereby returning to the objectivism of hermeneutic criticism, which sees the critical subject only as a medium. The unresolved contradictions of these years are reflected in Höllerer's belief that Curtius's methodological principles could alleviate the obvious crisis and his recognition of the dilemma of empathetic criticism—the very method that Curtius had prescribed.

The discussion initiated by Höllerer's lecture also showed that the call for a self-reflective criticism left room for a variety of interpretations. Arguing from a historical perspective, Edgar Lohner took issue with Höllerer's mistrust of the seemingly objective immediacy of the literary work[35] and insisted anew on an objectivity directly related to the text. Like Curtius, he blamed the present-day chaos on the movement away from Romantic criticism and the intrusion of the political public sphere. This stance was an expression of the historically accumulated tension within criticism, a tension between social and literary development. Lohner's statement, however, merely attempted to ban this problem from discussion once and for all. Criticism was directed very strictly back to its traditional intrinsic rules, and all reference to its public function was cut off. Lohner's suggestion of returning to the materials themselves was essentially a rejection of Höllerer's questioning of the critic's standpoint and role. Lohner suspected that this critique would lead to an intrusion of

---

[35]Edgar Lohner, "Tradition und Gegenwart deutscher Literaturkritik," *Sprache im technischen Zeitalter*, no. 2 (1962), pp. 238–248.

arbitrary aesthetic taste and political ideologies.[36] His worried attitude points both forward and backward. It articulates once more the shock experience of the generation that had seen National Socialism turn the entire literary realm into ideology. At the same time it seeks to fend off the pressure from anticipated political conflicts upon literary criticism. The lasting effect of this fixation on Nazism can be seen in Walter Boehlich's 1964 essay condemning German literary criticism. He charged that the aftereffects of Fascist perversion were responsible for its miserable condition. "Even today," he argued, "German criticism has not recovered from this disaster. We have a criticism, but only an anemic one, which seems to bear no relation to the literature it refers to."[37]

Boehlich's tirade is symptomatic in another regard of the self-image of criticism in the early 1960s. Like the basic arguments of the preceding decade, Boehlich's position was rooted in Curtius' definition of criticism as the form of literature whose topic is literature itself, in order to establish criticism as an immanent guiding mechanism for literature. Yet this task includes a political function, albeit a very cautiously formulated one, since literary criticism in post-Fascist Germany cannot completely do without the critique of ideologies.[38] Boehlich quickly headed off any overly radical development of this concession, however, by rejecting as too one-sided Franz Schonauer's demand for a criticism that is explicitly didactic and critical of society. Boehlich saw the critic as an honest broker between authors and readers. Ideally, this involves the mediation of ideas in a literary public sphere free from all domination. Consequently, when Boehlich dealt concretely with the weaknesses of the book-reviewing system, he deplored the mutilation and distortion of criticism

[36]"The decisive factors are no longer the immanent law of the poetic work but the mood and taste of the public sphere, no longer the object itself but the *Weltanschauung*. Criticism is predominantly uttered as a political statement or a pamphlet.... The relativism of critical standards is beginning—a relativism which until now we have not yet overcome" (ibid., p. 240).

[37]Walter Boehlich, "Kritik und Selbstkritik," in *Sind wir noch das Volk der Dichter und Denker?* ed. Gert Kalow (Reinbek, 1964), pp. 43-44.

[38]"There are things permitted by the Constitution that no longer belong in the state, things that everyone has a guaranteed right to say, but which the critic, if he wishes to give the state and himself a chance, cannot support when they take the form of literature" (ibid., p. 47).

brought about by the commercialization of literary life. These observations, which touched upon the weakest point of the liberal model, nevertheless did not confront the causes of these disturbances. Since in 1964 Boehlich still considered Fascism to be primarily responsible for this aberrant development, any analysis of the social situation remained peripheral. He revised his position four years later. Having lost his faith in the potential for realizing the liberal model, he attacked bourgeois literary criticism. Like Enzensberger and Karl M. Michel, he called unequivocally for its abolition. This change is indicative of the radicalization of the discussion in the sixties.

When we order this process chronologically, we encounter three basic stages—the liberal phase, represented by writers like Höllerer, Boehlich (prior to his conversion), and, above all, Marcel Reich-Ranicki; the phase of cultural criticism, in which Adorno's theory was appropriated and applied by such younger writers as Enzensberger and Reinhard Baumgart; and finally the phase of social criticism, where, under the influence of Brecht, Benjamin, and Marcuse, every form of aesthetic criticism was challenged. Liberal criticism proceeded from the assumption that although West German society was in need of reform it was nonetheless acceptable in principle, having reached a requisite level of political maturity. This attitude bred a certain mistrust of the use of literature for the purposes of social criticism.[39] Though it assumed a different function, the autonomy of literature and criticism was no less solidly anchored in the liberal conception than in the concept of hermeneutic criticism which dominated the 1950s. This connection can be seen most plainly in Reich-Ranicki's contributions to the criticism of criticism. Although Reich-Ranicki is fond of referring to Friedrich Schlegel, his position is actually quite far removed from the Romantic idea of productive criticism, which sees itself as its own end. Reich-Ranicki reaches back to the magisterial

---

[39]As Peter Demetz stated in 1963, literature and politics ought to remain apart: "As long as there are functioning parliaments, a civil press, trade unions, and active, free citizens, it is more practical to undertake the necessary changes in the society by means of legitimate political institutions. I am almost afraid that the constant call for a theater of change is nothing other than a sign of political impoverishment" ("Gedanken zu einer Kritiker-Tagung," *Sprache im technischen Zeitalter*, nos. 9–10 [1964], 820).

function of the critic which arose in the eighteenth century along with the literary public sphere. The audience grants the critic the role of public spokesman. Although he is a private citizen, he fulfills a public function that would be unthinkable to remove from society. Reich-Ranicki takes literally a phrase that the followers of Curtius considered a metaphor: Literary criticism is a social institution. Thus he continually comes to its defense when its functioning is questioned. He stood up for the Gruppe 47 when it was attacked by Friedrich Sieburg and Blöcker;[40] he defended the critical establishment against the polemics of Boehlich and Walser.[41] The debate with Walser merits special attention, for it allows us a closer look at the neoliberal conception. In 1964 Walser, irritated by the jargon of journalistic criticism, supported the idea of an intimate, subjective procedure in which the critic discusses himself as well as the literary work.[42] The idea of the critic as a public office holder, as it were, or even as a literary referee, seemed to Walser irreconcilable with the subtlety of the object under consideration. Reich-Ranicki must have felt attacked by these objections, for they called into question precisely that element which was most essential to him. In his reply he seized the opportunity to expand his ideas on the procedure and role of criticism. He rejected Walser's call for subjective criticism and again affirmed the concept of the public agent: "Of course the critic functions as a public spokesman. He ought to. He has to. He is fulfilling the duties of his office."[43] As a result, he may not write for himself, as Walser suggested; he must bear in mind his influence on public opinion and consider the possible impact of his criticism. Reich-Ranicki was so sure of his cause that he did not even raise the question whether this office was still legitimate. The business of criticism may be difficult in some individual details, but in principle he sees no problem in it, for he considers its institutional basis and social context

---

[40]Marcel Reich-Ranicki, "Die 'Gruppe 47' und Günter Blöcker," in his *Literarisches Leben in Deutschland* (Munich, 1965), pp. 273–277.

[41]"Kritik der Kritik der Kritik," ibid., pp. 217–220. "Ein bisschen Amtsarzt, ein bisschen Moses," ibid., pp. 273–277.

[42]Martin Walser, "Tagtraum, dass der Kritiker ein Schriftsteller sei," *Süddeutsche Zeitung*, 31 December 1964: reprinted in Peter Hamm, ed., *Kritik—von wem/für wen/wie: Eine Selbstdarstellung deutscher Kritiker* (Munich, 1968), pp. 11–14.

[43]*Literarisches Leben*, p. 277.

to be secure. He did not suppress this context as the mainstream of the fifties had done; rather, he openly espoused it.[44] Criticism is an instrument of the public's search for truth, and criticism of criticism is therefore to be welcomed, for "critics exist in order to saw away at the limb they are sitting on. They need not worry about doing so, because . . . the more one saws on it, the sturdier it becomes."[45] Obviously Reich-Ranicki felt sure of his partner in dialogue and never questioned the existence of a public assembled for critical discussion. His position postulated functioning democratic political institutions which supported literary criticism, with criticism contributing to the functioning of these institutions in return.

5. The restoration of the liberal model, in which the critic serves as a mediator between literature and the public and as the rational voice of the public sphere, could not dampen the smoldering crisis. The unquestioned acceptance of the institution was undermined by tensions in the West German political system, which for the first time led to a permanent polarization of public opinion. The political crisis influenced the dialogue of literary criticism and forced an examination of its liberal premises. This process began around 1961 but did not achieve a noticeably widespread effect until after 1965. The literary intelligentsia became polarized in the dispute surrounding the student revolt and the criticism of Germanistics which stemmed from it. A kind of anticriticism arose within the generation born after 1930, and was also supported in part by those born in the 1920s.

When an earlier volume of Hans Holthusen's essays was republished in a new edition in 1964, he noted that the intellectual climate had changed so drastically that his critical postulates seemed out of date. "Sociology is the trump card, Marx is again an urgent problem, dialectical thinking is practically a *conditio sine qua non*."[46] His past explanation for the "radical change of backdrop," however, was hardly relevant to the core of the matter, for it merely named the intellectual leaders of the new trend, such as Adorno, Ernst Bloch, and Brecht. This shift can be fully

---

[44]"Anyone who presents one's literary works to the public grants the public, whether one wants to or not, the right to decide the value of those works" (ibid., p. 155).

[45]Ibid., p. 217.

[46]Hans Holthusen, *Der unbehauste Mensch* (Munich, 1964), p. 10.

understood only by examining the accumulated questions of journalistic criticism in an industrialized mass society, problems that remained undiscussed because of theoretical fixations. The dubious nature of literary self-sufficiency became exposed as soon as the institutional, societal character of this journalistic criticism was emphasized (in part by liberal critics) and as soon as the mediations between author and public in an age of mass communication were more closely examined. The claim of established theory to have ready answers for all situations was exposed as a debt that could not be paid. As a solution, after 1945 a model was introduced in which criticism functions as the regulatory principle of a literature that is subject exclusively to its own laws of development. The debate during the 1960s made it clear that pat answers concerning the task and purpose of book reviewing contained questions of their own which contributed to an atmosphere of uncertainty and division. In the words of Hans Blumenberg: "There are problems that can be posed only after their supposed solution—or what afterward appears to have been a solution—has been offered. They then become stabilized as unsolved problems."[47]

After the building of the Berlin Wall in 1961 and the initial proclamations of emergency ordinances, conditions in the political realm helped to promote a fusion of literary theory and social theory. The political actions of the extraparliamentary opposition and the student movement since 1964 both fueled the process of self-examination and dictated its course. The revolt against established literary criticism culminated in 1968 and owed its vitality along with most of its arguments to these political movements. After 1965 literary and sociopolitical rebellions could scarcely be separated. In the early 1960s the liberal and the leftist critics were still working together against a common opponent, the conservative critics, as the controversy surrounding the Gruppe 47 illustrates.[48] After 1964, however, these groups became polarized. Within the Left, the grounding of literary criticism in criticism of culture took a radical turn toward social criticism under the banner of Marxism. An indication of

---

[47]Hans Blumenberg, *Die Legitimität der Neuzeit* (Frankfurt am Main, 1966), p. 43.
[48]See Reinhard Lettau, ed., *Die Gruppe 47: Bericht, Kritik, Polemic* (Neuwied and Berlin, 1967).

the sharpening of political perspectives is the Benjamin controversy of 1967–68, in which the Marxist writings of the mature Benjamin were used polemically against the Critical Theory of the Frankfurt School (Horkheimer, Adorno, Rolf Tiedemann).[49]

The belatedness of the literary revolt demands an explanation. By 1960 the political opposition had taken shape, in response to the Social Democrats' falling in line with the government's foreign and military policies (as the emergence of the SDS shows). Though in succeeding years this movement discussed alternatives to the official policies of the Federal Republic,[50] no similar confrontation took place in literary criticism. One chief reason, it seems to me, was the lingering influence of Adorno's theory of art on the younger literary intelligentsia. Adorno's theory reconciled social and literary criticism in the aesthetic realm, but set itself apart from the Left movement of the 1920s and its concept of engaged literature. In both Enzensberger and Baumgart, to name two examples, we see the impact of this theory which contends that it is not literary activism but the method of writing which breaks down ideologized consciousness. The Old Left is depicted not without a certain amount of pity in Baumgart's "Plädoyer für eine linke Literatur" (Plea for a Leftist Literature): "Testy in its political conduct, pious in its literary affectation, it inherited an already bankrupt bourgeois realism and applied it to new proletarian milieus. These settings deprived it of its old form but provided no new one until the theoretical crown of thorns of socialist realism was pressed onto its already dead forehead."[51]

Baumgart concluded that Leftist poetics faced the task of translating protest—which had previously relied on its message—into formal criteria. For the real foe was no longer material misery but the total envelopment of literature by the consciousness industry. "Only new methods can depict in a poem, play, or narrative the clouds gathering above our heads."[52] These overdue

---

[49]See the two special issues of *alternative* on Walter Benjamin: 56/57 (1967) and 59/60 (1968), as well as the literature listed there.

[50]See Ernst Richert, *Die radikale Linke von 1945 bis zur Gegenwart* (Berlin, 1969), est. pp. 85–103.

[51]Reinhard Baumgart, "Plädoyer für eine linke Literatur," *Literatur für Zeitgenossen* (Frankfurt am Main, 1966), p. 121.

[52]Ibid., p. 127.

reflections on the historical conditioning of literary forms had the presumably unintended side effect of sealing off theory and criticism once again from the social realm. Only an art that rejects any complicity with practical social interests can be safe from the ubiquitous suspicion of being ideology.

This attempt to assert the autonomy of theory by integrating the sociocritical impulse into it could not withstand external pressures. Aesthetic criticism that could not be converted into social praxis was abandoned, and the hope placed in the critical function of Modernist literature was written off as an illusion. This radical shift is illustrated by Enzensberger's positions. The main point of his 1968 essay "Gemeinplätze, die neueste Literatur betreffend" (Commonplaces On the Newest Literature) was the formulation "Literary works cannot be assigned an essential social function under present conditions."[53] This thesis retracts what its author had believed in the early 1960s. Both the essay on the universal language of poetry as well as the Neruda essay derived the sociocritical function of the lyric work of art from its aesthetic autonomy.[54] According to those essays a poem, to the extent that it is successful, does not allow itself to be reduced to a commodity, for its aesthetic self-containment it is more deeply engaged than political art. Aesthetic and social evolution are thus related to each other, in that the process of formal innovation corresponds to the progress of social liberation. Poetry anticipates and redeems the promise of humanity.

In 1968 Enzensberger renounced this belief in the emancipatory effect of poetry's power to anticipate social change, and he no longer identified with the "mission" of modern literature. He thus reformulated its history, specifically retracting the thesis that formal innovation and political emancipation were one: "This means the end of an equivocation that has ruled progressive literature for fifty years: the parallelism or even equation of formal and social innovation."[55]

The theoretical basis for this change of stance had been pre-

[53]Enzensberger, "Commonplaces on the Newest Literature," in *Consciousness Industry*, ed. Michael Roloff (New York, 1974), p. 92.
[54]Enzensberger, "The World Language of Modern Poetry," ibid., pp. 42–61). The essay on Neruda is in *Einzelheiten*, pp. 316–333.
[55]Enzensberger, *Consciousness Industry*, p. 91.

sent for some time in the theory of the consciousness industry.[56] Although poetic literature had been lauded in 1962 as being incommensurable to the system of the culture industry, since it was not reducible to commodity form and consumption, Enzensberger in 1968 condemned even the advanced poetic structures as a part of the system, since they could not overturn it. He argued that formal innovation and literary criticisms of society prove to be capable of integration into the status quo: "the more West German society stabilized itself, and the more urgently it asked for social criticism in literature, the fewer results the writer's engagement produced, and the louder the clamor for it. This mechanism secured literature an uncontested place in society, but it also led to self-delusions that seem grotesque today."[57]

The self-deceptions were Enzensberger's own. His bitterness over the ineffectiveness of poetic protest resulted from them. Critical Theory could not be transferred into practice. Because Enzensberger had placed all his hopes in modern literature, because it seemed to him (as to Adorno) practically the only possibility of formulating truth beyond ideology, it was scorned and rejected when it proved incapable of fulfilling this promise in a short time. Despite acknowledging the potential for continuing aesthetic change, Enzensberger no longer believes in its absolute legitimation, which Adorno had always affirmed. Such is the context of the following apodictic statement: "Hence a literary criticism which tries to do more than belch forth its personal preferences and which could regulate the market is not possible."[58] Literary criticism has lost its chance to serve as the training field for the political public sphere.

Sociopolitical constellations in West Germany transformed the crisis of immanent methodology into a crisis of the institution. Its opponents were well aware of this context.[59] The formation of the Great Coalition in 1966 clearly exposed a political crisis

[56]Enzensberger, "The Industrialization of the Mind," *Consciousness Industry,* pp. 3-15.
[57]Ibid., p. 87.
[58]Ibid., p. 92.
[59]In 1968 Enzensberger wrote, "When the totality of imperialism became evident, when social contradictions could no longer be covered up, when politics took to the street, the cracks began to show through the cultural façade" (ibid., p. 87).

within the Federal Republic. The subsystem of literary criticism, too, was drawn into the mire of political conflict, for the most part against the wishes of its most prominent spokesmen. The extraparliamentary opposition, because of its justified misgivings about the functioning of parliamentary democracy in West Germany, undermined the liberals' confidence in the separateness of literary and political debates. Political demonstrations and student revolts heightened the tension and pushed the discussion once and for all beyond the scope of mere methodology.[60] In Berlin in the summer of 1967, a few days after the murder of the student Benno Ohnesorg, the students' demand that science be politicized was applied directly to Germanistics.[61] The dispute over the proper tasks of academic criticism became a test case for the impending confrontation with literary criticism in general. The charge that Germanistics continued its traditional role of service to ruling forces by declaring itself apolitical reaffirmed the position of such liberal critics as Eberhard Lämmert, Karl Otto Conrady, and Walther Killy.[62] With some modifications, this charge could be made against professional book criticism as well.

6. The New Left's assault on literary criticism was no longer directed toward its improvement but toward its liquidation, thus exposing a protracted structural crisis. This assault arose from a rediscovery of problems that had been debated in the 1920s between Leftists and established literary criticism. They had remained unresolved, however, when the onset of National Socialism broke off the discussion. One can speak, as Jauss does, of a "shifting of position in regard to questions and solutions, a position that was conditioned and imposed both internally and

[60]The initial difficulty of this step is visible in Peter Schneider's critique of the reviewing system. In a 1965 analysis (considered radical) of five reviews of a novel, he was still holding fast to intrinsic criteria of information, consistency, and linguistic portrayal. He found the essential weakness to be that the critics failed to reveal their point of view, no matter what it was, so that the criteria applied to the literary object could not be clearly distinguished. "Die Mängel der gegenwärtigen Literaturkritik," *Neue deutsche Hefte*, 12 (1965), 98–123.

[61]See Heinz-Dieter Kittsteiner et al., "Germanistik, Reform oder Politisierung," *alternative*, 55 (1967), 141–183.

[62]*Germanistik—eine deutsche Wissenschaft* (Frankfurt am Main, 1967). The essays represent talks given in 1966 at the Deutscher Germanistentag.

externally—that is, by forces and impulses of the sociohistorical situation."[63] The confrontation with a sociopolitical position that was considered revolutionary led to a change of perspectives. As a result, Critical Theory, which had heretofore insisted on the independence of the aesthetic realm, was replaced by a materialistic approach with ties to Brecht and Benjamin.

Brecht's theses on the capitalist reviewing system and Benjamin's later works directed attention to the connection between the factors conditioning the production of a work of art (shown in the possibilities of technical reproduction) and its social function.[64] According to Benjamin, art in modern society has irreconcilably distanced itself from the concept of the genuine work of art, protected by its aura. This was the beginning of an outspoken resistance to existing literary criticism. Book criticism in leading newspapers and magazines continued to use the obsolete principle of contemplative absorption in the text as its basis for judgment. Furthermore, Benjamin's writings made the possibilities for political application apparent, which Adorno's theory had rejected: "But at that moment when the criterion of genuineness proves inadequate for the production of art, the entire function of art is altered. In place of its foundation in ritual comes a foundation in a different praxis—a foundation in politics."[65]

When Hamm accused Adorno of being allied with the idea of culture for its own sake, he may have pronounced only the *communis opinio* of the New Left.[66] Karl Marcus Michel formulated the same objection more cogently by dealing with the tension between aesthetic theory and the sought-for political praxis: "It is not Ernst Bloch, that atavistic monument to the 'not-yet,' who stands behind their [the New Left's] actions; it is far more the hermeneutic thought of Adorno, which cannot be translated

---

[63]Hans Robert Jauss, *Literaturgeschichte als Provokation der Literaturwissenschaft* (Constance, 1969), p. 61.

[64]Brecht, *Schriften zum Theater*, 2: 235–64, as well as Benjamin, "The Work of Art in the Age of Its Mechanical Reproduction," *Illuminations*, trans. Harry Zohn (New York, 1968), pp. 217–251.

[65]Ibid., p. 224; translation modified.

[66]Hamm, "Der Grosskritiker. Literaturkritik als Anachronismus," in *Kritik*, p. 35.

into political praxis but has nevertheless been transformed into concrete protest."[67]

The arguments of the anticriticism movement can be ordered according to four aspects: (1) the social position and role of the professional critic; (2) the communication between the critic and the public; (3) the social function of criticism; and (4) the position of literary criticism within the cultural system. The fourth aspect encompasses the central objections to the institutionalized reviewing system. Current book reviewing relies on the mass media to reach its audience. As a result, critics are subservient to the well-established mechanisms of the consciousness industry, even if they refuse to admit it. As the New Left justly insisted, the status and role of the critic, the conditioning factors of communication, and the social efficacy of criticism can be understood only within the context of the media industry. Meanwhile, this argument took on a strong emotional coloration. The consciousness industry assumed the role of the archenemy, responsible for everything. Its mechanisms were portrayed not only as the manipulators of public opinion but at the same time as unreachable, omnipotent forces. Direct action was urged against these demonized organizations, even when it offered no hope of success. "To escape the grip of the cultural apparatus and its unlimited capacity to swallow and digest any criticism which arises"[68] —this was stylized as a fight for survival.

The material circumstances of the professional critic and his social position were interpreted in a contradictory way. Obviously he is dependent on fees for writing and is therefore economically bound to the apparatus of the media. Yaak Karsunke notes, "Since critics have to live off their fees, they are forced to write prodigiously. After hasty reading comes a hastily written review. The system successfully prevents those serving it from engaging in more exact analyses which might ultimately turn back on the system itself."[69]

The picture sketched here is that of a literary lackey. Hamm pursued this perspective further with Brechtian arguments: the economic conditions under which the critic must operate permit

[67]Karl M. Michel, "Ein Kranz für die Literatur: Fünf Variationen über eine These," *Kursbuch*, 15 (1968), 185.
[68]Ibid., p. 184.
[69]Yaak Karsunke, "Uralte Binsenwahrheiten," in *Kritik*, p. 46.

him only the illusion of a freedom of opinion. He must therefore compensate for this through the postulation of aesthetic autonomy. The illusion of aesthetic freedom provides an absolute (though objectively false) legitimation of criticism. Yet Hamm's argument subtly turns into its opposite, for he wants to deal not with material dependence but with usurped claims to dominance. The successful reviewer, as a "major critic," belongs to an elite. Two contradictory diagnoses are thereby juxtaposed— first, the image of the functionary as a tool of the system; second, the image of the star whose commentaries control public opinion. Apparently Hamm, who scarcely differentiates between conservatives and liberals in his polemic, has confused the elitist attitude of the critic with social reality. This logical leap from self-image to objective situation is, however, dangerous. Some signs do indicate that a few critics may belong to the communications elite, but this by no means applies to the majority. Those belonging to the elite have solved the problem of material dependence touched on by Karsunke by reaching a higher status. Their bondage is linked to factors other than honoraria. They, like their less prestigious, less influential colleagues, are subject to the laws of the communications apparatus, which regulates their access to the public.

This brings us to the second point: Criticism is bound to the channels at its disposal and therefore reaches only the bourgeois public. Karsunke notes, "It makes no difference whom criticism seeks to reach; it will always reach the same audience of the Sunday editions, magazines, and educational radio networks (along with the evening programs in general). As a critic, one finds oneself in the cultural ghetto of the educated bourgeoisie; those who leave it find no buyers for their wares."[70] Because of the structure of the mass media, journalistic criticism must fail in its primary task of providing information to a wide audience.[71] With their fixation on superseded theoretical positions, profes-

---

[70]Ibid., p. 45.

[71]This dangerous reduction of the realm of communication was pointed out by Baumgart as well. He considered the only relevant question to be "what a book contributes to the further development of literature, to its future," and added, as a correction to his earlier position, "and that occurs by no means only through examining new ways of writing, but also through reaching a new public or achieving new political results using new methods" ("Vorschläge," in *Kritik*, p. 42).

sional critics have neglected to recognize their altered position in a changed society. In the words of Hans Helms: "This resolute abstinence of the critical faculty from any insight into processes occurring in the social base, in the sphere of production, is cause for concern and of grave consequence."[72]

Although repeated demands were heard for an analysis of the social base, however, writings in this area remained abstract and vague. The anticritical movement concentrated on an illumination of the ideological function of "bourgeois" literary theory. The postulate of aesthetic autonomy, which was used by the literary criticism of the 1950s as a source of self-justification and which remained untouched even in the liberal model, is suspected of no longer effecting emancipation in the present-day situation. Instead, it merely stabilizes a cultural superstructure that has accommodated itself to the social system. As an institution, literary criticism accepts the specialization of society and limits itself to literary evaluation. In doing so, it renounces the possibility of recognizing the forces that condition literary production—including its own. As a result, it ends in affirmational commentary. Helms states: "A literary criticism directed toward repeatedly burdening the reader with the same false information is nevertheless capable of sustaining, within its modest means, the existing power structure. It does so insofar as it diverts the reader away from the social factors conditioning artistic production and directs him constantly toward the ideological playground of Fascism—the origins of being."[73]

Or as Karsunke puts it: "Basically, critics as a whole are creating an illusion—namely, that of a value system independent of money."[74] Baumgart makes a similar statement: "For the most hypocritical aspect of the current reviewing practice is this: It is an instrument of the market, or, more harmlessly stated, of literary politics, but it feigns innocence in regard to its power, makes a pretense of pure objective interest, and claims to be creating order, critically and expediently."[75] Reviews, Baumgart concludes, actually function as unpaid book advertisements. The

---

[72]Hans G. Helms, "Über die gesellschaftliche Funktion der Kritik," in *Kritik*, p. 134.

[73]Ibid., pp. 137–138.

[74]Karsunke, "Uralte Binsenwahrheiten," p. 48.

[75]Baumgart, "Vorschläge," p. 43.

organized system of book discussions is exposed as an appendix of the book market, even though it will not admit it.

The New Left was united in its claim that the critical establishment, from Hohoff to Mayer, had abandoned its sociocritical function through its collusion with the apparatus. Boehlich summarized the general view when he wrote in *Kursbogen*, November 1968: "It [bourgeois criticism] has allowed itself to be exiled to the last pages of the newspapers, the weekly magazines, the journals. It knowingly accepts that the politics described on the first pages contradict the criticism it practices on the final pages. Still it continues to believe that it can have an effect. It accepts itself as the liberal ornament of a no longer liberal force."[76]

On the other hand, there were varying answers to the question whether a legitimate function of criticism could still be formulated. Whereas Boehlich, Baumgart, Hamm, and even Helms still considered such a function feasible (though not in the current state of specialization), Enzensberger and Michel in 1968 denied the possibility of a critical institution. They did so for two reasons. First, the apparatus of the culture industry hinders any substantial change through its omnipresence and wide control. Second and no doubt more important, modern postsymbolist literature has reached its historical end. At the same time, this has eliminated the legitimate function of progressive literary criticism, which entered the scene as a corollary of that literature. The indictment of progressive literature included an indictment of its criticism, which was dissolved by its most radical members.[77] Enzensberger predicted in 1968 that this judgment could not be carried out, for the convicted institution did not respect the jurisdiction of the court. In addition, the case (to remain in legal terms) was being retried.

Though the rebellion took place only a short time ago, its

---

[76]Boehlich, "Autodafé," *Kursbogen*, supplement to *Kursbuch*, 15 (1968).

[77]"Modern literature acted in a similar way—it bound and satisfied intellectual interests as though they were immediate social and political ones, thereby obscuring the latter. It took dissatisfaction and unrest (which it nourished) and placed them in a cage where mock battles were fought and the illusion of victory was achieved, while in the real world it was business as usual" (Michel, "Ein Kranz," pp. 178–179).

weaknesses can readily be pointed out. The demand to abolish literary criticism *in toto* and unconditionally was related to a yearning for spontaneous action after so many frustrating experiences with the apparatus of the culture industry. There was a great need to break loose from its grasp at any cost. Thus the protest served as a type of catharsis for the New Left. In 1968 their hope for an immediate change was nourished by a domestic political situation that seemed to point toward an imminent restructuring of social conditions. To be sure, no adequate replacement for bourgeois criticism was suggested. The revolt counted on the spontaneous emergence of new forms after the dissolution of the corrupt, worn-out institution. This juxtaposition of bourgeois and antibourgeois criticism is open to the charge of being empty rhetoric, as Boehlich's own pamphlet makes evident. Liberation from eroded formal and organizational mechanisms could not be accomplished through anarchistic protest, but only through a restructuring of the existing means of production. Here, no less than in the incriminated bourgeois criticism, there was a lack of precise analyses of the reading public and the media industry.

The critique of the present reviewing system overshot the interests of the masses. The debate over the function and purpose of literary criticism remained a matter for the literary intelligentsia and was therefore practically meaningless for the broad public.[78] This public was not interested in the abolition of an institution so unrelated to it. Even the Left now looks back on this phase of spontaneous action with a certain uneasiness. Such self-criticism nevertheless does not make the revolt of the sixties superfluous. The challenge to contemporary literary criticism

[78]With some justification, Karl H. Bohrer ("Zuschauer beim Salto mortale," *Merkur*, 23 [1969], 170–186) pointed out that the elimination of literature and criticism attempted by the authors of *Kursbuch* had itself been a contribution to literature by continuing the traditional dialogue on the function of literature. Bohrer was correct in relating the liquidation of literary criticism to excessive expectations, but he was wrong in asserting that the crisis was merely an ideological one that could be resolved through an adjustment of attitudes and positions. Bohrer, who criticized the Leftists for interpreting their models (primarily Benjamin) too literally, approaches the crisis far too narrowly in his view of the formulations of the discussants. What should have astonished him was not that such an "old" writer as Benjamin had been chosen as a spiritual leader, but that Benjamin's insights, though again available since 1955, could have been overlooked for so long.

revealed the long-present structural crisis that in the 1950s had been hidden once more by the restitution of Romantic theory.

It is impossible to predict the evolution of literary criticism in the coming years, for the process is determined by too many factors. We can, however, outline the problems inherited from the 1960s which it must confront. Some prognoses are thus possible.

(1) The schism between liberal criticism and that of the New Left will continue to exist. The conflicts between the two camps cannot be traced to particular differences of interests, which solve themselves, as it were, when access to the apparatus of the media is assured to the younger generation. There may be individual renegades for whom protest, as Horst Krüger has conjectured,[79] was nothing more than a means to express a personal grievance about the literary market. But aside from the personal aspects, the unsolved institutional and theoretical questions guarantee that the gap will remain. Even when the two sides seem to be working toward the same goal (the democratization of literary experience, for example), they really mean different things.

(2) We can expect the Left to revise its assessment of literary criticism. The idea of the end of art was still under the influence of classical aesthetics, which conceives of the work of art only as a coherent structure. With the overdue restructuring of aesthetics, which Benjamin anticipated a generation ago, the task of literary criticism will have to be redefined. The declaration of its death was an overreaction; not only because the reviewing business has continued to exist, but because the fate of literary criticism was made too exclusively dependent on a certain phase of literature and aesthetics.

(3) Within the Left, the discussion concerning the role of the consciousness industry and its influence on literary criticism will not be able to dwell on the essentially negative manipulation thesis. By now it has become clear that this thesis was ineffective in the form used during the sixties. Enzensberger (revising his standpoint once again) noted, "The current theory of manipula-

---

[79]Horst Krüger ("Hastige Ermordung der Literatur," *Neue Rundschau,* 80 [1969], 191–195) explained the revolt against literature as an uprising of communicators who had not been sufficiently recognized.

tion on the Left is essentially defensive; its effects can lead the movement into defeatism." And "A socialist perspective that does not go beyond attacking existing property relationships is limited."[80] Diminished resistance to the mass media—still shared by bourgeois and Neomarxist intellectuals in the 1960s—will perhaps also lead to a more precise understanding of current book criticism, which is dependent on these media.

(4) Finally, it is not out of the question for criticism to develop new organizational forms. The individual critic has been placed in a weak position in regard to the book and media industries and their seemingly unlimited production. Criticism can regain its function of information and mediation only by building collective organizations which, rather than discussing more or less randomly selected books, examine the guiding mechanisms of literary production and reception closely and critically.

[80]Enzensberger, "Constituents of a Theory of the Media (1970)," in *Consciousness Industry*, p. 101.

4 The Task of Contemporary Literary Criticism

After the "Death" of Literary Criticism (1974)

Everything is back to normal: literature is being produced—to judge by the statistics, more abundantly than ever—and books on the market are finding reviewers. The situation is no different from ten, twenty, or fifty years ago. The predicted demise of literature and literary criticism never did happen. Or so it would seem. Only occasionally do we recall 1968 and the horror with which one viewed the prophets predicting the destruction of the literature industry and the birth of a new and better literature. Gone are the New Left's dreams of restructuring advanced capitalist society through cultural revolution. Also forgotten, it seems, are the critical assaults on the institution of literary criticism.

Was the so-called crisis of criticism nothing but a momentary collapse? A number of the more recent statements on the subject suggest as much. Joachim Günther asserts: "Books are being written and printed, and, despite all the crises of authors and publishing houses, of a satiated public and overfilled libraries, it looks as though this unending process in the underground of the psyche and society, in the depths of the economy, culture, history and human life were not to be deterred or blocked, much less ever eliminated.[1] The appeal to the eternally human, so familiar to us from pronouncements of the 1950s, finds its place

Translated by David Bathrick.

[1]Joachim Günther, "Literaturkritik?" in *Die Literatur und ihre Medien*, ed. Ingeborg Drewitz (Düsseldorf, 1972), p. 114.

once more in the arsenal of this "surviving" criticism, and already they are saying that criticism *is* indeed as necessary as sun and rain. "A newspaper would simply not be able to compete financially if it let itself think that it could discard its literature and review section as antiquated and irrelevant."[2] It is safe to say that this professional self-assurance will probably not be deterred by indications that American newspapers by no means sell fewer copies simply because they do not review books regularly; nor would they be bothered by the fact that even in West Germany the public demand for literary criticism is not all that great: the literary section of large newspapers is, on the average, read by only 9 percent of their readers.

Some commentators even regard it as success that peace and quiet prevail at present, as though the arguments against the institution of literary criticism had somehow lost validity because ideological struggle has abated. All that can be concluded from such a view is that those critics have never really understood the meaning and consequences of this much discussed crisis of criticism; that they view objections to literary criticism as minor disturbances that have fortunately been eliminated once and for all. And yet, if we distinguish between immediate cause and deeper structural grounds of the crisis, there is no reason to assume that the pressing problems of a few years ago have been solved. For the most part, efforts of the New Left to destroy traditional criticism through a comprehensive cultural revolution have failed. The institution of literary criticism today is not much different from what it was ten years ago. The eloquent pleas for a new kind of literary criticism have brought about no change, precisely because they appealed to the subjective consciousness instead of transforming the institutional basis. In truth, the self-help measures of literary intellectuals have only scratched the surface. Thus traditionalists have had an easy time pointing out to the prophets of the new criticism that except for few name changes all has stayed the same. Of course, it should be remembered that this is the bad old, and not the sudden renascence of, literature and criticism.

Any reassessment of the future of literary criticism will have to begin with the unsolved problems of the past. Contrary to the prevailing tendency to repress such things, the only hope for

[2]Ibid.

their resolution lies in recognizing these problems as having accumulated over a period of time, as the product of a given social situation, and not as something that can be done away with exclusively within the realm of literature. Short-term solutions will accomplish nothing. This was one of the failings of the early New Left (1967–70), which in attempting to provide remedies through change of consciousness and by challenging rigid attitudes, failed to see that the business interests sustained by the literary criticism were not to be swayed by verbal appeals. Nor were they to be disarmed by daring violent actions. In fact, to a certain extent the demand for liquidation on the part of the New Left even obscured the underlying structural problems in the enterprise of literary criticism. Personalized attacks on big-name critics or individual publishing concerns, or even generalized assaults on the whole "system" (theory of manipulation) distracted from the larger context and, in so doing, focused on illusory solutions. A classic example of this was Boehlich's postulation of a new movement beyond the realm of bourgeois criticism—a criticism that would reclaim everything which bourgeois criticism had forfeited, that would rise like Phoenix from the ashes to gratify genuine human needs.[3] That criticism had completely lost its function, as Boehlich and Enzensberger claimed in 1968,[4] can be demonstrated only if one uncritically accepts certain premises. Only by equating the actual end of Modernism with the end of literature itself can one conclude that literary criticism has entered its final phase. Enzensberger, who offered the sharpest formulation of this problem, was also the first to recognize the limits of the thesis and consequently, with his theory of the media in *Kursbuch*, 20 (1970), the first to proclaim the resurrection of literature and criticism.[5] This theory of the media suggested at least tentatively that the much heralded crisis originated not in literature but rather in the problematic of an altered public sphere. The notion that a revival of criticism could be achieved only by restructuring the mass media brought us considerably closer to the essential problem. Only a theory that locates literary criticism—and

[3]See Boehlich's poster supplementing *Kursbuch*, 15 (1968).
[4]Hans Magnus Enzensberger, "Commonplaces on the Newest Literature," in *Consciousness Industry*, ed. Michael Roloff (New York, 1974), pp. 83–95.
[5]Enzensberger, "Constituents of a Theory of the Media," in *Consciousness Industry*, pp. 95–128.

literature—as part of a socially rooted hence socially regulated system of communication makes possible an understanding of its historically structured relationships. The Neomarxist Left's condemnation of bourgeois literary criticism in West Germany (1965-1969) uncritically laid claim to what in reality was in the process of perishing—the bourgeois public sphere. The emancipatory demands, the attempt to do away with the apparatus and its rigid roles and models, presupposed an interest in literary criticism *within* society as a whole, even though for decades it has been limited to one social class, namely the educated bourgeoisie. A critique of criticism remained a matter for intellectuals, a matter in which the masses, whose cause was supposedly being defended, had very little involvement. The valid claim that bourgeois criticism did not reach the masses (and did not want to reach them), that the media erected insurmountable barriers between classes, was equally true for the Left's own position. It was forced, no less than its adversary, to make use of the same apparatus. Ultimately the cultural revolution was to remain very much a question of superstructure (i.e., ideology), and one avoided analyzing the processes at the base which formed the background of the crisis. It certainly should not surprise anyone that the literary establishment ignored the crucial changes in the field of book production and consumption as long as possible and even today chooses to adapt itself to the changed relations rather than deal with them critically. Much more serious, it seems to me, is the fact that even the Left has not adequately taken into account the increased tendencies of concentration within the book market as well as the restructuring of production and distribution; or, at least, has failed to grasp the connection between these factors and the crisis of literary criticism. In so doing it has held bourgeois critics or criticism in themselves responsible for a deplorable situation which far transcends the (limited) scope of the accused. Thus it seems of little value to rehash the debates around this problem in order once again to refute the representatives of established criticism. Whether Günther hails the unfathomed mysteries of book reviewing or whether Heinrich Vormweg,[6] arguing formalistically

---

[6]Heinrich Vormweg, "Literaturkritik retrospektiv?" *Die Literatur und ihre Medien*, pp. 121-136.

against the cultural revolutionary attacks, demands that knowledge of the literary system in its diachronic and synchronic aspects be a prerequisite for reviewing—little is achieved. Obviously we are dealing with a rerun of positions which even in the 1960s could not be successfully defended. The controversy can only be fruitful if it focuses on problems which have been avoided and if it approaches the substantial issues which were still covered up in the late 1960s. Only then can the contours of an epoch emerge which will mark the end of bourgeois criticism. The value of such deliberations are not in the least diminished by the fact that they do not automatically transform the present conditions. That is to say, they should not be confused with actions. Such a misunderstanding would not be without its dangers, for it could lead one to the hasty conclusion that everything will change in the near future.

Accumulated Problems

A prognosis can be reached only if one recognizes not only the phenomena but also the causes underlying them. Thus literary criticism must be viewed within the entirety of its historical context. It should not be overlooked that in advanced capitalist societies literary criticism as an institution has by and large lost the mandate once given it by the public. Since the eighteenth century aesthetic criticism has legitimated itself before a public in which the readers congregated as free and discerning citizens. Yet from the very outset it was a fiction that everyone took part in critical discussion, although up to the middle of the nineteenth century one could at least hope to realize a liberal model of the public sphere. In the ensuing period the development of industrial capitalism made the fulfillment of this early bourgeois model impossible. The undeniable increase in formal education for the masses (the elimination of illiteracy through state schools) was not to be equated with cultural emancipation. What was said to be the democratizing of literary experience (entertainment through mass media, book clubs) proved upon closer examination to be the institutionalization of cultural barriers that have taken hold in the consciousness industry. In literary criticism these barriers are reflected in the fact that prominent professional critics have almost completely excluded those areas of literature which subsequently have come to be known as *Trivialliteratur* (popular literature). On the other hand, the majority of readers is no longer considered the recipient of literary essays and book reviews. Literary criticism is to be regarded as that part of literary production which is consumed by only the narrowest circle of the initiated. The more general accessibility of information by means of mass media should not obscure the fact that literary criticism reaches only very specialized groups, not a general public. Put more pointedly, the production and reception of literary criticism has become the concern of an exclusive circle and in the process has lost the very foundation that would legitimate its public distribution as part of the mass media.

The latest developments on the book and media market have also decidedly contributed to limiting the importance of book reviewing. Since the eighteenth century the book market and criticism have been closely linked; yet the commodity aspect of literature has been strictly excluded from criticism. Traditional publishing concerns have fastidiously respected this separation: the priority of the aesthetic qualities of a work was the unwritten law. On the basis of it, critics have assumed their judgments to have a direct influence on the literary market. Suffice it to say, only a minority of the profession clings to the illusion that such an influence still exists.

The material demands of the book industry—that is, total use of its capacities, the amortization of invested capital, etc.—have dealt a deadly blow to the autonomy of literary-aesthetic value judgments. Production, distribution, and consumption are determined according to criteria that are foreign to the literary critic—according to economic criteria. Any protest against this perversion of "true" relations must forever remain powerless in the face of a book industry that has long since found the ways and means to circumvent the institution of literary criticism or to make it adapt to its own goals. From the perspective of the big publishing concerns, literary criticism appears as a type of unpaid public relations, part of the requirements in any large corporate undertaking. In certain areas—for example, in book clubs—the industry has actually taken criticism into its own hands. In the magazines and newsletters distributed by the clubs, book reviews and advertising have become part of a package.

This is but one illustration of the process which Habermas has called the decline of the bourgeois public sphere.[7] Just as the model of literary criticism upon which the bourgeois-liberal press bases the validity of its literature section is indebted to the public sphere in the eighteenth century for its development, so its present crisis rests in a causal context with the fusion of the public and private sphere in late capitalist societies, as described by Habermas. Given the fact that these changes had already begun in the latter part of the nineteenth century, the structural crisis of criticism can by no means be considered simply a product of the 1960s. The influence of the German Left's extraparliamentarian opposition (APO) only brought out into the open what had long been smoldering beneath the surface.

The inclusion of the public sphere in the circle of production and consumption—that is, the determination of public opinion by the literary market—has undermined those principles which endowed literary discussion with its public significance. "When the laws of the market which govern the sphere of commodity exchange and social labor also penetrate the sphere reserved for private people as public, *Räsonnement* (critical judgment) transforms itself tendentially into consumption, and the context of public communication breaks down into acts that are uniformly characterized by individualized reception."[8] The dialogue of literary criticism loses its representative character as communication of human values that are valid for the entire society. Literary criticism is faced with the choice of either adapting to commercialized culture, thereby forfeiting its original claim, or choosing the esotericism of the literary avant-garde and thus giving up any universality of *Räsonnement*. In the developed forms of the consciousness industry both positions evolve side by side. One and the same organization plans both mass entertainment and elitist cultural programs. In this context we encounter the so-called star critic, whose name serves to guarantee that the new literary product is in step with the latest trends. Regardless

---

[7]Habermas, *Strukturwandel der Offentlichkeit,* 2d ed. (Neuwied and Berlin, 1965).
[8]Ibid., p. 177.

of how much the appearance of fame might seem to speak to the contrary, it is also true that the star critic as independent subcontractor of the literature industry is "inexorably pulled into the sphere of power dictated by companies with the larger capital investments and consequently becomes part of the market."[9] The freedom to form opinion is limited by one's public image. Self-censure confines the judgment of the critic to what corresponds to the public's preexpectations. The critic is paid not for *Räsonnement* but for the product, "renowned opinion." Here it makes no difference whether the critic still believes in this task, constituted as it once was by the bourgeois public sphere. The reliance on the liberal model, according to which the critic speaks in the name of an enlightened literary public, only makes the contradiction between the self image and actual situation more evident. Even the critical writer who takes his or her task seriously and wants to resist the impact of the literature industry gets caught by accepting premises that are no longer valid. The semblance of universal accessibility to critical judgments and to equality, at least in intellectual debates, ultimately hinders insight into the anachronistic nature of one's own intentions. With good reason Gerhard Bauer notes: "Today's critical author is still providing enlightenment in every sense of the word. In the face of a massive counterenlightenment that controls most of the channels of the consciousness industry, the critic thus fulfills an important task, as endless as that of Sisyphus."[10] These relationships were certainly not unknown to leftist anticriticism, and the demand was for a new kind of critic. Of course, this did not solve the dilemma as to how this new critic was to function under present conditions. Would it not be more likely that a change of those conditions would itself bring about a new type?

A New Criticism?

It is no longer reasonable to hope for the restoration of a liberal public sphere, as advocated by progressive critics in West Germany after the Second World War. Such a reconstruction can only be realized in certain limited, if not marginal, areas of

---

[9]Gerhard Bauer, "Zum Gebrauchswert der Ware Literatur," *Lili: Zeitschrift für Literaturwissenschaft und Linguistik* (1971), p. 49.

[10]Ibid., p. 53.

social communication. The fact that one would even consider its reinstitution within the field of literary criticism directly reflects the relative social insignificance of literature itself. For over two decades a kind of free space has existed here, completely unavailable to other sectors of the superstructure. If literary criticism is to regain a real critical and evaluating function, it is necessary to understand that a new, and by that I mean an activating and socially constructive, literature requires first of all changed methods of production and distribution in order to escape control of the consciousness industry. That the role consciousness and self-image of critics will change in accordance with these alterations is secondary in importance to changes of the basic model itself (even though they may be the most visible signs). Only by freeing itself from polemics against superficial phenomena and directing itself to the underlying structural problems will the discussion of the crisis of criticism make any meaningful progress. The hope for sudden transformation through spontaneous actions (graffiti, posters, wall writings, etc.) is illusory, simply because this counterpublic sphere cannot combat the influence of the advanced capitalist public sphere. The hegemony of the capitalist public sphere becomes apparent in its ability to neutralize anything said or written against it and turn everything to serve its own ends. The broad masses whose interests are controlled from above are unable to articulate their experiences, and their real needs are distorted and twisted by the consciousness industry. But it is precisely the expression of these needs in literature which cannot be achieved through a reinstitution of the liberal public sphere, since from the very outset it has equated general interest with bourgeois interest. "The degenerated forms of the current bourgeois public sphere cannot be salvaged or interpreted by looking back to the idealized concept of public sphere in the early bourgeois period."[11]

We must begin with the idea that at present the public dialogue about literary experience, organized as it is in bourgeois society as literary criticism, is of little use to the working classes. Although in a formal sense this dialogue may be generally acces-

[11]Oskar Negt and Alexander Kluge, *Öffentlichkeit und Erfahrung: Zur Organisationsanalyse von bürgerlicher und proletarischer Öffentlichkeit* (Frankfurt am Main, 1972), p. 20.

sible through the media, in fact the masses are prevented from taking part in it. If in the final instance the goal of this discourse is the exchange of opinion about subjective experiences and human interaction, then we can say that the masses are prevented from participating precisely because they remain alienated from the literature under discussion.[12] The well-intentioned and indeed progressive attempt to democratize culture ultimately failed because there was no effort to question the concept of culture in the light of the qualitatively different experience of the proletariat. The most glaring symptom of this failure is the language used in aesthetic discourse. It has been repeatedly pointed out how, in the literary sections of bourgeois newspapers, language has been distorted into a jargon that is almost incomprehensible even to the educated middle classes. And yet this elitist manner of expression identifies only one extreme. Even where critics make an effort to write clearly and comprehensively, they use a language which in choice of vocabulary and syntax lies outside of the experiential sphere of the masses. To this extent, the exchange of critical judgment remains blocked off. Where the lower classes do express themselves directly, they tend not to attain the linguistic standards upon which the public sphere has founded its discourse. This unequal relationship can be expressed more specifically as follows: where the masses, who themselves have not adequately been reached through formal education, do make literature their own, they tend to relate it directly to their own life experience without holding to those rules of an appropriately aesthetic attitude—a prerequisite for bourgeois discussions of art. This appropriation process usually ignores the aesthetic character of a text, thereby violating the rules of literary discourse. On the

[12]Bourgeois attempts in the nineteenth century to raise the level of education of subbourgeois classes through the formation of culture or reading clubs or by reducing the price of books have always stumbled on this hurdle. For they operate on the assumption that the accessibility of cultural privileges, the opportunity to read and discuss, will automatically integrate the underprivileged classes into the existing audience of the public sphere. Although these efforts have altered the situation of literature—the expansion of the reading public is an empirically proven fact—in terms of their intention they remain without consequence. The masses have not become real members of bourgeois culture. Even in its "democratic" advanced forms, the literary public sphere has been incapable of removing its ties to a bourgeois-determined concept of culture.

other hand, the attempt of literary critics to clarify the rules is met not so much with opposition as with lack of comprehension, and this precisely because it is difficult for the uninitiated masses to reconstruct the underlying separation between real experience and fiction lying at the core of literary discourse. These abstract rules cannot be absorbed by the more immediate experience of the lower classes.

Given that the structure of a postbourgeois public sphere can be grasped only in its barest outlines and even in socialist societies has in no way been realized, the possibilities and forms of expression for a new literary criticism can at best be only tentatively sketched out. They in turn have been obscured to a large degree by those forms and methods of criticism which have arisen within the framework of advanced capitalist sectors of production. Just as the advanced capitalist public sphere has been directly connected to market areas, so literary criticism has become an appendix of the culture industry. While the latter does preserve the appearance of a universal dissemination of information and of the accessibility of knowledge to everyone, it nonetheless reinforces in its very structure those barriers between the critical judgment *(Räsonnement)* of the avant-garde and the entertainment of the masses. Can this wall be broken down? Hardly under conditions of advanced capitalism. Adorno and Horkheimer were correct in making this assessment, based as it was on their analysis of the United States.[13] We cannot expect any interest on the part of the media industry in democratizing cultural production and reception, since this industry considers the population as an object to be administered and not a participant in the discussion. This is the relevant aspect of Enzensberger's media theory—it draws attention to the discrepancy between the potential and actual use of mass media and postulates the restructuring of the apparatus in such a way as to mobilize the masses and make them the subject of the apparatus.[14] According to Enzensberger, only through an open, permeable system of communication can the promise of democratization possibly be met. Moreover, Enzensberger is right in

---

[13]Max Horkheimer and Theodor W. Adorno, *Dialectic of Enlightenment,* trans. John Cumming (New York, 1972).
[14]See above, n. 5.

saying that the elimination of capitalist relations of ownership is a necessary but not sufficient condition for such a process. The control of the mass media by the state and party in socialist countries is not the same as socialization of the mass media. More questionable, it seems, is Enzensberger's assumption that the democratic potential of the media will in and of itself prevail against the conditions of production in advanced capitalism. In this he shows too much trust in the spontaneous advances of the masses and too little sensitivity to the current curtailing and crippling of experience. Before the masses can really appropriate the media, they must gradually overcome these deficiencies through a gradual learning process. Here one might confront him with his own statement on the subject: "Precisely because no one bothers about them, the interests of the masses have remained a relatively unknown field."[15] This is by no means limited exclusively to capitalist countries. In looking at more recent literary theories and policies in the German Democratic Republic, it becomes clear that mass needs, specifically in the cultural sector, have remained unsolved problems for socialist societies as well. Subsequent to the 8th Party Congress of the Socialist Unity Party of Germany (SED) in 1971, cultural political discussions focused particularly on the question of how literary criticism on the one side and the appropriation of literature by the working masses on the other could be meaningfully combined.

The Example of the German Democratic Republic

At this point let us examine more closely the social function of literary criticism in the GDR, a society that can well serve as a model for the study of possibilities and problems of a post-bourgeois public sphere. The concept of a socialist literary society, first introduced by Johannes R. Becher, defines its goal in a threefold way: the participation of the working masses in the literary process; the elimination (*Aufhebung*) of elitist and mass culture; and the appropriation of the literary heritage by the working class. Of central importance are the 5th Party Congress

---

[15]Enzensberger, "Constituents of a Theory of the Media (1970)," in his *Consciousness Industry*, ed. Michael Roloff (New York, 1974), p. 111.

(1958) and the First Bitterfeld Conference (1959), where the tasks of the East German cultural revolution were formulated. As we are not concerned here with the development of cultural policy, let us focus on key policy statements. It was Walter Ulbricht who called for "overcoming the gap still existing between artists and the people" and for "breaking down the barriers of the traditional division of labor."[16] Workers were urged not only to take part in the reception of literature, but also to partake actively in producing it. Obviously this attempt to have workers "storm the heights of culture" (Ulbricht) could not bypass the institution of literary criticism. In the Bitterfeld model the role of mediator necessarily fell to the critic. It was a time to develop a discipline that would make workers' needs the basis of one's work. In the introduction to his anthology of literary criticism, Klaus Jarmatz speaks of the "ensemble character" of the new literary criticism and emphasizes its collectivity: "This collectivity assumes the already mentioned leading role of the party of the working class in this area as well but includes all levels *(Schichten)* of socialist society; in short, readers are codeterminants of literary criticism. It is clear that they, too, are involved to an increasing degree in the development of new artistic conventions, in the formation of standards that are appropriate for our society."[17] Horst Oswald emphasizes the importance of reader and lay criticism: "Readers' opinions enter into the ensemble of critical possibilities for our socialist literary society. At the same time reader criticism becomes an expression of the new quality of this literary society. The formation of standards for judging literature occurs with the help of readers. Reader discussions—just as much as literary criticism— become the mediator between literature and reader."[18] With good reason Oswald insists that Marxist criticism is unthinkable without reader discussions. In the final instance, the process of reaching critical judgment must be founded on the intercommunication of the masses themselves. It certainly should not be concluded from this that lay criticism will finally have reached its humble place next to professional criticism, but rather that this dichotomy—a vestige of a past social

---

[16]Quoted from *Materialistische Geschichtswissenschaft*, Vol. 1 (Berlin, 1971).
[17]Klaus Jarmatz, *Kritik in der Zeit* (Halle, 1970), p. 19.
[18]Horst Oswald, *Literatur, Kritik und Leser* (Berlin, 1969), p. 99.

form—must be overcome. Criticism is always, of course, reader criticism, for even the specialized intellectual is a reader—a privileged one, to be sure.

As one can readily demonstrate on the basis of concrete literary debates, these demands were more easily voiced than put into practice. In the extensive public discussion around Christa Wolf's *The Divided Heaven* (1963), professional and lay criticism coexisted in an uneasy relationship.[19] In the long run the professionals had the final word, whereas, because of their unliterary character, the suggestions and objections of the amateurs were not taken all that seriously. It was quickly pointed out to workers that they had not yet acquired the prerequisites for discussion, that they still did not have the proper conceptual apparatus at their disposal. Nevertheless, that such reactions were even officially recorded must be regarded as significant progress. Among the critics, Günther K. Lehmann was the first to comment critically on this unequal relationship between the reading interests of the masses and the aesthetic as well as ideological norms of the specialists: "It was often the case that books were praised which virtually nobody read because they were boring, unrealistic and irrelevant. . . . And critics also frequently rejected fresh and unconventional works which interested people and gave them new food for thought, either because those books seemed to violate some supposed purity of genre or because the logic of the plot, the typology of the hero, or the tragedy inherent in the solution of the conflict contradicted theoretical models or ready-made critical norms."[20] From this Lehmann drew far-reaching conclusions for the restructuring of literary criticism. In place of a systematic, speculative criticism based primarily on textual analysis, he called for a science of communications that would "explore the degree of social efficacy of art works."[21] The model proposed here is connected to the problem of literary criticism insofar as it presented for the first time a theory of literary communication capable of analyzing the social function of literary criticism. The numerous works published in the GDR since 1965 which deal with the impact of art and with reader

[19]See Martin Reso, *"Der geteilte Himmel" und seine Leser* (Halle, 1964).
[20]Günther K. Lehmann, "Grundfragen einer marxistischen Soziologie der Kunst," *Deutsche Zeitschrift für Philosophie*, 13 (1965), 933–934.
[21]Ibid., p. 937.

interests attest to the growing interest of East German criticism in evaluating changing relations. Since 1970 these empirical studies have been complemented by theoretical exploration of the meaning of literary reception.[22] At the center necessarily stands the question of the possibilities of literary criticism within socialist life relationships.[23] For GDR theoreticians, the socialization of the means of production itself is seen as sufficient cause for the changes demanded. It is anticipated that a new type of reader will be developed—one who will be able to appropriate past and present literature on the basis of his or her experience in a socialist society. An end point of this development is a universal reading of culture which would encompass all members of society; thus the proletarian public sphere would emerge as a necessary component of the actual realization of socialism. Manfred Naumann underscores this achievement: "The ensemble of socialist life relationships, in particular the socialist educational system, has contributed to a continual improvement of the cultural level of the citizenry [GDR] and furthermore to a stimulation of its literary interests and needs."[24]

The key question, of course, is whether this development can occur as unproblematically as is suggested here. The recent discussion concerning the function of literary criticism in the GDR still suggests that the overcoming of cultural barriers is not without its difficulties. Although democracy has been instituted on a formal level, it has not been realized and guaranteed experientially. For instance, during the *Sinn und Form* debate of 1972 a number of problems emerged which were not in accord with the premises of official cultural policy. In what seemed to be a conscious attempt to provoke, Wilhelm Girnus spoke of the in-

---

[22] See *Sozialgeschichte und Wirkungsästhetik: Dokumente zur empirischen und marxistischen Rezeptionsforschung*, ed. Peter U. Hohendahl (Frankfurt am Main, 1974).

[23] Thus Manfred Naumann contrasts the determinants of a socialist with those of a capitalist society when he writes: "The collapse of the public into 'experts' and consumers is a result of the capitalist social order in which the cultural privilege of the owning class sees to it that the contradiction between the 'experts,' whose needs are served by literature for 'experts,' and the consumers, for whom a literature for the 'masses' is served up, constantly reproduces itself. . . . The ensemble of socialist life relationships, in particular the socialist educational system, has led to a continual elevation of the cultural level of its citizens and, connected to that, to a stimulation of their literary interests and needs" ("Literatur und Leser," *Weimarer Beiträge*, 16 [1970], 113).

[24] Ibid.

adequacies of literary criticism: "We simply cannot be satisfied with the present state of literary criticism or with the training in this profession."[25] Girnus pointed particularly to the fact "that despite repeated urging from the party, the working class, which has the power in its hands, does not carry weight in literature commensurate with its historical mission and social force."[26] What is missing is its collective involvement in public discourse. In this context, Girnus criticizes the lack of public discussion around problems of literature, without however giving any reasons for this phenomenon. It is only indirectly that fundamental problems are voiced when the conditions of public *Räsonnement* are presented. Then it becomes quite clear that the liberal public sphere is still the paradigm that shapes the mode of criticism. The desired discussion is defined as a dialogue among specialists. The audience gathered here as the public sphere is in reality a socialist republic of scholars whose experiences are not necessarily the same as those of the working class.

The writings of Friedrich Möbius point in a similar direction.[27] His attempt to define art criticism within the ensemble of social productivity is directed toward systematically designating the scope of criticism by assigning to it specific audiences and functions. Distinctions are drawn between the promotional function of criticism (in relation to the artist), the educational function (in relation to the audience), and administrative functions (the concerns of the social contractors)—that is, "the editorial staffs of mass communications, associations of artists, and the party and state apparatus."[28] Here the apparatus envisages itself as the contractor of a public that appears only as the sum of malleable individuals. Decisive theoretical and practical decisions are relegated by Möbius to the area of administrative function, which characteristically is reserved for the party apparatus; whereas the public—the working masses—is considered only from the vantage point of education. The critic defines himself or herself vis-à-vis the masses as expert and pedagogue; his or

[25]Wilhelm Girnus, "Erste Gedanken zu Problemen der Literaturkritik," *Sinn und Form*, 24 (1972), 443.
[26]Ibid., 445.
[27]Friedrich Möbius, "Zwei Kapitel zur Kunstkritik," *Weimarer Beiträge*, 18 (1972), 166–174.
[28]Ibid., 167.

her goal is the aesthetic education of individuals. "An art critic . . . must guide readers, listeners, viewers to identification or disagreement, even regarding the 'attitude' of a work of art."[29] The masses are not considered as the actual contractors of critical *Räsonnement*. Relations between them and the critic remain one-way communication.

Möbius is certainly not blind to the inclination of professional critics to isolate and make themselves self-sufficient. Although he critically analyzes the "ivory tower of academic contemplation,"[30] the overcoming of this condition is still conceived in terms of individual contact between critic and artist, teacher and student, etc. This means, however, that the structure of the dialogue itself remains intact. The professional role of the critic in the GDR differs significantly from similar roles found in capitalist societies; yet the status of expert remains unquestioned. The production of book reviews, critical essays, and historical works remains in Möbius' model a matter for trained specialists; and no demands for greater contact with the masses can hide that fact. The basis for the function of the expert is still a restrictive public sphere in which the masses primarily remain receivers. The stimulus for action lies with the party apparatus; the policies laid down (articulated) at party conventions are designed to initiate activity among work collectives. Hannelore Vierus describes the effects of the 8th Party Congress in the following way: "Just as the Kirov workers emphasized the role of art and literature in the development of a socialist personality for the importance of forming a cultural environment and cultural relations within the work collective . . . so after the 9th Party Congress of the SED numerous work collectives struggled to achieve a living relation to culture and its enrichment."[31] A statement like this does not make clear whether the "struggle" has been decreed by the party apparatus or whether the seed of a proletarian public sphere—one in which literature would become the subject of discussion directly related to common everyday experience—is emerging from within the collectives. The 6 percent cited by Vierus as that segment of the population

[29]Ibid., 170.
[30]Ibid., 172.
[31]Hannelore Vierus, "Über kulturelle Lebensgewohnheiten der Arbeiterklasse," *Weimarer Beiträge*, 18 (1972), 32-33.

actively and creatively engaged in culture is a clear indication that the desired democratization is still very much in the inception stage.[32] The dilemma of the GDR is that the state and party apparatus still cannot do without intellectuals as specialists, and this in turn makes the juxtaposition of lay and professional criticism part of the system itself. This contradiction makes itself felt within the structure of the mass media; the media not only permit but actually demand that the public articulate its needs. At the same time they continue to remain the means of communication for the party apparatus and its specialists, only occasionally being placed at the disposal of the lay person.

The Democratization of Literary Criticism

What does the democratization of literary criticism really mean? The answer to this question will decide the future of criticism. A meaningful answer is by no means obvious and can only be given in relation to a concrete social situation. In this regard it is easier to say what democratization cannot mean: it cannot mean the separation of literary institutions from everyday life in order to prevent the further incursion of socioeconomic interests. The critic as spokesperson for an educated reading public or as discerning mediator between artist and reader is no longer a viable model because the model's underlying conception of democracy is tied to a certain class structure. In other words, the literary public sphere cannot be democratized by merely using the media and other institutions to draw in lower classes previously excluded from such privileges. The history of book clubs provides ample evidence why this does not work. Initially established to enable the underprivileged to participate in literary life, they soon became instruments in the hands of private capital for keeping the masses in a state of cultural dependency. Attempting to organize the cultural needs of the proletariat through institutions of the late bourgeois public sphere is problematic, for the consciousness industry will usually succeed in channeling and thereby neutralizing these efforts. As long as current social conditions in the Federal Republic prevail—more specifically, as long as the media can be used as

[32]Ibid., 39.

instruments by dominant social groups against the interests of the masses—the socialization of literary criticism can only be prepared for. A first step in this direction would be a praxis-oriented didactic criticism which, by analyzing distortions and promoting legitimate needs, could begin to do away with professional isolation in bourgeois cultural ghettos and direct itself consciously and intentionally to broad social groups. It is not simply a matter of knocking down language barriers; we must also expand the scope of the subject matter. The present focus of the book review industry on innovative literature might be replaced by an emphasis on the impact of literature. One cannot conduct a discussion about so-called "good" literature if no one has knowledge of the subject. Obviously popular literature and best-sellers would be a priority concern, since here there is an impact that must be critically examined.[33] Of course any such revision of critical tasks will necessitate another kind of training for the critic. It is astonishing how little attention has been given this problem in recent literary debates. The unsatisfactory state of academic criticism and, more specifically, the assumed irrelevance of academic training for the practice of literary criticism, have hindered the necessary reconsideration of how critics are to prepare for their tasks. Based as it is on established norms of aesthetics, the constant emphasis on literary quality is nothing but a hidden defense of the status quo. A truly popular criticism would first and foremost attempt to provide the lower classes— under the conditions of a diffuse public sphere—with the opportunity of coming to terms with their own situation, one which they themselves did not create. This can only be achieved if the machinations of the culture business, of which they are the objects, are gradually made visible. (The warning against "bad" literature will have no effect as long as it is unclear what the needs are which have led to the reading of this literature.) The proper place for such a discussion would not be literary magazines or the book review section of nationally syndicated

[33]The academic complement to such a popular criticism would be a critical— that is, a social and historical—investigation of so-called *Trivialliteratur*. Such a study would have as its first task the destruction of the traditional classification of literature. For a discussion of research in popular literature, see Joachim Bark, "Popular Literature and Research in a Praxis-Related Literary Scholarship," *New German Critique*, No. 1 (Winter 1973), pp. 133–141.

newspapers but local or factory newspapers, mimeographed newsletters, or even programs of educational radio and television.[34]

These few efforts will, of course, soon run up against the limits of what the system will tolerate. The competing industrial and commercial interests will exert their influence to thwart and control democratic efforts. For that reason it will be necessary for a popular literary criticism to make maximum use of areas of communication in which the classical principle of the public sphere is still operable. Public control of some mass media in West Germany (radio, television), compared to the United States, provides shelter in a limited sense, as does the relative autonomy of schools and universities vis-à-vis private interests. Anyone familiar with these institutions knows very well how precarious their situation is in regard to outside pressure. For all that, the ultimate goal remains a movement in the opposite direction; the public sphere is to be extended into the area the bourgeoisie has defined as private—namely, control over the means of production. Consequently, a second step would consist of workers gaining a share in the decision-making of the press and major publishing houses. Here labor organizations and unions would play a crucial role, for their influence on the structure of the media is anything but secondary. Of course we cannot expect that the masses will have a clear perception of the problem. This is not only because the consciousness industry has attempted to hinder such insights, but, more importantly, because the proletarian public sphere cannot be simply transferred to a mass media developed by the bourgeoisie. Adapting to the forms of the bourgeois public sphere will be paid for through separation from the very subculture that heretofore has lent identity to the proletarian classes. Qualitatively new ways of producing and living can be developed only subsequent to overcom-

---

[34]Such a didactic criticism, which at this time is only in its beginning stages, should not be confused with the attempts of the nineteenth-century liberal bourgeoisie to bring culture to the people. Although certainly well intentioned, in the final instance these efforts ultimately led to the culturally deprived lower classes giving up their own experiences in favor of models found in literature. Here culture remained an instrument of domination for the ruling class. The masses to whom it was directed could not eliminate the contradiction between their own social situation and the human values found in the literature made available to them.

ing capitalist relations of production; prior to this there exists a contradiction between political goal and everyday life. The worker "must choose between his or her own, present identity and a historical, characteristic quality as a proletarian and revolutionary force that would transform the totality of society into new means of production."[35] Hence Negt and Kluge are right in calling the present form of proletarian counterpublic sphere a "self-defense organization of the working class,"[36] which while creating enclaves of solidarity to counter bourgeois interests must at the same time sacrifice any claim to universality because of its integration into late capitalism's public sphere of production relations. Thus at the very moment when the proletariat wishes to realize its claim to universality, it finds itself thrown back upon the liberal public sphere. This is also what characterizes the current difficulties of popular literary criticism: either it makes use of bourgeois institutions, or it is driven back to areas of communication that are not public in the sense of the entire society. As Enzensberger has clearly demonstrated in his discussion of the New Left, the price for undermining the bourgeois public sphere is self-exclusion from forms of communication directed at society as a totality. On the basis of that he came to the following conclusion in his theory of the media: the mass media must be refashioned in such a way as to become the masses' means of production—and this not only in a formal sense, through nationalization, but through actual appropriation of tools and technology. Enzensberger's proposal is itself not entirely free of the *Aporie* it describes, for it assumes a condition which the masses have not yet reached and fails to show how the prevailing structure of the public sphere is to be overcome. The question of what the basis of experience should be from which the masses are to learn an emancipated use of the media if the intelligentsia does not assume the task of organizing new forms of decentralized communication remains unanswered. Yet, more than any other social group, the intelligentsia is inextricably bound to the consciousness industry. In this it retains its freedom to critique the system, but not to abolish it—an act that would amount to economic suicide. Where the intelligentsia suc-

---

[35]Negt and Kluge, *Öffentlichkeit und Erfahrung*, p. 113.
[36]Ibid.

ceeds in establishing contact with the masses, it is able to function in an advisory and enlightening way, but it can hardly constitute a counterpublic sphere.

The beginnings of a socialized literary criticism have begun to emerge in the most recent forms of self-organization among writing workers. Whereas Gruppe 61 was still conceived as a bourgeois association that chose the working world as the subject of study, within the workers' literary workshops *(Werkkreis)* forms of organization have developed which break through the context of the bourgeois public sphere (without being, of course, immune to getting pulled into it). They thereby destroy a definition of literature, peculiar to the bourgeois public sphere, which sees itself as a form of communication divorced from real life experience. The workshops no longer wish to provide insights into the living conditions of a particular social class but rather seek to mobilize this class for its own literary activity and thereby construct a literary dialogue in which those being depicted comprehend their own situation. "Workers and white collar workers write as 'wage earners' for workers and white-collar workers, in order to promote and develop class-consciousness and bring about the solidarity resulting from it."[37] Clearly this program contains the call for a new conception of literary criticism. Further development is yet to come. If the movement is not to be confined merely to primary groups where personal contact and communication are possible, new forms for establishing dialogue in literary criticism must be considered.

[37]Reinhard Ditmar, *Industrieliteratur* (Munich, 1973), p. 75.

5 *Promoters, Consumers, and Critics: On the Reception of the Best-Seller*

There was a time—some look back on it with longing, others with abhorrence—when the world of literature and literary criticism was still in good order, when literary historians and reviewers still knew (or seemed to know) exactly what they were supposed to be doing, when one could speak with a clear conscience about "poetic literature," and when such profane topics as the mass distribution of books were examined at the very most by a few specialists in library science. It was well known, to be sure, that best-sellers existed and that they were on occasion reviewed in newspapers and journals. Nevertheless, the critical attitude toward these phenomena of the book market was fixed a priori: it seemed obvious that mass distribution of literature and aesthetic quality were mutually exclusive. Accordingly, best-sellers could only be discussed in depreciating terms. Anything that pleased the taste of the broad reading public was automatically excluded from the canon of serious literature. Worthwhile literature is accessible only to small circles of readers within modern mass society; it achieves no high sales figures and is not absorbed by the market. Any work, therefore, which attains an unusual success in sales is somewhat suspect and is quite possibly no longer worthy of critical analysis.

This is not the place to analyze the birth and development of this attitude, and I will restrict myself to an examination of its

Translated by Ronald L. Smith and Henry J. Schmidt.

results.[1] This self-image of criticism and literary research, rooted in the aesthetic distance from the broad reading public which is the stamp of the modern literary age, results in a horizontal apportionment of critical endeavors. Producers of literature have a label of quality attached to them in the literary marketplace, a label that determines the future extent and type of reviewing. A mediocre novel by Heinrich Böll is nonetheless a Böll novel, and as such receives wide attention in the national press, while a novel by Johannes Mario Simmel remains a Simmel novel, and thus is reviewed primarily in local newspapers. The extent to which this concept of "niveau" has hindered criticism and literary research was demonstrated again a few years ago by Helmut Kreuzer in his critical contribution to the examination of "trivial literature": despite researchers' efforts to broaden their subject matter and to include so-called trivial literature in their field of research, the traditional differentiation between "serious" literature and "trivial" literature remained for the most part intact, so that the advance into uncharted literary regions was again checked.[2] Some critics sought to destroy this polarity by expressly denying any aesthetic element in entertainment literature and assigning it other functions. But even they remained caught in time-worn categories; the denial of aesthetic merit in popular literature and the emphasis on its communicative function served to affirm the dichotomy between poetic and trivial literature. Only when we divorce ourselves from the prejudices of our literary tradition, when we resolve to examine the process of literary communication in its entirety, will we be able to subject the relationship of best-sellers and literary criticism to a critical analysis that can accomplish more than the perpetuation of rigid cultural values.

The first task would be to take stock of the present situation. Which newspapers review best-sellers? Who, in fact, writes about a novel by Hans Habe, Johannes Mario Simmel, or Hans Helmut Kirst when major critics like Reinhard Baumgart and Walter Jens

---

[1]For a further investigation see Jochen Schulte-Sasse, *Die Kritik an der Trivialliteratur seit der Aufklärung: Studien zur Geschichte des modernen Kitschbegriffs* (Munich, 1971), esp. pp. 63–129.

[2]Helmut Kreuzer, "Trivialliteratur als Forschungsproblem. Zur Kritik des deutschen Trivialromans seit der Aufklärung," *Deutsche Vierteljahrsschrift für Literaturwissenschaft und Geistesgeschichte* 41 (1967), 173–191.

remain silent? Who provides critical information to the prospective buyer about this field of literature? Or is it simply left to the publishers' advertising agencies to describe the strengths—though hardly the weaknesses—of the writer in question? Do reviewers have any influence at all on public opinion? With what criteria do critics approach best-sellers and their authors? To whom do they direct their statements of opinion? Questions upon questions, which have found few answers. To my knowledge, only Peter Glotz has dealt with these processes of communication and formulated hypotheses based on hard evidence.[3] According to him, literary criticism is carried out in various realms of communication, depending on whether it concerns a best-seller categorized as serious or as trivial literature. Although a book by Uwe Johnson, as one might expect, is reviewed by prominent critics and authors in the national press, Kirst's books are reviewed chiefly in second-rank provincial journals and local newspapers.

Until now, the term "best-seller" has been used as though it were self-explanatory. We call a book a best-seller when its sales are extraordinarily high.[4] Since the concept is based on quantity, it seems less of a problem than the concept of trivial literature. The troublesome question of value is excluded; statistics alone decide whether a book is a best-seller. But the impression that there is a clear demarcation is deceptive. All statistics must incorporate boundaries. Is a book a best-seller when it sells twenty thousand copies, or must it reach five hundred thousand? Such distinctions are arbitrary, especially when one compares different book markets and different eras.[5] Although one needs statistics in dealing with best-sellers, statistics alone do not provide a clear genetic and structural explanation of the phenomenon. It is worth noting that the term appears to have been in use

---

[3]Peter Glotz, *Buchkritik in deutschen Zeitungen* (Hamburg, 1968). See also my review in *German Quarterly*, 44 (1971), 441–450.

[4]In earlier investigations the best-seller was often equated with the trivial novel and thus defined in psychological terms (oriented toward the reading public) or aesthetic terms (kitsch). Cf. the findings of Sonja Marjasch in *Der amerikanische Bestseller* (Bern, 1946), pp. 23–24.

[5]Frank L. Mott, for example, proceeds from the idea that a book is a best-seller when the number of copies sold equals one percent of the total population of the decade of its publication. See his *Golden Multitudes: The Story of Bestsellers in the United States* (New York, 1947), p. 7.

only since 1895, when the journal *Bookman*, using empirical methods of research, began to print regularly a list of "books in demand."[6] This concept is thus inextricably bound to the methods of book production and consumption in the age of high and late capitalism. The interest in exact numbers began at a time when the book trade was assuming a more active role in directing the literary market. What was previously left for the most part to the natural growth process of production and consumption was now used—though at first in a very modest form—as a means of advertisement: success in terms of quantity served as an index of quality.

The best-seller is a product of the twentieth century, sociohistorically as well as economically. In the nineteenth century certain preconditions for this phenomenon were developed: first, the reading public expanded through the inclusion of social strata below the educated bourgeoisie,[7] for whom books had previously been economically out of reach (we should not be too easily deceived by reports from the early nineteenth century; regular purchases of books were possible then only for the upper classes); second, reading habits developed that were based on the continuous consumption of literature (resultant to some extent, no doubt, from the introduction of serialized novels in magazines and newspapers in 1840);[8] third, the technology of book production advanced, permitting the rapid printing of large numbers of books at low prices.[9] The interdependence of these factors led to what we now call best-sellers. The contemporary best-seller is no longer an accidental success, as it was in the nineteenth century, but a planned one, using all the marketing and promotional techniques at its disposal. This means that only publishing houses with great capital resources can produce such

---

[6]Alice P. Hacket, *70 Years of Best Sellers: 1895–1965* (New York, 1967), p. 2.

[7]For the sociohistorical background, see Richard D. Altick, *The English Common Reader* (Chicago, 1957).

[8]See Eva D. Becker, "Zeitungen sind doch das Beste. Bürgerliche Realisten und der Vorabdruck ihrer Werke in der periodischen Presse," in *Gestaltungsgeschichte und Gesellschaftsgeschichte,* ed. Helmut Kreuzer (Stuttgart, 1969); and Nora Atkinson, *Eugène Sue et le roman-feuilleton* (Paris, 1929).

[9]From the introduction of the rotary press in 1811 to the Walter press in 1866, which could print 12,000 double-sized eight-page sheets per hour; in addition, the possibility of mass production of cheap paper since 1840.

a commodity. The tendency toward planned best-sellers was strengthened by the transition from middle-class family enterprises to a large-scale book industry. And today the giant publishers can no longer do without best-sellers if they are to remain financially successful.[10] In order to avoid going into the red, they must push a big money-maker through the market at regular intervals in order to cover the cost of numerous unsuccessful ventures and their high operating expenses. This is not to say that the production of best-sellers is without risks. Managers and chief editors are well aware that even today, despite sophisticated market research, the success of a book with a large printing cannot be safely predicted.

The seemingly irrational element in the calculations of publishing houses and book retailers can be fully explained in retrospect. In terms of the sociology of the reading public, the best-seller represents the special case of a book which surpasses its intended readership. In the words of Siegfried Kracauer, "Huge sales figures are the mark of a successful sociological experiment, the proof that once more a mixture of elements has been found which corresponds to the taste of an anonymous audience of readers."[11] Robert Escarpit was correct in pointing out that the best-seller is defined not by the amount, but by the pattern, of sales.[12] The usual sales chart of a book of belles-lettres shows a sharply rising curve which then falls slowly until sales reach a near halt after approximately a year. The curve of a best-seller differs from the expected pattern by rising once again. Its sales graph exhibits a wave pattern; the number and height of these waves reflect the extent to which the book has reached beyond its original circle of readers. The breakthrough can come about in several phases. The crucial boundaries in the German and French book markets are 10,000, 50,000, and 100,000 copies. Only when sales surpass 100,000 copies can we speak of a true

---

[10]See Dieter Wellershoff, "Literatur, Markt, Kulturindustrie," in his *Literatur und Veränderung* (Cologne, 1969), pp. 123-247; and my essay in this volume, "The End of an Institution? The Debate over the Function of Literary Criticism in the 1960s."

[11]Quoted from Siegfried Kracauer in *Tendenzen der deutschen Literatur seit 1945*, ed. Thomas Koebner (Stuttgart, 1971), p. 331.

[12]Robert Escarpit, *The Book Revolution* (London, 1966), pp. 117, 119.

best-seller that is reaching the broad reading public—that is, even readers who only occasionally purchase a book.[13] The sales pattern outlined by Escarpit can serve as an index to the sociology of the reading public. The best-seller is a book that finds strata of readers beyond the group to which the author initially directed his work. In contrast to the novels written for serialization in magazines, and to the schematically produced entertainment novels for lending libraries, which are written for a known public (the right length of a serialized novel is judged, for instance, by the continuing sales of the magazine), a consensus among readers in the open book market, the basis of any best-seller, must be recreated each time. The task of the publishing firm is to establish the book as a topic of conversation. In a highly specialized society based on division of labor, the best-seller fulfills an important function in providing the potential for social contact.[14] It supplies its readers with a special gratification in offering a ready topic of conversation with other readers, with whom they have little else in common.[15] In this process the

[13]One should not be fooled by the best-seller lists of *Der Spiegel* and *Die Zeit*, for they are based on surveys of selected bookstores and not, as should be absolutely necessary, on confirmed data from the publishing houses. The lists in the press provide only an approximate index to the popularity of literary works. The advertising departments of the publishing firms concede that these figures can be manipulated.

[14]Experienced publishers who know their authors have a feeling for the originally intended reading audience. They intuitively know its specific reading needs, desired and forbidden themes, and preferred writing styles. They can advise their authors in this regard. Beyond that they depend on the observation of trends in the various realms of literary communication to seek out new readers. The Rowohlt firm, for instance, speculated on the audience of the Sunday magazines and family journals when it decided to market Eric Malpass' book *Morning at Seven* as a best-seller (it had not been very successful in England, selling only 5,000 copies). Although the conditions in England described by Malpass are not identical to those in Germany, there was a foundation on which the publishing firm could build, namely the milieu of the rural family—that is, distance from modern society with its burdensome problems. With this they could attempt to reach that considerable portion of the German population which still yearns for the harmony of the pre-industrial world and rejects such literary tendencies as the depiction of sex and crime. The success of the book was thus based on its repudiation of a certain fashionable trend and its likeness to a genre with an established audience, the *Heimatroman* (novel of the homeland). The mild departure from the basic pattern through the English milieu may have helped the novel to find readers who would have ignored a similar German product.

[15]Cf. Wellershoff in *Literatur und Veränderung*, p. 140.

institutions of the culture industry, such as the press, radio, and television, serve an indispensable function, as publishers are well aware. Except in the case of a few authors whose sales come automatically, as it were, only the use of the mass media can bring a work the degree of attention in the public sphere which is needed to achieve high sales figures. In the past ten years the creation of best-sellers has entered a new stage. The tendency is toward programing, a process in which the transition from the originally intended readership to other groups and finally to the general public is no longer left to chance but is carefully planned. Once the path to a programed best-seller is taken, there is no turning back, for the resulting expenses can be recovered only by sales that would be considered astronomical by traditional standards.

For the best-seller industry, authors and their works are interchangeable. Aesthetic criticism is thus inappropriate. The best-seller does not belong *eo ipso* to the category of trivial literature. In the past culture critics made the error of constructing a logical, immanent contradiction between aesthetic quality and printing quantity.[16] "Social uplifting," the transfiguration and harmonization of reality, the psychological facilitation of reading by fulfilling the public's expectations—these factors can contribute to the success of a work but are not, in my opinion, necessary conditions. Otherwise it would be impossible to understand how works of "high literature" can appear on the best-seller lists.[17] Interchangeability means that the original characteristics of a work and its author are replaced by secondary ones. This image-building is not confined to popular literature, however. The daring, if not indecent, tone of Günter Grass's writing certainly helped the sales of *The Tin Drum,* though it has nothing to do with the structure of the text. Of crucial importance for mass

---

[16]For example, Q. D. Leavis, *Fiction and the Reading Public* (London, 1932).

[17]Too narrow is a definition that emphasizes the psychological facilitation provided by a particular writing style, as stated, for example, by Marjasch, *Der amerikanische Bestseller,* p. 23: "The modern best-seller is characterized by a typical element of style, the 'particular touch' of best-selling authors, which is achieved through constant, conscious repetition, so that the reading public, once it is familiar with certain authors, can recognize it immediately." That statement applies to Simmel and Kirst but hardly to Thomas Mann, whose *Buddenbrooks,* it must be remembered, was also a million-seller. For America see also Roger Burlingame, *Of Making Many Books* (New York, 1946), pp. 136–137.

selling power is the creation of reading attraction that can be attached to the text. The planning of a best-seller must incorporate the current conversational topics of the public sphere in order to emphasize the up-to-date nature of the article being sold. This interchangeability of author and work underscores the often observed fact that the publisher is primarily responsible for the success of a book. Only a work with the highest level of marketing and promotional techniques can survive in the competition among new titles. It is the publisher who provides the book's marketable "finish." The reader knows what to expect from Rowohlt, Molden, or Droemer. What Escarpit vigorously disputed has now become a fact—production and merchandising of literature have taken on the forms used in the auto industry. This involves making the sale of a product independent of its use value. Various means are available to accomplish this: (1) market research into the needs of the audience[18] (the Bertelsmann publishing firm, for example, engages at regular intervals respected organizations which analyze the impact of its production); (2) the entire arsenal of advertising ploys, from in-house articles to carefully arranged publicity tours for authors;[19] (3) complete exploitation of rights in the media market.

The chief difference between the modern programed bestseller and its nineteenth-century predecessor lies in the utilization of the media "network"—that is, passing the same material through various media to exploit fully its profit-making potential. In contractual terms: the subsidiary rights are often more important than the original book edition. To exaggerate only a little, the original edition is merely a display window in which the publishing house exhibits its wares for other purposes. In the traditional book trade, the sales of the original edition were calculated to cover costs and secure a profit. In the programed best-seller, however, the further sale of subsidiary rights is anticipated from the outset. For the Rowohlt publishing firm, the latest book by C. W. Ceram, *Der erste Amerikaner* (The First American), will barely turn a profit even if more than 125,000

---

[18]Cf. Klaus Ziermann, *Romane vom Fliessband: Die imperialistische Massenliteratur in Westdeutschland* (Berlin-GDR, 1969), pp. 171, 168.

[19]Cf. Hartmut Panskus, "Buchwerbung in Deutschland," in *Literaturbetrieb in Deutschland*, ed. H. L. Arnold (Munich, 1971), pp. 78–90.

copies are sold.[20] The purchase of the rights and the advertising costs were so exorbitant that only the succeeding paperback edition or the sale of the rights to a book club will make it a profitable venture. Since the subsidiary rights are so important, the programed best-seller must reach its predicted sales figures, for if it should fail, the profit potential of those subsidiary rights would be endangered. As a result, the sales figures must be driven upward at any cost, or at the very least the impression must be created that the book is selling well. The publishers are by no means averse to using, on occasion, various tricks of the trade that may help them gain an advantage in their dealings with book clubs or the film industry.

Under these circumstances, advertising (in its broadest sense) attains an importance completely alien to the traditional book trade.[21] Since large amounts of capital are at stake, which must be amortized rapidly, the reception of a novel cannot be left to the usual needs of the audience. The public must be conditioned, even though it has already been largely disoriented by a flood of advertising stimuli. This conditioning begins with such seemingly innocuous matters as the design of the jacket and its blurb. It includes an intensive and extensive advertising campaign in newspapers and magazines carefully chosen for their particular readership, and also involves a planned release of information to the mass media, so that even before the book appears, public interest is aroused by provocative statements.[22] Such new best-seller advertising replaces slow, cumulative effects

---

[20]According to a statement to me from Dr. Matthias Wegner, director of Rowohlt Verlag.

[21]Under Samuel Fischer, the Fischer Verlag restricted its advertising to notices in the *Börsenblatt* and an occasional prospectus. The advertising budget was small. Collective advertisements were placed in the national newspapers twice yearly to promote new titles. Cf. Gottfried Bermann-Fischer, *Bedroht—Bewahrt: Wege eines Verlages* (Frankfurt am Main, 1967), p. 33.

[22]It is with good reason that the manager and chief officials of such a publicity-conscious publishing firm as Rowohlt seclude themselves for several days when planning a best-seller in order to produce the most effective jacket blurb possible. For the jacket blurb represents the book's calling card, heavily relied upon by the specialists of the media industry, who insist on quick information. If they succeed in finding the appropriately enticing phrases, they can be sure of having supplied a good many of the critics with the formulaic expressions that will appear in their reviews. A well-written jacket blurb multiplies its effect through the numerous reviews for which it serves as a model.

by a comprehensive strategy that coordinates individual initiatives in such a way that each reflects back on the others. When the film rights are sold, the publisher can take advantage of the publicity from the filming, and the film studio, of course, benefits from the book advertising.

The promotion of Erich Segal's *Love Story* has become a classic example. To a lesser extent, Rowohlt's advertising department utilized this effect during the filming of Eric Malpass's *Morgens um sieben ist die Welt noch in Ordnung* (*Morning at Seven*). In an interview with Dieter E. Zimmer, advertising chief Eric Merwick remarked: "The Constantin studio bought the rights, and from that moment on, the publisher, the film producers, and the rental agency worked together in the advertising sector. All the competitions we held—the search for a child star, for locales—everything you could imagine, we did it together, in the press, for the public. And naturally there were new peaks of interest, and people talked about the book again and again."[23] They did not seek the cooperation of the literary critics so much as that of the local news editors—for stories about the selection of the star, the work on the set, and so on. These reports in the local news sections were usually replete with photos, and the advertising agencies were correct in anticipating very effective results from them, since the local section of a newspaper is read more extensively than the literary page.[24] The culture editors are not consulted again until the finished movie or television film is ready for release to the public. In principle, of course, this achieves the same effect—the multiplication of publicity through the network of media. "With a few exceptions," Zimmer notes, "the bestseller today needs the help of other media, of the interlocking media network. A book can hardly succeed by itself any more."[25] This judgment has to be modified. The cooperation of the media is indispensable if the publisher wishes to surpass the 100,000

[23]Dieter E. Zimmer, "Die Herren grosser Publikumszahlen ... Über die Karriere eines Bestsellers, am Beispiel von Eric Malpass," *Literaturbetrieb in Deutschland*, p. 107.

[24]According to Glotz (*Buchkritik*, p. 214), reviews are read by fewer than 10 percent of the readers, while the local news section is read by nearly 80 percent. See Peter Glotz and Wolfgang Langenbucher, *Der missachtete Leser* (Cologne, 1969), p. 101.

[25]Zimmer, p. 112.

mark—that is, if he seeks to tap the reservoir of passive readers who only seldom decide to purchase a book.[26] The modern best-seller business cannot do without the aid of the mass media. Conversely, the media profit from the publicity accorded best-sellers. In a highly differentiated realm of communication, in which isolated, specialized groups of readers exist side by side, the best-seller provides a potential crystallization point for public discussion. It is worth noting that *Der Spiegel,* which offers a popular, simply written form of literary criticism, reviewed in its own pages no fewer than thirteen of the thirty-four titles appearing on its best-seller list of 1970. And obviously the *Spiegel* list serves more than its own staff as a guide for books to be reviewed: the local and provincial press gladly follow its lead.

One group of periodicals, to be sure, stubbornly resists the media resonance of the best-seller—the literary and cultural journals. Of the thirty-four books on the 1970 *Spiegel* best-seller list, *Der Monat* reviewed three, *Neue Rundschau* one, and *Akzente* none at all. The barrier between "highbrow" and "middlebrow," about which Q. D. Leavis wrote so confidently some forty years ago, still exists here. The price of this abstinence is low circulation. Not one of the above-mentioned journals (one of which has since ceased publication) reached more than 5,000–10,000 readers.

---

[26]Promotion departments, in the traditional publishing firm of earlier times merely an appendage for collecting and transmitting reviews, are now highly developed and equipped with sizable budgets. Their functions include guiding the initial readings, the proofs, arranging interviews, communiqués, and organizing radio and television discussions. The traditional allocation of 5 percent of the total costs for advertising purposes is no longer adequate to establish a best-seller. To cite some examples: the Molden Verlag guaranteed Hildegard Knef DM 250,000 for advertising alone for her memoirs; Hoffmann and Campe spent DM 120,000 on the German edition of *Love Story;* and the Droemer Verlag paid DM 100,000 to promote Irving Stone's biography of Freud. These sums necessitate a programed promotion campaign like the one mounted by the Molden Verlag for Hildegard Knef: The first readings were conducted seven months before publication; four months later came the onset of an intensive ad campaign in the press, accompanied by a "promotion package" for bookstores, consisting of a complimentary copy of the book, a record, and an autographed postcard; also regular communiqués to radio and television stations, a renewed ad campaign shortly before the appearance of the book, and finally a well-publicized tour for the author, with "gala evening receptions for book merchants and the press." Cf. Panskus, "Buchwerbung," p. 79.

Thus I return to my first question: Who reviews best-sellers? If 18.9 percent of book purchases are stimulated by the press, one must concede a significant influence to literary criticism. This view is not shared by the market experts who maintain that reviews exert for the most part no great influence on the total sales of a book. I would like to pursue this issue, using the example of Habe's novel *Das Netz* (*The Net*, 1969). There are a number of reasons for this choice. Habe is not content to be known as an author who provides cheap entertainment to the masses. He wants to be taken seriously and to be noticed by the leading newspapers and literary critics. A good deal of Habe's vehement aggressiveness toward the liberal and Leftist West German intelligentsia can be explained by his fear of rejection. This is not entirely unfounded, for there does exist in West German book-reviewing a tendency to avoid the sphere of popular literature. To be legitimatized, German critics who value their reputation must discuss literature of the most experimental sort. It is no coincidence that Marcel Reich-Ranicki noted in regard to Habe's book: "Certainly a decidedly 'trivial' novel is analyzed occasionally, and its reviewers try hard to give their work a highly scientific flavor. But when it comes to books that might possibly be worth discussing as entertainment, German criticism always gives them a wide berth."[27] By writing this and extensively discussing *Das Netz* Reich-Ranicki did not absolutely disprove his own assertion, but he did contribute somewhat to making it obsolete. For this novel by Habe gained more than attention from the local and provincial press; it was found worth reviewing by such leading national newspapers as *Die Welt,* the *Frankfurter Allgemeine Zeitung, Die Zeit,* and *Christ und Welt,* not to mention *Der Spiegel,* which made this reviewing phenomenon the subject of a critical commentary. Thus in Habe's case we have an opportunity to study the reception of a best-seller that reached out into several realms of communication. We can investigate the launching of a best-seller, the unfolding of public debate, the role of advertising, and the significance of the mass media. And finally, the Habe case illustrates the possibilities of external influence on the institution of literary criticism.

Although the jacket blurb's reference to Habe as "one of the

---

[27]"Seelen von der Stange," *Die Zeit,* 20 June 1969, p. 19.

most admired and most controversial authors of our time" belongs to the advertising clichés used by every firm for its best-selling author, the exaggeration contains an element of truth: the publicist Hans Habe, experienced in dealings with the mass media, made sure that his novel remained a topic of conversation. Never burdened with false modesty, he voiced his own views of his work both before and after the publication of *Das Netz*. The moralistic-allegorical interpretation of this novel, mentioned repeatedly in numerous later reviews, originated with Habe. Even before the public could obtain the book and form its own opinion, Habe let it be known in an interview with *Welt am Sonntag* (27 April 1969) how the text should be read: "In an age of confusion, I believe the hour of clarity has arrived. I must exemplify the sickness. Of all the sicknesses that society cannot accept, cannot tolerate, the use of force is the most intolerable of all. The use of force is symbolized most clearly in murder. In opposition to unrest for its own sake, I have tried to establish tragic unrest."

The troublemakers were clearly identified in the interview—the Leftist writers who, according to Habe, control West German literary criticism. His literary tirade is political in this instance, for the literature written by the Leftists contributes, he claims, to the confusion of public opinion. It hinders the propagation of an easily comprehensible writing style and, with its experiments in form, dissolves the sociopolitical order that Habe declares inalienable. Habe's assertion in this interview is used by editors as a headline: "Literary Cliques as Arsonists." Habe, who feels he has been boycotted by the national newspapers ("I yield only to the terror of the literary *apparatshik*"), turns instead to the millions of silent readers of his books ("There is no serious conflict between the German reader and myself") and recommends his novel quite openly as an ideological support of law and order. He suggests that groups that are dissatisfied with the "corrupt world" may find help in his novel. In another interview he refers to himself as "an angry old man" who speaks for the oppressed majority of persons over thirty years of age.[28] As elements of oppression he lists the corruption of the mass media, the demands of confused, demonstrating young people, and the

---

[28]Manuscript of an interview with the *Allgemeine Jüdische Wochenzeitung*.

power of the Leftist intelligentsia, which serves the interest of Communism. It is not surprising that part of the West German and Swiss press printed these views in four- to five-column articles. Both sides found this pact beneficial—Habe created an atmosphere conducive to reading his novel, and this faction of the press (namely the Springer publications) found a prominent spokesman for its ideas.[29]

All too conspicuously, these Springer publications made sure that Habe's new novel became well known. A three-column article in the *Hamburger Abendblatt* (27 March 1969) was the start. And ironically, it involved precisely what Habe had denounced in *Das Netz*—the article's lead-in was the murder of Habe's own daughter in Hollywood on December 12, 1968. In April Habe was interviewed by the correspondent of the *Welt am Sonntag*. On May 17 even the *Bild-Zeitung*, which seldom deals with literature at all, printed a report *cum* interview under the heading, "The Book That Wasn't Supposed to Be Published," in which once again the novel was linked to the incident in Hollywood. Whereas the *Welt am Sonntag* spoke of "compelling reading," the *Bild* went a step further: "Hans Habe's *Netz* is as gripping as a detective story." A few days later, on May 22, two Springer newspapers dealt with the novel once again. The *Abendblatt* followed its article with a book review, and the *Welt* printed a positive review by Willy Haas, who wrote, "Its structure is so unified that it finally becomes a portrait of the morality of an entire epoch."

If the tortuous style of the review is any indication, Haas was not fully at ease praising the novel, though it appears he had no choice but to write it: Editor-in-Chief Herbert Kremp had given him the assignment. The *Welt am Sonntag* also took up the theme

[29]The alliance between Hans Habe and Springer goes back to 1967, when he wrote an open letter to the newspaper publisher in which he defended Springer's press empire, which was under heavy attack at the time. In his letter, printed in the *Welt*, he wrote, among other things: "Not their [Springer's] newspapers but their enemies are the real sources of danger to German democracy, which is already in a precarious position. They thereby endanger the democracy of Europe as well, which was placed in a basket and abandoned by its parents." And: "They have not subjected German cultural life to the rule of a clique; . . . they have merely realized a small part of their dreams; they have not established a bogey man or set up idols, either in the political or the cultural realm, as their opponents have." Quoted from *Der Spiegel*, 16 June 1969, p. 163.

once more—three weeks after the interview it printed an extensive review of the book. And in Berlin, the *Berliner Morgenpost* spread the corporate opinion by accenting the book's "passionate social criticism." The stance taken by every Springer publication was positive. Of primary interest was the ideologue Hans Habe, whose "healthy" views could now be circulated in literary form. Even the review written by Willy Haas, otherwise far more differentiated than the rest, was no exception in that regard. The picture of Habe drawn by the Springer newspapers was identical to Habe's self-image even in its nuances. Although Habe had vehemently criticized the mass media, along with other things, in *Das Netz* (the publisher Carlo Vanetti, unscrupulous owner of the magazine *Quest'Ora,* could remind German readers of Axel Springer), this obviously did not influence their accord. Hans Habe did not feel compromised by the advertising strategy of the Springer empire, and its editors obviously were correct in their assessment of the direction of Habe's social criticism.

By virtue of its discussion in influential, widely circulated newspapers (in some instances, even before it was released to the public), *Das Netz* avoided the fate of many best-sellers which achieve high sales figures but are ignored by the national and international press. Habe thus gained something generally denied to Kirst and Simmel, since they had been stamped as "magazine novelists"—the attention of at least a few prominent critics. The extensive review in the *Welt* was a provocation that was answered by *Die Zeit,* the *Frankfurter Allgemeine,* and *Der Spiegel.* The initial impetus provided by the Springer press was certainly useful to the Walter Verlag, which published the novel, but it was not the only means used to gain publicity. All forms of sales promotion were utilized. Effective cover notes which cleverly summarized the contents and theme of the novel were composed. The sentence "Eight people do business with death" was frequently quoted by reviewers. Personal endorsements and praise were solicited for quotation on the jacket. Complimentary copies were widely distributed to reviewers so that the first reviews would be ready as soon as the book was available to the public. But the Walter Verlag, to which Habe had switched after a previous association with the Desch Verlag, paid particular attention to the regional Swiss press. The new author was depicted as a friend and admirer of Swiss democracy and a victim of alleged oppression in West Germany. The purpose was to establish Habe, who had lived in Switzerland since 1960, as a Swiss literary figure as well. This gambit was a success, as the numerous reviews in the local Swiss press attest.[30] It cleverly played on the patriotic pride of the Swiss people and their feeling of superiority over the surrounding democracies by virtue of the age and maturity of the country.[31] A gala reception for the press, held in an elegant Zurich hotel on May 19, 1969, and attended by prominent visitors from Switzerland and abroad, gave the media a welcome excuse to report on both the book and the author.[32] Though the English edition had already appeared in London (it was later given a negative review by the *Times Literary Supplement*), this did not detract from the excitement of the premiere; on the contrary, it contributed to the "international" atmosphere of the book being promoted. Few press accounts failed to mention that several foreign editions were being prepared. Although these observations in the mass media could not be verified by the newspaper reader and were not at all relevant to the quality of the novel, they seemingly enlarged the extent of the book's reception and provided the air of cosmopolitanism so suited to the modern best-seller.

We will characterize briefly the details of the press reaction—the number and length of articles, the types of newspapers, and the influence of certain evaluations on other reviews. Most revealing is a comparison with another best-seller of the same category: Kirst's *Fabrik der Offiziere* (*Officer Factory*, 1960). Peter Glotz wrote about the impact of this novel: "Kirst's book was analyzed in the German press 53 times. Newspapers with national circulation, however, almost never dealt with it. The only

[30]"Diskussionen um Selbstverständlichkeiten. Anette Freitag sprach mit Hans Habe," *ZW-Sonntagsjournal*, 19–20 April 1969; also Habe, "Ich bin ein liberaler Konservativer," *AZ-Solothurner Ausgabe*, 9 July 1970.

[31]This was very clearly expressed in a full-page interview with Franz Disler, who was often referred to in the press as Habe's biographer. Habe's opinion of Switzerland: "It is a good country and it is good to be a citizen of this country." On the form of government: "I believe that plebiscite democracy is the only modern, viable form of democracy. Every time the Swiss vote on a new schoolhouse, democracy is born anew" (*AZ-Solothurner Ausgabe*, 9 July 1970).

[32]"Premiere eines Bestsellers," *St. Galler Nachrichten*, 23 May 1969; "Habes neuer Roman *Das Netz* wird vorgestellt," *Solothurner Nachrichten*, 24 May 1969.

exceptions were *Die Zeit,* which printed an extensive and in many ways interesting report by Robert Neumann on *Fabrik der Offiziere,* and the now defunct *Deutsche Zeitung.* A great number of the reviews appeared in very small newspapers, including weekly ones and ones containing local news only.”[33]

Habe's novel, too, was discussed in very small newspapers, not only in Switzerland but in West Germany and Austria. As a rule we find short critiques, which generally rely on jacket blurbs. There are exceptions, to be sure—for example, the *Wetzlarer Neue Zeitung* (21 August 1969), the *Badische Neueste Nachrichten* (16 October 1969), and the *Wolfenbüttler Zeitung* (22 October 1969)—which had a fresh approach to the novel. Habe's impact differs from Kirst's in regard to the newspapers of national circulation. In addition to the ones already mentioned, *Die Rheinische Merkur* and *Die Tat* took part in the discussion. The only major newspapers that did not were the *Süddeutsche Zeitung,* the *Allgemeine Sonntagszeitung,* and the *Deutsche Allgemeine Sonntagsblatt.* We have already mentioned one reason for this difference: the strategy of the Springer Press gave rise to the critical report in *Der Spiegel* (16 June 1969), whose promotional effect was very likely much greater than the lukewarm review the *Spiegel* gave *Das Netz* on July 7. Editors of newspapers representing a different viewpoint may have felt compelled by this report to take a stand against the Habe euphoria that was being spread by the Springer organization. In fact, the first cool or adverse reviews of the book appeared after June 16. On June 20 the *Nordseezeitung* printed a decidedly negative review, and a few days later the reviewer in the *Saarbrücker Zeitung* (21/22 June 1969) expressed strong reservations about the new best-seller.

A second probable reason is the changed literary climate of the late 1960s. Given the influence of elitist-oriented literary theory in the 1950s, it was difficult to justify dealing with a so-called entertainment novel. But in the 1960's, novelists like Habe benefited from the literary revolution, which broke down the literary canon. Marcel Reich-Ranicki, for example, claimed, if belatedly, to be the discoverer of the popular novel. But in *Die Zeit* he was by no means the first to deal with this genre. The increasing interest of academic criticism in trivial literature, itself

---

[33]Glotz, *Buchkritik,* p. 191.

responding to aesthetic realignments during the sixties, definitely affected contemporary literary criticism. In each period, the state of academic discussion was reflected in the book-review section of the newspapers by the delay that arises (as would be expected) in the transition from one realm of communication to another. Whereas Robert Neumann in his series of articles in *Die Zeit* entitled "Kitsch as Kitsch can" (21 September–5 October 1962) used the concept of "kitsch" without questioning it, basing his work on Walther Killy and Walter Nutz, Wolfgang Rieger in 1970 based his discussion of Simmel's novels on a critique of ideology.[34] Toward the end of the sixties the demand that the literature consumed by the broad public be given critical attention had not yet been generally accepted; nevertheless, critics were more open to the idea.

A graph of the number of reviews per month does not show Habe's novel to have been treated in a way markedly different from other best-sellers. *Das Netz* did, however, remain an item of discussion somewhat longer than usual, thanks in part to the repeated attention it received in the Springer press. After its initial success in May, it showed a dropoff in the dog days of summer; then came its period of most intensive reviewing in October. After that the interest curve fell slowly; in the spring of 1970 there appeared only occasional short critiques in provincial newspapers. After a year the book's publicity was exhausted. This closely follows the pattern of such best-selling novels. What is not evident from an analysis of press attention is the lucrative business which the publisher reaps long after the public has turned to other subjects. The special book-club editions go unnoticed by critics even though by virtue of these editions the work is just entering its phase of widest distribution.

One statistic, noteworthy if compared to the novels of Kirst or Simmel, is the number of extensive reviews—three to six columns long. In this aspect Habe compares favorably to successful authors from the Gruppe 47. Uwe Johnson's *Zwei Ansichten* (*Two Views*), for instance, received 72 reviews and discussions, 34 of which can be classified as extensive articles (150 cm² or more), 15 as short critiques, and 19 as reviews of average length (50–150

---

[34]"Fluchtburgen vor der Wirklichkeit: Politisches Bewusstsein und Trivialliteratur," *Die Zeit*, 17 April 1970, p. 23.

cm [2]).[35] According to the material available to me, Habe's *Das Netz* was accorded 33 extensive analyses, 25 short critiques, and 24 average-length reviews, whereas Kirst's *Fabrik der Offiziere* received only 14 extensive reviews. Habe, then, had no ground for complaint about the amount of press coverage. His assertion that he was treated unfairly by the critics proves to be a myth. The numerous positive evaluations far outweigh the few negative reviews. The rejection by the literary elite which Habe anticipated never materialized. In *Die Welt,* Haas (perhaps under pressure) found nothing objectionable in the novel. In *Die Zeit,* Reich-Ranicki found fault with some aspects, but emphasized Habe's masterly craftsmanship. In *Christ und Welt* (5 December 1969), Giselher Wirsing wrote approvingly of the book's message, and *Der Spiegel,* from which one might have expected a scathing review after its June article, took a neutral stand. Only the *Frankfurter Allgemeine Zeitung* (26 July 1969) printed a strongly negative critique. Among the Swiss newspapers, *Die Tat* (25 April 1969) and *Der Bund* (6 June 1969) were on Habe's side, while the *Neue Zürcher Zeitung* wrote a purely descriptive analysis. Overall, Johnson's *Zwei Ansichten* was no more favorably reviewed (*Das Netz* 59 percent positive, 26.6 percent neutral, 14.4 percent negative; *Zwei Ansichten* 66 percent positive, 19 percent neutral, 14 percent negative).

These perhaps surprising findings need, of course, to be analyzed more thoroughly; it is a question not of describing Habe's impact, but of exploring the conditions behind the phenomenon. What acounted for the wide agreement among critics? Was it the message that made the novel so attractive? Were the positive reviews evoked by the narrative style of the author? Or were nonaesthetic considerations within the institution of literary criticism of greater importance? It should be noted in this context that statistical studies reveal in general more positive than negative book reviews. Still, this does not fully explain the case of Habe's novel. Had *Das Netz* appeared two years earlier or two years later, the book probably would not have had the same success. The novel came at the right time—its theme was already filling the pages of the press. In other words, this was an instance of a "relevant media event." There was no need for a prestigious

[35]Cf. Glotz, *Buchkritik,* p. 191.

literary magazine to write about *Das Netz.* The connection between its fictional world and the reality experienced by the
reader was so obvious, it seemed, that a specifically literary approach was not necessary—one could write about this book even
in the local news section. This is apparent in the tenor of the
reviews. The provocative social message forced the literary-
aesthetic problematic into the background. This was, it seems,
fully in accord with Habe's intentions.

This observation may appear at first glance rather odd, since
Habe had chosen a narrative form that does not lend itself to the
direct communication of a message. Since the narrator steps
back completely behind his characters in *Das Netz,* we cannot
examine the empirical reception of the novel without considering its structure. We must show how the reader necessarily becomes involved in the literary realization of the work, which
becomes complete only through the reading process. By involvement we mean the acceptance or rejection of the role projected in the text, not individual reactions or reactions of specific
groups, though the novel, of course, provoked these as well, as
we will see in our analysis of the reviews.

The plot of this novel, 560 pages long in the original edition,
can be summarized quickly. I intentionally quote the synopsis
that appeared on the dust jacket, prepared by the publisher and
presumably cleared with the author:

> Call girl Hertha Enzian is murdered in Rome. A search for the
> killer? A search for success and fame. Eight people do business with
> death. The reporter, cynical in spite of his youth. The magazine
> publisher, who hides the murderer until he has written his
> memoirs. The publisher's son, a rebel with ambition. The attorney,
> who buys the life of the dead girl. The dead girl's father, who picks
> flowers from graves. The swinger from the Via Veneto, who turns
> sex into numbers. The chief of police, who wants one more big one
> before he retires. And finally the murderer, a broken-down writer
> who uses his reprieve in his own way. Aurelio Morelli is a rapist and
> killer who believes that fish, not humans, are the only creatures
> with ethics. Like all other figures in the novel, he seeks to justify the
> unjustifiable. His excuse is the "youth of today"—they must be
> done away with; older people are threatened and cannot begin this
> task soon enough. Aurelio thinks he has done his part for the
> "revolution of age."

Obviously this summary contains hints for interpretation and evaluation which are designed to prod the potential reader into purchasing the book. The fictionalized events seem to offer material for a detective story—the murder, the search for the killer, the finding of clues, the relentless pursuit by the police chief, and so on. But Habe reverses the pattern of the detective novel. The discovery of the murderer takes place not at the end of the story but in the first chapter. The search for the killer is of secondary importance. In its place, in a modern-day transformation of the model, stands a commercial exploitation of past events. The action in the present stretches between the accidental discovery of the murderer in the autumn of 1967 and the publication of the Enzian story—that is, the confession of the murderer—in the Christmas edition of Vanetti's magazine *Quest'Ora.* This action in the present is broadened by the thoughts and comments of the characters, in which they justify their actions. There is only one connection between these various experiences and reflections of the figures, namely that each of them has something to do with the death of Hertha Enzian. The traditional plot, which carefully integrates all elements, has been broken into fragments. It is no accident that this is reminiscent of the way the *nouveau roman* transformed the model of the detective story and used it as a new form of fictional narrative which no longer provides the reader with an answer, but instead poses a question. Conceived as antinovels, the works of Michel Butor and Alain Robbe-Grillet contradict conventional preconceptions. Habe was known from his earlier novels as a traditional storyteller who remained in control of his narrative. In *Das Netz,* he applied for the first time the formal methods of the modern experimental novel. The action is no longer entrusted to an auctorial narrator. The total picture is assembled through eight different first-person accounts; they overlap one another, but also to some extent contradict one another in their interpretations of the events. The reader must immediately assume the task of comparing the various narrative strands, each offered in segments, and examining them for accuracy. We seem to have a situation analogous to the modern novel whose text does not offer the reader a definite meaning but forces the reader to participate in the search for this signification. This narrative method is based on the idea that reality cannot be recreated

201

mimetically, nor can it be depicted as an objective unity. We do not need to delve into the historical reasons for these premises here; suffice it to say that this concept is decisive for the poetics of the novel of the modern, postrealistic era. It is important, however, to examine the changed relationship between the textual structure and the reader which resulted from the modern poetics of the novel. Klaus Netzer noted in regard to the *nouveau roman*, "The old habits of the reader must be broken, and the reader must make a considerable effort in order to come to a new concept of literature which is at the same time both epic and didactic."[36] But how can this exertion be demanded of a broad public with well-established reading expectations? Must not the modern narrative method frighten away the very readers whom Habe could previously count on, those who seek a tightly knit, suspenseful story filled with themes of current relevance?

The popularity of the novel, evidenced by its sales of over three hundred thousand copies, proves that Habe's plan worked, that one can tell a story in a "modern" way and still reach a wide readership. His readers obviously withstood the shock created by the new form. But now comes the second question: How deep was this shock; how much adjustment did it actually require for the reader to adapt to the structure of the novel? Habe places unaccustomed demands on his readers in *Das Netz*, but at the same time he carefully provides aids within the text to help orient the uncertain reader. For instance, the sudden beginning of the first first-person report—Emilio Bossi's account of his conversation with the publisher Vanetti—is quickly explained by Bossi's description of the first meeting with Morelli, during which the contract for the murderer's memoirs is signed. In case the reader is still confused after this first segment, the immediately following passage by Morelli helps to explain the background and origin of the action. If it is true that one of the assumptions of the modern novel is that reality can no longer be depicted by traditional epic narration, and if therefore the expectation of the reader is soon confused by modern texts which no longer offer a definite meaning, we can only conclude that in Habe's novel the form has been divorced from its original function. For the author does not attempt a disorientation of the

---

[36]Klaus Netzer, *Der Leser des Nouveau Roman* (Frankfurt am Main, 1970), p. 21.

reader in its deeper sense. To be sure, the division of the action into numerous perspectives requires a greater degree of participation on the part of the reader, who must compare the versions offered and decide which interpretation to accept. But the "reality" of the world of the narrative is never seriously placed in doubt.

The framework of the action could be put together piece by piece, for Habe made sure that all the elements could be found somewhere in the puzzle. He uses stereotypical characters—the careful, legalistic attorney, the millionaire's son vainly fighting the establishment, to name two. Each presents his actions and viewpoints, and the reader is able to choose from among them. These possibilities for identification with a character are, however, set up in such a way that the revolutionary young Vanetti is revealed as an opportunist as soon as the leadership of the firm is handed over to him, and the ambitious lawyer Zempach summoned his courage too late to inform the police about the murderer. These types are morally negative, and the reader is not inclined to identify with them. Habe has openly conceded the weaknesses of this one-dimensional characterization. In the case of the three older male figures—the writer Morelli, the police chief Canonica, and the publisher Vanetti—he uses a more differentiated method. These men are so nearly alike in their attitudes that the value judgments anticipated by the reader seem to be thrown into question. This shocking similarity is, however, a superficial one; it exists on the level of opinions behind which the initiated reader can recognize the author himself. In this way Aurelio Morelli, the washed-up, forgotten novelist, can speak for Habe with his commentary on the problem of narration:

> The writer is a vigilant god whom nothing surprises. By no means does he experience the action he describes, though younger writers would have us believe this. In looking back, rather, he reports, summarizes, and comments on things that have long ago taken place before his omnipresent eyes. The architect, a lesser artist, builds from the bottom up, pedantically placing each stone on the next; but the writer, in a divine way, builds from the top down— from a roof hovering in the air he sets his stones row by row. [pp. 154 f.]

Habe is far less removed from these creative artists, the *alter deus* of Shaftesbury and Herder, than he admits. He too guides the events according to a prepared plan and knows how to construct a realistic fictional world. The confusion introduced by his technique and the absence of a narrator touches the surface of the novel, but not its deep structure. Habe's first-person voices, his witnesses, give the reader the impression of being directly addressed. Like the epistolary novel of the eighteenth century, which also utilized this device of interruption through multiple perspectives, the various first-person personae carry on an intimate conversation with the reader, who can then feel empathy with the figures. A number of reviews made note of this effect—the reader gains the impression of dealing with people very much like those he might meet in real life. Now perhaps we might answer the question of how Habe could borrow so much of the form of the modern novel without losing his readers. Devices that served to disrupt the illusion of realism in the *nouveau roman,* as well as in other examples of the modern novel, are used by Habe to contribute to the semblance of reality. There arises finally before the reader's eyes a homogeneous entity, no longer a world of unbroken ideals but an intact picture of reality with which the average reader is familiar.

Using two examples, I would like to demonstrate how the criticism verbalized the horizon of expectation of the reading public. I shall quote Hans Helmut Kirst, author of successful war novels, whose review appeared in the *St. Galler Tagblatt* on May 18, 1969, and the critic Hermann Lewy, who published his critique in the *Allgemeine Jüdische Wochenzeitung* of June 6, 1969. It is not surprising, we might note, that Kirst, who had often been praised by Habe, returned the favor with a positive review. Lavishing superlatives, he calls the book "the most interesting, most amusing, and most daring book that Habe has ever produced," and adds apodictically, "And there is probably no one else in the German-speaking world who could bring off anything like it." Habe is celebrated as a deeply perceptive critic of society who is at the same time a brilliant master of the literary craft. For Kirst it is not a question whether Habe has correctly analyzed social reality: "This is a novel that probes a society in which only such a novel could appear probable." The intent never seems problematic, so that Kirst is able to say, "It is soon perfectly clear what Habe is after this time: ... what primarily interests him, the author, is this: What profits can be made from murderers and their victims?" That summarizes, for Kirst, the core of the novel. Even Hans Habe had not considered the matter to be so simple; with the Enzian case he intended to deal with today's youth, Marxism, the teachings of Freud, and the commercialization of the mass media, among other things.

Lewy takes a broader view of the novel's message. Like Kirst, he distinguishes between the events of the novel and its theme: "For Habe, the murder itself is merely an excuse to castigate a society that pretends to be more than it really is, to pillory the machinations . . . which have taken root in certain illustrated magazines and the boulevard press." Concerning the meaning of the book, he writes, "But this latest book also shows the author's bitterness, his dissatisfaction with the development of mankind, which is certainly making progress in technical and scientific fields, but by no means in the spiritual realm—indeed, it seems to be moving backward." Lewy completes this identification with the ideological message of the novel (seen, by the way, in the light of Habe's own commentaries) with praise for the author's narrative art: "Habe has depicted men as they actually live in our society, characters of flesh and blood, replete with the faults evident in a self-indulgent society where might is more important than right." This praise of Habe's realism—realism in which society, unconditionally and *in toto*, fits neatly into the epic method, in which reality is dissolved into independently existing figures and events—legitimates at the same time the implied social criticism. It presupposes the success of the writing style (the plausibility of the contexts and the credibility of the figures) in order to prove the accuracy of the message. For a story told in such a way that it really could have happened carries the measure of its truth within itself. Neither Kirst nor Lewy asks whether contemporary reality actually corresponds to its depiction in *Das Netz*, nor do they ask how this reality might have been fictionally confronted.[37]

Kirst's and Lewy's reviews are representative of that group of critics who more or less agree with Habe's evaluation of the

---

[37]Even Willy Haas, who speaks of a "moral portrait" of an entire epoch (*Die Welt*, 22 May 1969), and Kurt Riess, who calls the novel a "comédie humaine" (*Tat*, 25 April 1969), hold fast to this pattern of interpretation. Riess's reference to Balzac and Dickens makes the poetological context clear historically as well.

social and cultural situation and thus view the novel as a reflection of reality. Therefore they see no serious difficulties in conveying their criticism. The reviewer and the reading public comprise an unquestioned unity. Criticism could assume, however, both the task and the opportunity of explaining to the reader how the novelist fictionalizes social criticism. The beginnings of such a confrontation can be found in the reviews of three local newspapers. Their analyses of Habe's ideology proceed from a critique of form. The three reviewers set high literary standards; they take Habe's attempt at "modern" writing seriously and come to the conclusion that the novel falls short of the goal it set for itself. In the *Bonner Generalanzeiger* (19 September 1969), Paul Hubrich points out the discrepancy between the narrative mode and the theme: "And it is precisely at this point that Habe, it seems to me, is resting on a huge poetological error—blending techniques and other such formalism are legitimate in the modern novel only when they necessarily emerge from the theme itself, unnoticed by the reader."

Judged by the standards of the modern novel, *Das Netz* remains a mediocre product, a "cheap jumble of platitudes," making any serious consideration of its message superfluous. The critics for the *Wolfenbütteler Zeitung* (22 October 1969) and the Berlin *Telegraf* also explicitly connect the twisted social criticism with the work's formal deficiencies, though they do not document this connection in detail. They fail to go beyond general formulations or such individual observations as those by Heino Eggers in the *Telegraf* (18 January 1970): "Habe loses all touch with reality when he attempts a critique of our age, in depicting, for instance, a student demonstration. He saves himself with modernisms that do not fit him at all. It is apparent that his experience with the youth rebellion has come from his summer house in Ascona, not from the street."

The general reader, who is not so familiar with the aesthetic standards of the modern novel, may have trouble seeing why this failure of form must have a negative effect on the message, the social criticism. But if the literary discussion is carried on without regard for the competence of the public, the discussion risks being confined to experts, with no chance for the broad public, namely Habe's readers, to participate. At that point one reaches the esoteric formalism censured by Peter Glotz in German literary criticism. Hans-Joachim Broihan's review in the *Wolfenbütteler Zeitung* offers a good example of this tendency. His introductory sentences, which obviously refer critically to Haas' review, distinguish theme and content from poetic relevance: "This new book by Hans Habe has been called a portrait of our time and a passionate criticism of society. I do not take issue with that. We need to ask, however, whether a novel can be judged merely according to its intent, or whether we must consider the more stringent criteria of what makes a good novel."

This opening suggests that the author's intention of social criticism is unimportant to the value of the novel. But that is not Broihan's view: he establishes the discrepancy between the message of cultural criticism and the narrative mode but does not explain its cause to the reader, for he considers the poetic norm of the modern novel to be an absolute. The book's success with the general readership, proved by the best-seller lists, is ignored or, as in the review in the *Bonner Generalanzeiger,* dismissed as the "fame of mediocrity." Here are three instances of rigorous criticism of both form and content which proceeds from the aesthetic premises of the experimental novel and does not take into consideration that these premises are not self-evident to the average reader. It fails to show the reader how Habe's narrative strategy is actually designed to take away the reader's freedom of choice, despite the seemingly wide selection of characters and views offered. Habe takes care to ensure that the reader does not misread the message. Despite the use of modern narrative techniques, the intellectual scope is limited to a mere cataloguing of clichés. Habe's novel (setting aside the author's own views) is not directed toward mature, independent readers, but toward those whose perception is molded by the information industry. It offers a collection of stereotypes corresponding precisely to the mass media's codified demand for "true-to-life" figures. "What is expected to happen does happen, thus assuring the readers that they belong to a world in which, no matter how perverse and decadent it may be, everything functions in an orderly fashion (although in reality only clichés function)," wrote Peter W. Jansen in the *Frankfurter Allgemeine Zeitung* (26 July 1969). The reader is offered clichés that help soothe the worries of the 1969 public: "But the cliché world betrays its cosmopolitan figure. The millionaire's son, naturally a young protester (cliché), shaves

207

off his beard (cliché) when he has to assume control of the publishing firm after his father's heart attack (cliché)—the cliché expectation of society is fulfilled, the cliché hope that the extra-parliamentary opposition will become 'reasonable' as soon as it assumes responsibility."

We see here the beginnings of the idea of a metacriticism to Habe's social criticism—a metacriticism that does not restrict itself to pointing out shortcomings in the artistic form, but demonstrates that both the success and danger of Habe's ideologized novel are predicated on its use of questionable artistic means. Yet Jansen, in the final analysis still a prisoner of the literary coterie, tosses *Das Netz* into the bin of trivial literature, as though by doing so he can overcome the danger it presents. A familiar matrix shines through: trivial literature presents a system of false values because its customers are the masses.

It is worth noting that among the more lengthy discussions, only two deal with the problematic theme of best-sellers and trivial literature, namely Reich-Ranicki's review in *Die Zeit* (20 June 1969) and Peter Meier's essay in Zurich's *Tagesanzeiger*.[38] Only twice are questions raised regarding the function of a novel like *Das Netz* in the literary world, and the proper evaluation of that function. Two typical positions are assumed by the reviewers (consciously or not), each reflecting certain attitudes which in fact appeared rather early in the history of literary criticism. Reich-Ranicki uses Habe's novel to initiate a cultivated discussion with the readers of *Die Zeit* concerning the uses and the possibilities of literature as entertainment. His defense of entertainment novels is directed not toward those who read them but toward those who scorn them, who reject the genre as being alien to art. He appeals to a reading public that thinks in terms of hierarchical norms and in accordance with its self-established boundaries excludes any Habe novel from the world of true literature. Thus the prefatory remark: "It is sad but true: Anyone who praises a popular novel (*Unterhaltungsroman*) in Germany supplies easy ammunition to his opponents. For no matter how one twists and turns the issue, an entertainment novel remains a kind of half-breed, a more or less questionable item,

---

[38]Peter Meier, "Einblick in die Bestseller-Fabrikation," *Tagesanzeiger,* 13 December 1969.

always easy to attack. But it is also true that one can never quite get at it with strictly literary criteria." Despite this statement, Reich-Ranicki uses extraliterary criteria only to a minor extent, noting that an author of best-sellers must necessarily strike a compromise between what is desirable aesthetically and what is desired by the public. This plea for a higher class of popular novel treats the reading needs of the broad public as well-known fact which needs no further investigation. For Reich-Ranicki a writer such as Habe fulfills an important function by offering a product on the middle ground between "high" literature and trash, engaging in the business of entertainment in a manner that is intelligent and not literarily objectionable. To belabor the title metaphor ("Souls off the Rack"): Habe provides not a custom-made suit but a solid, ready-made garment for mass consumption. The norms of high literature, to summarize Reich-Ranicki's position, are suspended on this middle level. Or better: they are applied less strictly. Literature operates on many levels, and it is unfair to demand that every novel meet the stringent criteria of belles-lettres. We should not begrudge the average readers their need for entertainment. It is understood, of course, that the genre cannot be included in the canon of serious literature. Nevertheless, entertainment novels perform a sociopsychological service that should not be underestimated—by verbalizing current issues, they help relieve the pressure of them.

If we assume this to be Reich-Ranicki's position, a number of questions arise: Why must works that obviously find their readership without the mediation of literary criticism even be reviewed? What good is second-class praise? Reich-Ranicki's review, aimed at an educated public familiar with the standards of contemporary high literature, ends in a pronouncement of literary status. Habe is held to be a master within a certain class of literature. This positive evaluation would turn into rigorous belittlement if Reich-Ranicki assumed its author to be a Böll or a Johnson.[39] His review does not eliminate literary classification; it

---

[39]When Reich-Ranicki analyzes Böll's *Ansichten eines Clowns*, for example, this kindness is no longer in evidence. Since the critic considers this author to belong to the circle of high literature, he formulates his evaluations sharply. In discussing Habe's novel, he barely touched on its myopic, clichéd criticism of society, but this aspect is brought fully to bear against Böll's work. Böll failed, according to Reich-Ranicki, on two levels. First, the object of his social criticism is too limited.

confirms it. That holds true for the critic and for his readers as well, since the article is directed toward a group for whom Habe's novels probably do not represent a serious topic of conversation. The critic comes to an understanding with his audience here: it is permissible for other, less competent groups of readers to occupy themselves with more refined sorts of entertaining literature. And if one should occasionally read a bestseller oneself, it is nothing to be ashamed of.

For Meier, unlike Reich-Ranicki, the question whether Habe's *Das Netz* is worth reading is not one of taste. Meier demonstrated something that Reich-Ranicki had only asserted abstractly: the impossibility of examining the novel fully through literary exegesis. The work must be seen in connection with Habe's newspaper articles and social criticism. Actually, Meier is merely taking Habe at his word—Habe never denied that the novel contained moral instruction for the middle and older generations. To that extent the literary discussion is also a political and ideological one. The coincidence of the author's political views and the thrust of the novel is the key to Meier's criticism. His pronouncements on Habe's writing capabilities, which are never disputed, are therefore more severe and more negative than those of Reich-Ranicki. He uses Habe's admitted technical craftsmanship as evidence against him and calls the author's use of shifting perspectives a tactic of concealment: "This procedure has several advantages. First, it achieves (nearly) authentic effects. Second, it provides color and the lifelike quality which novels of this genre are careful to cultivate. And third, it supplies its inventor with a (nearly) perfect alibi—what is spoken are not his own views, prejudices, sentiments, and clichéd ideas, but must be seen and understood from the perspective of the *dramatis personae;* thus they cannot be attacked."

This narrative technique, Meier concludes, appears to offer the reader a freedom that does not really exist. The views offered in the novel as those of a psychopathic writer, thus easy for the reader to reject, can be read also, in a milder form of course, in Habe's journalistic essays. The factual agreement cannot be

---

Second, his methods of presentation are no longer appropriate, given the degree of complexity of modern social forms. Cf. Reich-Ranicki, *Literatur der kleinen Schritte* (Frankfurt am Main, 1971), pp. 15-21.

doubted. Habe himself accentuated these ideas in various ways in his interviews. But there is no ready explanation for why an opinion from the mouth of a psychopath in a novel should be more influential or more portentous than the directly stated views of Hans Habe the publicist. Meier at least does not stringently pursue this connection, but offers a correct conclusion without having previously developed the corresponding premises. His final judgment is stated thus: "*Das Netz* is a dangerous book precisely because it does not openly announce its message . . . but propagates in a cleverly disguised form a mentality that stirs dimly felt emotions in a wide reading public; it does not reduce or even critically illuminate the prejudices of the masses—rather, it corroborates them."

There is a gap here between the evidence and the conclusion. It is not clearly demonstrated why the reader is manipulated by Habe's use of shifting perspectives. In Meier's review the literary elements and the critique of ideology are not sufficiently interwoven. Problems of literary technique are analyzed in such a cursory fashion that it is difficult for a reader unschooled in theory, who might well find *Das Netz* exciting reading, to understand where the danger of this book lies. It is probably no accident that Meier ascribes prejudices and "dimly felt emotions" to the broad public. No less than Reich-Ranicki, he directs his remarks to a group of readers for whom this novel is, at best, an example of the discredited best-seller. If one asks, therefore, what the purpose of this criticism is, the answer is that it affirms the standpoint of the critical intelligentsia—that is, a representative of this group has said what needs to be said regarding such a book as this. But Meier's well-founded warning does not reach the readers for whom it would be most significant, since these readers are written off as the "masses."

The restriction to a single example makes generalizing from the results problematic. Still, some hypotheses can be formulated, to be tested through an examination of comparable material, namely reviews of Willi Heinrich's novel *Geometrie einer Ehe* (Geometry of a Marriage, 1967) and Siegfried Lenz's *Deutschstunde* (The German Lesson, 1968). How does the critical establishment respond to the best-seller? Critics for the most part merely record best-sellers without reflecting on the existing mechanisms of production and consumption. But in the past few years a change has taken place in the cultural editorial staffs of some national newspapers. Some are beginning to realize that the best-seller is not merely a book that sells a great many copies. A certain interest in production methods and forms of distribution is gradually becoming evident, although local newspapers in general still tend to act as though the copy of the book sent to the editor simply fell from heaven. Symptomatic of this change in attitude is the extensive article by Dieter Kraeter in the *Rheinische Merkur* (19 February 1970) entitled "Alles über einen Bestseller: Der unaufhaltsame Aufstieg des Siegfried Lenz" ("Everything You Wanted to Know about a Best-Seller: The Irresistible Rise of Siegfried Lenz"). It deals with the economic side of Lenz's novelistic success, based upon publishing data. In addition, the same edition of this newspaper offers a second review of Lenz's *Deutschstunde,* in which Heinz Beckmann explores the question of why precisely this novel, which seems to contain so few ingredients of the standard successful novel, broke through the crucial one-hundred-thousand-copy barrier so quickly.

Signs of a new level of reflection in literary criticism can be observed. The literary elite's mistrust of the best-seller as a typical product of despised mass culture has not yet disappeared, but occasionally one finds a more carefully weighed, self-critical posture. Nevertheless, the well-worn dichotomy of serious literature and popular literature has by no means lost its hold. One approaches a novel by Lenz differently than a novel by Heinrich. This fact has less to do with the work in question than with common stereotypes. Although reviewers tended to accept Lenz's *Deutschstunde* a priori as a work of high standards and applied aesthetic as well as ideological criteria, there was an inclination (especially in the national press) to treat Heinrich with a certain kindly condescension. These differences are noticeable primarily in the neutral and negative reviews; the positive reviews show far more agreement in their conception and articulation. The qualities praised in Lenz were emphasized in praise of Habe and Heinrich as well. This tendency can be demonstrated in three examples from the local press. In the first case, the book is lauded as follows: "This is without doubt the author's masterpiece. A book such as this contains a tremendous energy. Behind the joy of narration lies a moral impetus. The author has created a distressingly narrow world of prejudices and stubbornness. With a gripping, powerful language and epic cleverness he paints a portrait of his era" (*Darmstadter Zeitung,* 14 August 1971, on *Deutschstunde*). In the second instance, one reads: "This book can be read simply as a suspenseful tale about people of our time. But it can also be seen as a challenge to look one's own life, including its more or less limited potentialities, soberly and without illusions right in the eye" (*Esslinger Zeitung,* 19 August 1968, on *Geometrie einer Ehe*). The third example: "A suspenseful and provocative book appeared which not only describes an exciting case, just as it happens a thousand times, but also forces the reader to think about the myriad attitudes and problems in today's society" (*Flensburger Tagblatt,* 15 November 1969, on *Das Netz*). The structure of each work disappears behind handy formulas that can be applied to many cases. We find here the platitudes spread by the advertising campaigns of the publishing houses, which recur later on in the program circulars of book clubs. The negative reviews and those which express reservations are more illuminating, for they reflect the typical positions more clearly.

Three patterns of criticism can be discerned—aesthetic discrimination, the suspension of strict aesthetic norms, and criticism of ideology. Aesthetic disqualification depends on the criteria (usually not expressly formulated) of a literary theory grounded in the notion of autonomy. Critics choosing this approach believe that the worthlessness or mediocrity of certain successful products on the literary market, whether called bestsellers or trivial novels, can be exposed through an analysis of the text. The discussion is supplemented by referring to other works that are firmly installed in the canon of great art. The question of why the work under examination became a bestseller poses no problem. The critic readily admits that the mass public has poor taste. His or her review is directed not toward the masses, but toward the "in" group, which feels an allegiance to the same norms. This is a pronouncedly literary-aesthetic discussion which intentionally stays away from extraliterary factors of influence. In the second group such rigidity relaxes into mild condescension, for the concept of a unified artistic literature has been loosened somewhat: popular literature follows its own laws, not primarily dictated by aesthetic considerations, and so should not be judged by rigid aesthetic standards. A reviewer of Heinrich's *Geometrie einer Ehe* in the *Süddeutsche Zeitung* (16–17 September 1967) states: "Heinrich occupies something of a middle ground between the novels of Walser and Max Frisch on the one hand and, on the other, the platitudes of women's magazines." This middle status diminishes the criticism to an ironic commentary: "But no matter how much sex goes on, the result of the exercises is meager—literarily, psychologically, even medicinally. More important for the action, which moves along at a lively pace, is an aspect Heinrich has chosen to explore extensively—the power of income. Where money is the weapon, Heinrich is a knowledgeable war correspondent." Jürgen P. Wallmann shows a similar friendly but ironic distance toward Lenz's *Deutschstunde* in the Berlin *Tagesspiegel* (8 December 1968). "The book will get along well," he notes as an introduction. "And that is nothing to complain about. For even those who take a critical stance toward this sort of novel, which is caught in the tradition of realistic narrative, will have to admit that Lenz understands his craft and reflects, in a rather accomplished manner, a laudable attitude." This liberal approach of live-and-let-live which seems not to insist on the application of rigorous standards to a notable, successful novel proves on closer examination, however, to be by no means a neutral evaluation. A popular novel, even when its author has good intentions, may effect a suspension of aesthetic norms, but not the abandonment of them. Aesthetic disqualification may be shown out the front door, but it makes its way in again through the rear, and not because the private morality of the critic is two-faced and disputable, but because the hierarchy of the literary canon is merely differentiated. The formula for this conditionally praiseworthy middle class is talented craftsmanship, borne by a decent viewpoint, usable as family reading matter.

This lack of commitment does not apply to the third position—the method that exposes the ideological bias of a work. It is not content with the formula "good attitude and solid handiwork," which leaves the potential effect of the text untouched. Nor does it accept the separation of theme and presentation, for the praise of good intentions can obscure the possibility of good intentions being converted into their opposite by the textual presentation. With the suspension of aesthetic criteria, concessions are made to the broad public to facilitate its access to literature, but the approach using criticism of ideology defines this public as a mass of consumers who do not perceive the true implications of the work. These critics should therefore not be indifferent about what audience is reached by their reviews. Nonetheless, their interest in communicating with the masses is not very pronounced. The group standpoint tends to predominate. Characteristically, the reviewer in the journal *konkret* (30 December 1968) uses the plural form in his polemic against the harmless nature of Lenz's social criticism: "After 23 years we have had enough of this sort of culinary, officious, outdated, internalized *Vergangenheitsbewältigung* (coming to terms with the past), which is surely a source of bourgeois reading pleasure even for old Nazis." The critic unmistakably distinguishes his readership from that of Lenz. There is no thought of speaking to the general public. Similar tendencies exist in national newspapers. For example, there are the critical reviews of *Deutschstunde* by Hans-Albert Walter in the *Süddeutsche Zeitung* (14 November 1968) and by Peter W. Jansen in the *Frankfurter Allgemeine Zeitung* (17 September 1968). Both deal extensively with the content and theme of the novel, with the narrative situation and the constellation of the figures. Both are critical of the same point—the overburdening of the youthful narrator with the task of producing a fictional world. For Walter and Jansen this is not merely a psychological flaw; they see in it the reason why Lenz did not do justice to his theme (German history under Hitler), why good sentiments did not lead to a good novel. Their doubts are directed toward the attempt to portray epically, using only a few characters, the history of the Third Reich. Walter writes: "The central injustice of the Third Reich is to be represented through peripheral events. So the dehumanized parents, the Jepsens, have to assume the form of nearly mythical monsters, while the painter Nansen swells into a monument to undaunted artistic freedom. Evil and full of insidious intrigues on the one hand, noble and full of defiant simplicity on the other—O Germany, if only you could be grasped so easily!"

Like Jansen, Walter endeavors to show how the narrative method selected by Lenz abbreviated the theme and reduced the constellation of characters to clichés inadequate for a complex reality. They object to this attempt to reconstruct fictionally the Fascist era, stating that the author did not "confront" the past, but merely transferred it to the personal, individual realm, thereby making it seem harmless. The position taken by Walter and Jansen leads to an unequivocal judgment; it makes no concessions to the reading public. The assertions of Jansen and Walter are absolute and specific, and they overlook, to be sure, the communicative aspect. They leave unexplored the connection between the literary characteristics of the novel and its unusual success, unanticipated even by its publisher.

If this case is to go beyond description and categorization, it must ask what conclusions can be drawn from this analysis for literary criticism. What should the task of current criticism be in regard to the phenomenon of the best-seller? To prevent expectations from becoming too exaggerated, it should be noted in advance that while such considerations do not alter the factors presently affecting book reviewing in West Germany, they may help to influence the consciousness of critics.

Professional literary criticism has not yet sufficiently realized that intrinsic literary discussion is inappropriate in dealing with best-sellers, because problems of economics and the sociology of the reading public are not merely peripheral to the concept of trivial literature. Since mass reception was frequently turned into an index of aesthetic triviality, critical attention was restricted to those authors and works which were discriminated against, for other reasons, in their own right. And the success of those authors who belong to the avant-garde (or at least are considered so) remained unexplored. Thus there are supposedly two types of best-sellers—those able to attract a sizable readership on the basis of their literary status, and those which as a result of adapting to the readers' taste are able to captivate and dupe the masses. Symptomatic of this schizophrenia (which is by no means the prerogative of literary snobs) are Meier's introductory remarks to his analysis of Habe and Willi Heinrich: "Not every successful, money-making book is inferior in a literary sense; there are also legitimate best-sellers. For example, when a writer of proven talent publishes a new work—every new book by Grass, Böll, Frisch, or Martin Walser (to name just a few

German speaking authors) is bound to grace the best-seller lists for a time."[40]

This position is poorly thought out. It presumes that these books become best-sellers on their own and that only bad novels ("trivial" novels) are manipulated through advertising campaigns, as though Grass's and Böll's publishers were less informed about the art of sales promotion. It is highly questionable to assume that recognized authors are not liable for their sales successes, while the others are relegated to second-class status precisely because of this success. If the best-seller is equated with the so-called trivial novel, the field of investigation is too quickly restricted to the segment of literary production which prominent critics do not take seriously even today.

The dependence of literary criticism on the theory of the trivial novel can be proven paradigmatically. Professional critics have loyally followed the academic discussion on the nature and function of trivial literature. The shift in attitude can be shown clearly by examining two essays that appeared in *Die Zeit*. The title of Neumann's 1962 essay, "Kitsch as Kitsch can,"[41] anticipates the beginning of the movement, namely the influence of the kitsch debate within literary scholarship in the fifties and early sixties. Neumann expressly based his statements on Killy's study of kitsch and the work of Walter Nutz on the serialized novel for lending libraries.[42] With his orientation toward cultural criticism, Neumann makes the Industrial Revolution responsible for an immature public searching for false images. The trivial novel's capacity to adapt to the varying conditions of the time is rooted in its amalgamation of fairy-tale structure and quasi-realistic accoutrements—the reader is shown a fantasy but is given the impression of seeing the true problems of real life. Kitsch as the fulfillment of the half-conscious wishes of a repressed readership—this summarizes Neumann's brilliantly written essay. In essence he offers an evaluation of taste supplemented by arguments from the sociology of the reading public. His examination of the programmed magazine novel is

[40]*Tagesanzeiger*, 13 December 1969.
[41]21 and 28 September, 5 October 1962.
[42]Walter Killy, *Deutscher Kitsch: Ein Versuch mit Beispielen* (Göttingen, 1961); Walter Nutz, *Der Trivialroman, seine Formen und Hersteller* (Cologne, 1962).

friendly and obliging; he calmly notes the manipulation of the public. The questions raised by Neumann in regard to future studies of the trivial novel have very little to do with the consumers of the genre. This rhetorical gesture, which speaks in a friendly, patronizing tone about both the trivial novel and its public, can also be found as late as 1970 in Wolfgang Rieger's investigation of the novels of Johannes Mario Simmel.[43] Other constants can be identified in this scholarly debate—a reprise of Nutz's argument that trivial literature is totally adapted literature, and a reference to the pseudo-realistic nature of trivial novels. Neumann had maintained that in the trivial novel, contemporary reality serves solely as an interchangeable background for stereotyped courses of action. Rieger's critical analysis of the patterns of action and character structures in Simmel's novels is more precise. Simmel's contemporary pseudo-reality, claims Rieger, is an invitation to dream. The readers are privy to the secrets of the mighty; they see the heroes of the novel with whom they identify suffer yet triumph in their suffering. Thus in the mind of the reader the world returns to order. Should one not ask how the reader, having closed the cover on Simmel's or Habe's novel, then engages in discussion, judges, chooses, or even thinks about the news on television?

Neumann suggested in 1962 that an academic institute be established to deal with kitsch and trivial literature. It appears to me that Rieger's critique is still directed toward the members of that select group. The broad public is treated as an object—it is analyzed as to why it has such poor taste and why it so readily allows itself to be deceived. The critics have become prisoners of their theories and concepts, even if, like Reich-Ranicki, they occasionally make fun of the scientific veneer of essays on the topic of trivial literature. No one seems called upon to explain to Simmel's and Heinrich's audience how they can become more critical readers.

It is worth thinking about the reasons for this failure. Helmut Kreuzer touched on some of the causes in his critical report on the state of research.[44] The inclusion of so-called trivial literature into literary research was poorly thought out, for the critics

[43]See above, n. 34.
[44]See above, n. 2.

unwittingly operated with categories that previously had served as an aesthetic evaluation of specific types of literature. Kreuzer is correct in pointing out that this attitude, no matter how progressive it might claim to be, ultimately affirms the orthodox position. Applied to the situation of literary reviewing, this means that it makes no real difference whether a novel by Habe, Simmel, or Lenz is aesthetically rejected or, within the context of a three-tiered model, is praised as solid consumer goods; the literary premises, the critic's evaluation, the reading public's judgment remain untouched by it all. Even Reich-Ranicki's praise merely attests to the traditional dichotomy between serious literature and something else. Professional critics, no less than literary scholars, are inclined to see popular and/or trivial literature as separate genres well suited to survey reviews with a bit of sociology of the reading public thrown in. Even the reviewers who employ arguments from the criticism of ideology are not always immune to this attitude insofar as they believe that trivial works are particularly suited to this methodology. Their standpoint is that what is not worth discussing aesthetically can still be discussed through criticism of ideology. The creation of an aesthetic canon, which is not rationally justified, dominates even those who would benefit from its dissolution. All in all, institutionalized book criticism is not yet in a position to break away from traditional, deeply entrenched modes of thought.

These modes of thought are powerful because in a process of accumulation they are continually presented to intellectuals in new variations. Literature classes at the *Gymnasium,* education at the university, the tradition of critical writing—all pointed to the separation between art and non-art. This dichotomy has been indispensable for the cultural elite's conception of itself since the late eighteenth century. With the expansion and differentiation of the reading public and the accompanying increase in literary production (especially in the realm of the novel), there emerged a defensive posture within criticism. Its best representatives felt compelled to protest against the lowering of literary taste, even the misuse of literature. The majority of current arguments against trivial literature can be found in the reviews and theories of the German Classic and Romantic eras. Seen historically, the Classical-Romantic tradition of literary criticism has blocked critical and analytical study of the best-seller.[45] Even well-meaning attempts to break out of the ghetto of literary criticism remain tied to the standard pattern of horizontal categorization. Thus Peter Glotz is correct in writing of a failure of professional criticism: "In this subjective sense, the books of Hans Habe, Willi Heinrich, Pearl S. Buck, Anne Golon, et al. are for millions of people far more 'relevant' than most products of high literature."[46]

Even if it is no longer true (as I was able to show in Habe's case) that the press pays no attention to the works of these authors, it still has not generally reached the stage of a literary discussion useful to the broad public. Neither snobbish attacks nor affirmational plot synopses and uncritical admiration in local newspapers can achieve that goal.

One possible solution to the aesthetic restrictions of contemporary literary criticism might be to pass over its aesthetic value when discussing a best-seller and concentrate instead on its analysis of current issues. That is to say, rather than dwelling on literary quality (presumed to be low, at any rate), the critic could discuss the contemporary problems that led the reader to buy the book. In this sense, Wolfgang Langenbucher has urged that entertainment literature be evaluated according to its social function, and therefore that it be exempt from literary discussion per se.[47] The discussion ought to concentrate on the impact of a best-seller on its readers. He uses an example to demonstrate the results of this change in attitude. Whereas professional criticism has either ignored Simmel's novels or aesthetically condemned them, a reader-oriented criticism would pursue Simmel's analysis of our age, would accentuate his political engagement, and would take into account his efforts to break down

---

[45]Cf. Klaus Berghahn, "Volkstümlichkeit ohne Volk? Kritische Überlegungen zu einem Kulturkonzept Schillers," in *Popularität und Trivialität*, ed. Reinhold Grimm and Jost Hermand (Frankfurt am Main, 1974), pp. 51–75; also my "Literary Criticism and the Public Sphere" in this volume.

[46]*Buchkritik*, p. 84.

[47]Wolfgang Langenbucher, *Der aktuelle Unterhaltungsroman* (Bonn, 1964); Langenbucher, "Robert Prutz als Theoretiker und Historiker der Unterhaltungsliteratur," in *Studien zur Trivialliteratur*, ed. H. O. Burger (Frankfurt am Main, 1968), pp. 117–136; also Langenbucher, "Im Banne eines Begriffes: Kritik der literaturwissenschaftlichen Beschäftigung," *Kürbiskern*, 4 (1966), pp. 90–97.

national prejudices.[48] Let us set aside for the time being the question whether a critic should be satisfied with merely determining the author's intentions. More important here is that not even this attempt by Langenbucher and other scholars to lift aesthetic restrictions is able to overcome the dilemma of the theory of division according to quality. The justification of entertainment literature and its public represents a return (without admitting it) to Friedrich Schlegel's differentiation of poetry and nonpoetry. It attempts to save the lower realm by ignoring its literary characteristics in favor of its use value. According to the logic of narrative theory, this is obviously a false conclusion. The assumed or conceded lack of literary quality does not categorically remove the work from literature so that a discussion of current issues can replace the literary or aesthetic one. Langenbucher's suggestion, which has much in common with the didactic legitimation of the novel during the Enlightenment period, deprives critical discussion of a decisive dimension. We lose the possibility of critically examining the uniqueness of the fictional world. Because Langenbucher (among many others), following Classical-Romantic aesthetics, equates the literary uniqueness of a work with its aesthetic quality, he separates structure and use value and fails to note that formal qualities such as the mode of writing, the narrative attitude, and so on are important for the work's effect. That is the only explanation for the way he praises the democratic political engagement of Simmel's novels without even asking whether the textual elements acting upon the reader (characterization, use of action, the epic portrayal of contemporary reality, etc.) actually serve the function he ascribes to them.

Popular literary criticism should therefore not repress the literary aspect, but should replace the horizontal model of evaluation with a vertical one. It should stop initiating survey reviews of works discredited as trivial literature and confront the phenomenon of the best-seller in its entirety. It is noteworthy that Böll's novels, which are classed as serious literature, scarcely lag behind those of Habe or Simmel in sales. The book clubs live just as much from Böll, Grass, Lenz, and Frisch as from Anne Golon, Annemarie Selinko, and the steady sellers of Luis

---

[48]Langenbucher, "Unterhaltungsliteratur als Märchen und als Politik," in Koebner, ed., *Tendenzen der deutschen Literatur seit 1945*, pp. 341–343.

Trenker and Ludwig Ganghofer. The question of which groups within the reading public turn a work of those authors into a best-seller has yet to be investigated. Given the imponderable size of the modern book market and the high degree of differentiation among reading groups, the usual (pejorative) reference to the mass reading public means little. It can only be seen as an expression of embarrassment. To what extent does the reading audience of Habe overlap with that of Lenz? Are Habe readers also Simmel readers? Do those who enjoy Lenz also reach for a novel by Peter Härtling or Peter Handke? Literary criticism's inability to answer these questions is less disconcerting than its apparent lack of interest. Most critics (with some notable exceptions) are satisfied with an aesthetic scheme of stratification which is not only alien to reality (in that it does not correspond to the reading habits of the audience) but actually hinders, with its inscrutable irrationality, the enlightenment of the reader.

The situation can be changed. The factors necessary for a more effective popular literary criticism can at least be outlined. The first of them would be for the feuilleton editors to gain a clear picture of the composition of their readership and the taste of those readers, in order to guarantee that their reviews are suited to the audience's level of competence. The elevated formal-aesthetic critique of Habe's *Netz* in the *Wolfenbütteler Zeitung* probably had little effect, for its readers were for the most part unacquainted with even the basic premises of the reviewer. A discussion needs to proceed from things familiar to the readers—other novels they have probably read, literary concepts that seem natural to them—not to confirm these expectations, but to illuminate them critically on the basis of the example given. The second precondition would be the destruction of the literary-aesthetic canon, which defensively perpetuates a dichotomy within both literature and the public. The opposition of art and non-art has social implications that are no less dangerous when they are unintentional. The critique of ideology includes approaches whose animosity toward the public jeopardizes their goal of an illuminating analysis. Certainly the literary canon should not be abolished so that in the future all books can be considered equally significant.[49] Opening up the encrusted

---

[49] In contrast see Helmut Kreuzer's attempt to trace value differences ("aesthetic discrimination") back to differences in taste. The differentiation between high

canon should not be used to justify a standpoint which the media industry has seized as a democratic banner—entertainment for everyone.

The third precondition would be a continuing concentration on literary-economic questions. So long as neither the critics nor members of the public are acquainted with the mechanisms of the literary market, there can hardly be any hope of understanding the phenomenon of the best-seller. This phenomenon cannot be studied through a hermeneutic analysis of the individual work. Such criticism can become exemplary only when it can explain the economic as well as the cultural-political context. It is inadequate, though currently chic, to produce occasional reports on the business of literature, such as the development of a best-seller business or the mergers of book clubs. It is far more important to educate the readership about the factors that determine the availability of books.

---

and trivial literature has, for Kreuzer, no basis in the matter itself; it is to be understood purely as an intersubjective agreement within a certain group of people sharing common tastes. His scientific interest is thus defined as a value-free investigation of the use of the concept in certain historical situations. "That a certain segment of literature, on the basis of historical conditions in addition to those related to the sociology of taste, becomes collectively canonized while another segment is flatly discriminated against; that a contemporary class or group of persons sharing common tastes develop a consensus regarding the literary boundary between these areas, and how they do so—these are phenomena of scientific interest" (p. 184). This theoretical attitude, which consciously excludes the practical aspect of the problem, is only partly helpful to the critic. It supplies a description of these taste groups and the demarcations of their tolerances, but it abandons critics when they must decide whether to respect an established canonization or disqualification. If in the case of trivial literature it were merely a question of taste, with certain groups of readers battling for leadership, there would be no set criterion for deciding the struggle. One could only state that a certain category of literature has been rejected by the dominant reading group; one could not establish whether this suppression had occurred with or without justification. An insight into the functioning of traditional patterns of thought and a consciousness of their historical relativity are without doubt a necessary precondition for a confrontation with the phenomenon of "trivial literature." In addition, this first step must be complemented by a critical analysis of the reading situation implied by the structure of the text. As readers, critics cannot remove themselves from the appeal of the text without limiting the significance of that text. They cannot pretend merely to register its characteristics and their correlation to the expectation horizon of the readers to whom it is directed without thinking about the practical function of the text and deciding whether to support or reject it.

6 *Prolegomena to a History*
of Literary Criticism

The title of this essay needs some explanation. It assumes that none of the existing histories of literary criticism is sufficient for our needs and that we are still developing a history of literary criticism. Such an assumption might indeed be called unfair given the accomplishments of international literary criticism. Also, the term "prolegomena" might seem inappropriate when one looks at René Wellek's five-volume history of modern literary criticism soon to be completed. This extraordinarily learned work presents the high points of European literary criticism, and it is highly unlikely that a more encompassing work than Wellek's will be produced within the next ten to twenty years. Of course, things are not as promising in the history of German literary criticism. For methodological reasons the important contribution of Anni Carlsson[1] cannot fill the gap. Moreover, the various anthologies containing selected documents from the history of criticism are not adequate substitutes for a general survey.

Could this be merely an insufficiency peculiar to *Germanistik?* Could it be that Germany must simply catch up with what has already been accomplished in other European countries? This possibility should not be taken lightly. Because of a more limited concept of literature (poetry or *Dichtung*) which includes nonfic-

Translated by Jeannine Blackwell.
[1] Anni Carlsson, *Die deutsche Buchkritik von der Reformation bis zur Gegenwart* (Bern, 1969).

tion only in part, literary criticism (in the sense of contemporary book reviews) long led a shadowy existence in academia. Only within the last few years have there been investigations that consider the form and function of literary reviews (*Literaturkritik*) as an object of scholarly research. In addition to the previously mentioned work by Carlsson, we might cite Glotz's polemical *Buchkritik in deutschen Zeitungen* (1968), the volume *Kritik von wem/für wen/wie* (1969) edited by Hamm, the essays collected from the Loccum Conference *Kritik der Literaturkritik* (1973), and finally various essays by Dieter Wellershoff (if he can be relegated to *critique universitaire* at all).[2] Although the self-analysis of West German Germanistics containing critiques of ideology has made significant contributions to a critical history of German literary analysis (*Literaturwissenschaft*),[3] the same strong impulses have long been missing in the area of criticism (*Literaturkritik*). Hence, we are still in the prestage of a polemical discussion that must precede a historical elaboration of this problematic.[4]

In order to explain the obvious tension between scholarly literary analysis and literary criticism, it is necessary to investigate the special historical conditions in Germany which have prevented mutual acknowledgment of the two fields. It can be assumed that the fundamental difficulties of a historical evaluation of literary criticism are not limited to Germany. These difficulties are more likely related to the fact that our concept of literary history has altered so much in the last ten years that previous investigations (or those begun before that time) can no longer fully meet our needs. It is not so much an insufficient knowledge of the material which keeps us from a suitable history of literary criticism (although there are still countless shady areas), but rather the problematic of the assumed premises. On the basis of the specialized investigations to date, a research team could probably produce a summation of German literary criticism within a few years; however, the unsolved problems that plague present studies would of necessity be carried over into such a work. At present, the history of literary criticism is still

---

[2] Wellershoff, *Literatur und Veränderung* (Cologne, 1969), and *Literatur und Lustprinzip* (Cologne, 1972).
[3] Bernd Peschken, *Versuch einer germanistischen Ideologiekritik* (Stuttgart, 1972).
[4] Cf. my book *Literatur und Öffentlichkeit* (Munich, 1974).

behind the more advanced level of scholarly literary analysis. This gap can be reduced only if the fundamental premises concerning the conditions for the feasibility of literary history are applied to the area of literary criticism.

The long overdue prolegomena must address two problems: first, there is the structural position of literary criticism as opposed to, or within, the totality of literature which must be critically questioned. Traditional literary histories and surveys have paid notably little attention to the participation and significance of literary criticism in literary life. To put it positively: a future history of literary criticism should be conceptually integrated into the history of literature, and its functional value should be established. What must be overcome is the present specialization, which, by tracing concepts, ideas, or persons, explains the history of literary criticism as a history comprehensible only through itself. This reintegration of criticism into the history of literature is the first step. It can be expanded by the elaboration of the historical-theoretical discussion of the last ten to fifteen years. One is reminded of Roland Barthes' polemical accusations against an academic literary history, which, in his words, "consists of a series of monographs,"[5] and which therefore deserves more the name chronicle than that of history. In differentiating between creation/work on the one hand and genre/tradition on the other, Barthes is able to separate the historical process from the psychological one. Literary history, for Barthes, in the period around 1960, is the history of the literary institution and not that of its works, which continue to be subjected to psychological or aesthetic methods. Under the historical aspect—and here he speaks to our topic—problems of the author's environment, audience, the level of education, and of rhetoric are included. Here the object of history (in the double meaning of event and representation) is the self-transforming system of literary production, distribution, and consumption together with its subsystems. Criticism belongs to these subsystems to the extent that it can be classified with the mechanisms that both stabilize and alter the total system.

This notion of a history of literary criticism as an integral part of the literary system has been further developed through the

---

[5]Roland Barthes, *Literatur oder Geschichte* (Frankfurt am Main, 1969), p. 12.

aesthetics of reception and also in the critical debate with structuralism.[6] Clearly this was brought about by the thorough critique of the historical-theoretical presuppositions of literary history. Hans Robert Jauss summarizes it in his most recent commentary: "The work does not exist without its effect. Its effect presupposes its reception. The judgment of the audience conditions, in turn, the production of the authors. The history of literature is, from this point on, a process in which the reader, as an active subject (despite its collectivity) confronts the single producing author. This subject as the mediating stage in the history of literature can no longer be ignored."[7] It is impossible to sketch even briefly the recent discussions about the theory of reception.[8] Let us confine ourselves to those aspects which apply to our topic. The status of literary criticism is altered by the concept of literary history in the aesthetics of reception, since if the historicity of literature is considered in Jauss as a dialectical process in which the recipient and the producer equally participate, then criticism, to the extent that it is a form of reception, proves to be an essential component of literature. Literary criticism has a vital function for the historical presentation of literary processes at the point where the historical existence of a work of art is understood as the relationship between text structure and concretization. Within the framework of this premise the examination of literary criticism is carried out on several levels. A first step would be the investigation of the review, the essay, the polemic, etc., as interpretations of a certain work—that is, as time-bound concretizations in comparison to others. On the second and higher level, the poetological and aesthetic norms which entered the text of criticism must be reconstructed in the sense of the Jaussian horizon of expectation. A third level of the analysis deals with the very concept of literature on which all texts are based. In each case, a historically indissoluble bond exists between the critical text and the work of art it addresses.

---

[6]Hans Robert Jauss, *Literaturgeschichte als Provokation* (Frankfurt am Main, 1970), pp. 144 ff.

[7]Jauss, "Der Leser als Instanz einer neuen Geschichte der Literatur," *Poetica,* 7 (1975), 335–336.

[8]Cf. my introduction to *Sozialgeschichte und Wirkungsästhetik* (Frankfurt am Main, 1974), pp. 9–48, trans. in *New German Critique,* no. 10 (1977), pp. 29–64; also Gunter Grimm, "Einführung in die Rezeptionsforschung," *Literatur und Leser* (Stuttgart, 1975), pp. 11–84.

Literary criticism becomes an integral component of literary history, an element that is indispensable for the reconstruction of past significance as well as for the explication of contemporary evaluation.

I

A critical look at the more recent studies reveals the extent to which reception theory created a new situation for the history of literary criticism. The questionable aspects of present histories of literary criticism are essentially related to the various ways in which they neglect the integral connection between literary criticism and the general reception of literature itself and thus underestimate the significance of the topic. From a methodological point of view, this deficit results from a conception of history which stresses the genesis of the work. In such a situation, criticism seems to be an opinion derived from hindsight, one which no longer influences the actual work of art. Furthermore, traditional literary scholarship handicaps and stigmatizes literary criticism for being unscholarly. Because of these presuppositions, three main types of criticism have developed: (1) history of taste and judgment; (2) conceptual history or the history of theory; and (3) the biographical approach which centers on the significant critic.

One example of a critic who defines his task as a history of judgment and taste is George Saintsbury, as evidenced in his *History of Criticism and Literary Taste in Europe* (1900–1904). He states in the introduction that "the criticism which will be dealt with here is that function of the judgment which busies itself with the goodness or badness, the success or ill-success, of literature from the purely literary point of view.... We shall meddle little with the more transcendental Aesthetics, with those ambitious theories of Beauty, and of artistic Pleasure in general which, fascinating and noble as they appear, have too often proved cloud-Junos."[9] This definition is to be qualified in two ways: it limits the task of the historian strictly to the area of literature, thus consciously omitting the complications of cultural back-

[9] *History of Criticism and Literary Taste in Europe* (London, 1900), 1:3.

228

ground, and it sets itself apart from the history of general aesthetics and literary theory. Saintsbury sees literary criticism as a specialized discipline, the development of which manifests itself as an expanded history of rhetoric. Its subjects are the ideas, norms, and methods with which critics have approached literary works. "In other words," Saintsbury notes on this topic, "the Criticism or modified Rhetoric, of which this book attempts to give a history, is pretty much the same thing as the reasoned exercise of Literary Taste."[10] It is noteworthy that what for Saintsbury was still totally unproblematic has become the central question for contemporary literary scholars—the presentation of history. Having protected himself from the demands of aesthetics and textual criticism, Saintsbury's method of organization is basically chronological. Critics are arranged according to a timetable; here the same organizational principles prevail as in positivistic literary history. History is reduced to a compilation of facts that does not elucidate the historical process. If we investigate the historical consciousness found in Saintsbury's study, we find "an objectivism which compensates for the lack of historical consciousness through an increase in historical knowledge."[11] Saintsbury also defends himself emphatically against interpreting the past from the point of view of the present and seeks a standpoint "which may enable him to see each period sub specie aeternitatis."[12]

Positivistic history of judgment, as it is exemplified in Saintsbury, distorts history of criticism by (a) narrowing criticism to a specialized history, that is, excluding the respective literary as well as sociocultural connections and therefore (b) merely registering changes in opinions without making the historical significance of these changes apparent. The historicity of criticism is not taken into consideration because it is tacitly assumed that literary-critical judgments are all constituted in the same manner and can therefore be treated as variations of an identical basic model.

New Criticism's polemics against Positivism are well known and

---

[10]Ibid., p. 4.
[11]Robert Weimann, "Gegenwart und Vergangenheit in der Literaturgeschichte," *Sozialgeschichte und Wirkungsästhetik*, p. 246.
[12]Saintsbury, p. 8.

needs no further elucidation.[13] Wellek's monumental *History of Modern Criticism* (1956) suggests that the New Critical reservations about positivistic objectivism were not capable of solving the deeper problems of the history of criticism. Although Wellek criticizes the objectivism of the positivistic method, which is interpreted as relativism, and thereby takes up the problem of approach, the historicity of literary criticism is only partially problematized. The presentation of material in a more or less chronological way is then legitimatized through an understanding of history which is grounded in the history of ideas. "We should first recognize," says Wellek in the introduction directed against the causal-mechanical explanatory attempts of Positivism, "that there is an inner logic in the evolution of ideas—a dialectic of concepts. An idea is easily pushed to its extreme or converted into its opposite. Reaction against the preceding or prevailing critical system is the most common driving force of the history of ideas."[14] Through this attempt at justification, however, the immanent literary reduction of the presentation is not eliminated, but actually emphasized, in spite of certain concessions to the sociohistorical aspects of theories. Wellek is thus of the opinion that the specific influence of general social and historical phenomena on criticism is difficult to understand and to determine. Like literature, criticism has its own worth, which should not be diminished by a causal treatment. The price Wellek must pay for maintaining such a critical standpoint vis-à-vis the past is nevertheless considerable. Not only does he banish historicism but ultimately even history itself. Of course, Wellek's study contains a wealth of insights about critics, critical theories, and connections between aesthetics and critical book reviews, etc. The insoluble problem for Wellek is of a theoretical-methodological nature. In order to avoid relativism, Wellek imposes an external set of criteria on his subject. The views under investigation are judged in the last analysis by their agreement with New Criticism. The dogmatic character of this position avoids critical self-reflection, since for Wellek literary criticism attained its historical goal in reaching the level of New Criticism from which

---

[13]René Wellek, "The Revolt against Positivism in Recent European Literary Scholarship," in his *Concepts of Criticism* (New Haven, 1963), pp. 256–281.

[14]Wellek, *The Late Eighteenth Century,* Vol. 1 of *A History of Modern Criticism: 1750–1950* (New Haven, 1955), p. 8.

it can be judged. To that extent, Wellek saw himself in the tradition of teleological historical writing. The direct result was a realization of the past in contemporary terms (the present-day problems of literary criticism in the past). Later, in the essay "The Fall of Literary History" (1970)[15] it became a position of resignation which relinquished the possibility and value of literary-historical research altogether. Here Wellek concludes that a convincing model for the evolution cannot be found and therefore its history can only be understood as a continuing discourse about fixed fundamental problems. It is not by coincidence that Wellek's presentation verges on being a closed essay dealing with one important critic because in that way the curtailment of the historical premises can be formally minimized.

Wellek's *History of Modern Criticism* assumes a typological position between a theoretical-historical and a biographical-individualistic approach. In order to be fair to the individual critic, Wellek must intentionally refrain from a purely idea-oriented historical construct. The loss in methodological consistency is counteracted by the pragmatic gain in this compromise (clarity and readability). The historicizing of theorems is not really accomplished. The model of a thorough functionalistic view in which the given perspectives and systems are radically examined for historical significance appears in the works of Hans Blumenberg. His premise is differentiated from the older intellectual history (to which Wellek is still bound in many ways) in that he is not satisfied with the descriptive reconstruction of ideas and theories. Instead he problematizes the conditions under which they might be valid. Consequently, he dismisses the idea that the theories described are valid *per se*. History of criticism is presented in this model neither as a mere reporting of opinion nor as the description of theories and concepts, but more as the opening up of questions to which the formulated literary-critical positions provide answers. Historical presentation does not limit itself to the ordering of perspectives and attitudes that have prevailed in the past and to the examination of their background. Rather, its goal is the reconstruction of

---

[15]Wellek, "The Fall of Literary History," in *Geschichte, Ereignis und Erzählung*, ed. Reinhart Koselleck and Wolf-Dieter Stempel, *Poetik und Hermeneutik*, 5 (Munich, 1973), pp. 427-440.

those human needs manifested in the question that aesthetic and critical theorems attempt to answer. Using the example of imitation of nature, Blumenberg shows that identically worded postulates have totally different meanings in antiquity and in the modern era,[16] and thus a method of inquiry which holds abstractly to identical formulations (imitation concepts of both Aristotle and of modern poetics) entirely misses the cognitive-theoretical sense as well as the practical sense of these statements. Blumenberg states: "We will have to free ourselves from the notion that there is an established canon of 'great questions' which have moved constantly through history and have stimulated human thirst for knowledge and the human claim for world and self-definition in such a way that the alternating systems of mythologies, theologies, and philosophies could be explained from their congruency with this canon."[17] In place of this canon, the history of criticism would present itself as the relationship of problems and possible solutions that take shape against the background of positions that have grown dubious. Methodologically, it follows that the historian analyzes the formal system of a period's criticism "in the structure of which changes can be localized—changes that constitute the process nature of history up to the radicality of the historical turning point."[18]

II

A history of literary criticism based on this model could be labeled critical but would still remain, of course, bound to the theoretical premises of intellectual history. The human needs and practical interests assumed from the beginning are abstractly determined. If the social mediation of these needs is to become comprehensible, the characteristic determination of historical processes, which is still formalistic, must be broken down. This can no longer be accomplished through traditional investigations of literary background. Rather, literary criticism itself

[16]Hans Blumenberg, " 'Nachahmung der Natur': Zur Vorgeschichte der Idee des schöpferischen Menschen," *Studium Generale*, 10, no. 5 (1957), 266–283.
[17]Blumenberg, *Die Legitimität der Neuzeit* (Frankfurt am Main, 1966), pp. 42–43.
[18]Ibid., p. 43.

must be understood as a *social institution* and particularly as an institution which, in a specific way, participates in several spheres. In regard to presentation, it is obviously a part of literature; in regard to communicative activity, it is, however, a part of the public sphere as forum in which literary-critical deliberation (*Räsonnement*) takes place. What Bürger notes about literary history in developing some ideas of Benjamin can also be applied to the history of literary criticism: "the periodization of the developments in art are to be sought in the realm of art . . . and not in the changes evidenced by the subject matter of individual works."[19] This position assures inclusion of that sociohistorical context in a consequent historization which is sketched out by Blumenberg and omitted by the history of taste and the history of concepts or theories. It would be the task of such a history of the institution to show how literary criticism (as a subsystem of the institution art) changes not only in its manifestations (attitudes, judgments) but also in its basic conditions (organization, social arrangement, nature of the public sphere)—and to show it in connection with the changing conditions of production and the societal needs they affect.

The first step is to define more precisely the institutional character of art and art criticism. The systematic-normative and the sociohistorical aspects must be differentiated. As Felix V. Vodička has pointed out,[20] we can understand literature as a complex which encompasses works as well as literary (and other) evaluations—that is, norms. With respect to their significance for the historical evolution of literature, these two components stand in a dialectical relationship to each other: through artistic innovation, norms are changed, and, vice versa. Through the (possible) anticipation of norms, a change in the canon is made possible. If this relationship were absolutely self-regulating, the literary system would seem to produce its own evolution. Vodička is, of course, aware that this literary evolution must have a foundation in order to avoid the irrational hypothesis of an independent literary dynamic. For Vodička, the system of literature is embedded in its reception (aesthetic perception) and

[19]Peter Bürger, *Theorie der Avantgarde* (Frankfurt am Main, 1974), p. 40.
[20]Felix V. Vodicka, "Die Rezeptionsgeschichte literarischer Werke," in *Rezeptionsästhetik*, ed. Rainer Warning (Munich, 1975), pp. 71–83.

elaboration by the reading audience: "Just as it is the task of literary history to encompass the plethora of relationships which result from the polarity of work and reality, so must the dynamic which is determined by the polarity of work and reading audience become the object of historical description."[21] This statement clearly indicates that the institution of literature not only consists of the complex of works and norms, but has a social aspect as well which, for Vodička, is expressed through the reading audience. The difficulty, of course, is in exposing the special relationship between these two aspects—that is, revealing the nature of the mediation because the concept of audience is too narrow and too vague to be brought into *direct* connection with the system of literature (works, norms, values). If one starts with the assumption that the norms as well as the artistic products are directly determined by the audience (as the empirically verifiable recipients), the system of literature necessarily falls into just as many parts as the society has social groups. This is precisely what happens with Levin L. Schücking, who transforms the function of literary history into a history of types arbitrating taste.[22] The needs of specific social groups manifest themselves for Schücking as preferences in taste which, in turn, effect the production of works answering these preferences. In the development of such a causality, the unity and relative independence of the literary system which should be analytically maintained get lost. For no matter how certainly social groups and classes ultimately influence literary production, it is still not directly dependent on them because previously available works as well as the predominant literary and politicoreligious norms determine production by limiting the possibilities and alternatives in each concrete historical situation. Moreover, there are unavoidable stages of mediation in the social sphere between the institution of literature and the literary system in a more limited sense. The category of taste, on which Schücking centers his argument, is constituted not ad hoc by social groups, but by specific organizations (salons, clubs, societies) which themselves

---

[21]Ibid., p. 73.
[22]Levin L. Schücking, *Soziologie der literarischen Geschmacks-Bildung,* 3d ed. (Bern, 1961).

are oriented toward a more comprehensive institution, namely the public sphere.

An essential category of mediation emerges between the audience and the system of literature, and this is the public sphere, which is only casually mentioned by Vodička and above all is not conceptually distinguished from the audience. However, the public sphere cannot be defined and explained by socio-empirical data. Rather, it is a construct whose function is to make the dynamic processes between the spheres of society, state, and culture describable.[23] Its more specific significance for scholarly literary analysis is that it brings the relationships between social and literary activity (which for a positivistic sociology of literature can only be considered separately) closer to a nonmechanical interpretation. The structure of the public sphere determines the type of literary discourse, initially influencing its form (means and organization of communication), but also its content, in themes treated or avoided. Since the structure of the public sphere is relatively stable, it reinforces the system of literature. By referring to public opinion (*Räsonnement*), the literary system becomes anchored in the entire societal process. Class character expresses itself indirectly, of course, in that the dominant class can impose its preferences (ideologies) with the help of the organizations serving the public sphere (the press, academies, clubs, etc.).

A sketch of such an institutional history of literary criticism was presented in 1953 by the American literary sociologist Hugh D. Duncan.[24] He argued that statements and texts, which can be formally considered literary criticism, can have a very differentiated function, and he came to the following methodological conclusion: "In the kind of analysis undertaken here, it is very important to discover who is assigned the right to criticize; what institutions assume the guardianship of criticism; how these institutions defend their guardianship in competition with other institutions; how those who are to criticize are selected,

[23]Levin L. Schücking, *Soziologie der literarischen Geschmacks-Bildung*, 3d ed. (Bern, 1961).
[24]Hugh D. Duncan, "Literature as a Social Institution," *Language and Literature in Society* (Chicago, 1953), pp. 58–74.

trained, and supported; to whom the criticism may be communicated; and on what occasions criticism is required."[25] This catalogue of problems relates (1) to the social role of the critic, (2) to the social organization of criticism (the press, associations, academies), (3) to the connections of these organizations to the institutions of the whole society (state, church, court, parties), and (4) to the significance and function of literary criticism in the system of the whole society (whether required for its functioning or not). Duncan rightly stresses that the forms of literary criticism familiar to us have a place only in a relatively differentiated social structure and in a highly developed public sphere: "For it is precisely when a society becomes differentiated within, as well as among, its institutions that the critic, as we know him in modern society, emerges."[26]

In conjunction with these fundamental considerations, Duncan develops a typology of literary criticism that is still worthy of consideration today. The point of departure is a model of communication in which author, audience, and critic are deemed the significant factors. According to the dominant relationship in each communication situation, Duncan differentiates five different types of socially institutionalized literary criticism. Oral literature in primitive society had little need for the critic. Here the bond between author and audience is strong; on the other hand, the relation to the critic is marginal. The spiritual literature of the Middle Ages and courtly poetry of the Renaissance and Baroque belong to a type in which the bond between author and critic (censor) is strong, while the general audience remains on the periphery. The third type Duncan describes is a situation in which the producer has a strong bond to both audience and critic but in which the critic does not speak on behalf of the audience. If, as in the fourth type, the impulse originates in the audience, in whose name the author writes and the critic judges, the bonds between author and critic are undeveloped while the lines between the audience and the critic or author are starkly drawn. Duncan presents a fifth type in which all three bonds are equally developed as the ideal: it forms a harmonious balance that secures the autonomy of literature. Duncan's preference is

[25]Ibid., p. 60.
[26]Ibid., p. 64.

obviously influenced by New Criticism, which dominated the 1950s and may be the least convincing today. His method allows (in a form that is still very simple) the elaboration of models of communication with which important contributory aspects of literary criticism's social basis can be analytically understood. Two further steps are necessary to add to the historical dimension. First, the typology must be differentiated according to its historical material so that not only epochal phases but also shorter time periods can be isolated from one another. Moreover, the evolution from one type to another is not merely to be described as a change, but the process by which it came to this change should be simultaneously reconstructed. The possibilities depicted in Duncan's typology must be presented in their historical context so that the significant alterations are made visible.

More recently Peter Bürger has developed a historical typology of literary production and reception which underlines the aspect of historical evolution not thematized by Duncan.[27] Within the sphere of reception he differentiates the collective-sacral appropriation of Medieval art, the social appropriation of courtly art, and finally the individual reception of bourgeois art. The corresponding forms of literary criticism can be extrapolated easily with the help of Duncan's model. Naturally, these broad frameworks are only of limited benefit for the history of modern literary criticism between the eighteenth century and the present, since the category of individual reception must cover very distinct types of appropriation which manifest themselves in various forms of criticism. When Bürger writes that "solitary submersion in the work is the suitable mode of appropriation of art works which have moved away from the daily life practice (*Lebenspraxis*) of the bourgeois,"[28] it must be added that this condition, generally speaking, is only possible in late bourgeois society. Early bourgeois art deals with an individual reception which is, however, brought back through public deliberation (*Räsonnement*) to a social type of appropriation. It is true, of course, that naive and direct daily life practice gets lost in the use of art (the loss can be traced back to the representative depletion of courtly art), but this loss is compensated by the

[27]Peter Bürger, *Theorie der Avantgarde* (Frankfurt am Main, 1974), pp. 49–75.
[28]Ibid., p. 65.

moral-aesthetic deliberation, in which art serves as a critical corrective to society.

III

The incorporation of literary criticism into the history of the institution of literature is best illustrated by the following example. Ever since the pioneering work of Lukács, the year 1848 has been rightly viewed not only as a political but also as an essential literary epochal dividing line.[29] This change is most obviously seen in the field of theory, where after 1850 the norms and evaluative criteria based on the Vormärz period were replaced by the concept of realism. It can be easily shown how this theory of poetic realism developed from ideas formulated before 1848 (Hegel, Schelling) and how it then once again affected the literary production of the 1850s and 1860s.[30] For instance, the most significant critics of the epoch tested out the meaning of the new criteria in exemplary reviews. As important as it is to elucidate and formulate this reciprocal relationship of altered theory and new literary production, the history of literary criticism cannot be satisfied with this discovery. The conditions determining the development of the new theory must be indicated. In other words, the connection between the formation of literary norms and political ideology must be explained. Moreover, it must be kept in mind that the function of literature has changed in a significant way. Only against this background can the proper place of literary criticism in the age of Realism be understood.

The structural change of the institution of literature can be discerned in several phenomena which obviously cannot be isolated from one another. Most importantly, a quantitative as well as a qualitative change in the reading public must be noted. In connection with the industrialization and urbanization of Germany, congested metropolitan areas developed in which literary communication was concentrated. For the majority of people, participating according to taste was made easier. From the 1860s onward, one can speak of a mass audience which did not absorb

[29]Georg Lukács, *Deutsche Realisten des 19. Jahrhunderts* (Berlin, 1952), and *Skizze einer Geschichte der neueren deutschen Literatur* (Berlin, 1955).
[30]Cf. Max Bucher et al., *Realismus und Gründerzeit* (Stuttgart, 1976), 1:13-20, 38 ff.

but changed the educated group of Vormärz readers. Indications of this change are the family journals created in the Nachmärz period, through which belles lettres reached the general public regularly for the first time in Germany. While book production was still declining during the 1850s,[31] new groups of readers were introduced to literature through the journals and newspapers. These groups are probably responsible for the expansion of book production in the 1870s.

The results of this change are: (1) the rise of a popular literature tailored to the needs of a wide audience; and (2) qualitative changes in the area of literary criticism. Indicative of this change is the fact that a journal such as the *Gartenlaube*, which definitely had a great effect on taste, dispensed with all critical deliberation. Literary criticism was offered only in the form of author portraits in which the literary as well as ideological processes were personalized. Opposed to this approach, the liberal journals like the *Grenzboten* and the *Deutsche Museum* maintained the critical dialogue about literature. In particular, the *Grenzboten* became the organ of the new literary theory. Thus the division of literature into avant-garde and popular literature had already begun but was still held back by the idea of realistic *Volkstümlichkeit*.

A history of literary criticism would have to take into account this transition from a public predicated on standards of cultural deliberation (*Räsonnement*) to one based on consumption—that is, a structural change in the literary public sphere. As a part of this sphere, criticism is affected, along with other areas, by the erosion of literary tradition. Where literature is primarily produced and distributed for entertainment, it is potentially threatened with elimination, and its preservation is entrusted to the media, which only reach certain areas of communication.

As the concept of the public sphere was being truncated by post-1848 liberalism (Alexander Baumgarten, August Ludwig von Rochau) and as those specific elements such as equality and social justice, on which the working masses relied, were being denied, the limitations of the new literary theory of poetic realism became increasingly visible. Between the contradictions of the liberal model of the public sphere and the theory of

---

[31]Ibid., p. 167.

realism, there is a relationship that was recently revealed by Helmut Kreuzer when he pointed out that poetic realism "cannot be separated from ideological-political motifs based on the historical conditions of the post-1848 epoch."[32] The battlefront against the proletariat and the legitimation of the alliance between culture and capital by critics such as Emanuel Geibel, Gustav Freytag, and Julian Schmidt were the manifestations of the horizon of expectation about what "realistic" depiction had to achieve. What is intended here is the idealization of the German bourgeoisie. Poetic realism finds its boundaries where the message criticizes the compromise of the middle class, a compromise disguised as the idea of progress. Poetic realism is meant to be a balanced representation that expressly separates itself from "crude" West European realism.

The position of the literary critic must be situated within the context of these conditions. Of primary consideration would be the change in the critic's professional role in relation to the change in the literary market, particularly in relation to the rise of the mass media (family journals, mass press). The Vormärz critic became a salaried copy writer who delivered what the medium demanded. The freedom of the press enacted in the interim did not have a major effect, as Heine pointed out in *Lutetia,* since the organization of the press came increasingly under the pressure of commercialization. On the whole, an increasing dependence of the critic and a corresponding decline in his social status could most likely be found. And finally, on the level of its function in the larger society, the legitimizing use of criticism should be investigated. The reviews of the Nachmärz period refer primarily to norms and criticisms which, in the final analysis, reinforce sociopolitical processes that eventually led to the conservative foundation of the Second Empire in 1871.

Let us return to our point of departure: there are little more than beginnings for a history of the institution of criticism. What such a history could accomplish can, however, be ascertained. Its goal would be: (1) to overcome the specialization and reductiveness of premises based on judgment and the history of ideas; (2)

---

[32]Helmut Kreuzer, "Zur Theorie des deutschen Realismus zwischen März-revolution und Naturalismus," in *Realismustheorien,* ed. R. Grimm and J. Hermand (Stuttgart, 1975), p. 50.

to end the purely chronological organization of material and instead to understand change against the background of institutional transformation; and (3) to take into account the interconnection between the literary and social processes from the beginning, so that monocausal relationships and mechanical correlations are not presumed, but so that the social factor can present itself in the institution of criticism.

7   Critical Theory, Public Sphere, and Culture: Jürgen Habermas and His Critics

Liberal theory, especially after 1848, tends to separate carefully the domains of culture and politics. Its notion of the autonomy of art is particularly indispensable for countering arguments that conceive the relation between culture and politics as historically changing. One of the essential achievements of Critical Theory has been to dissolve this seeming opposition and make visible the objective link between the two. The category of the culture industry, introduced by Adorno and Horkheimer in 1944, contains this very insight. What it does not deal with is the concept of the public sphere. This question was taken up by Habermas in his *Strukturwandel der Öffentlichkeit* (Structural Transformation of the Public Sphere, 1962) and has generally defined the debate over mass culture within the younger generation of the Frankfurt School. Even when Habermas has been contradicted, it is usually within the framework of his theory. The intensive and sometimes decidedly polemic argument about the history, present state, and future of the public sphere has always been at the same time a discussion about the conditions and possibilities of culture in an advanced capitalist society. Habermas' theory of the public sphere offered a model for unraveling the political and social element in the concept of culture. Yet this assertion is still too general. The essentially political character of culture was certainly familiar to the older

Translated by Marc Silverman.

Frankfurt School. One has only to recall Herbert Marcuse's essay "Über den affirmativen Charakter der Kultur" (The Affirmative Character of Culture, 1937)[1] and Benjamin's works from the 1930s in which the political function of cultural production was emphasized. Habermas' work presupposes these studies. His theory of the public sphere must be understood as an attempt to reformulate the dialectical relationship of the sociocultural and political system (to introduce his later terminology). The theory of the culture industry, as it was developed in the *Dialectic of Enlightenment,* needed historical grounding. The difference between the classical analysis of mass culture by Horkheimer and Adorno and the description of disintegration in the public sphere by Habermas is not so much at the level of subject matter and its critical evaluation as at the level of its systematic starting point. The theory of the culture industry remained abstract insofar as it assumed the existence and influence of organized capitalism without demonstrating it materialistically. The development of human history culminating in monopoly capitalism and its requisite mass culture was explained as the misguided dialectic of *ratio*—that is, less by means of social theory than by the principles of intellectual or ideological history. One could even say that the advanced phase of instrumental reason was projected back into early European history. Habermas, on the other hand, strives for a sociohistorical explanation that proceeds from the historical constellation of the early nineteenth century. His concern is to explain the transformation of cultural institutions through change in the political system, whose development in turn is conceived through changes in the economic system. This introduces, then, the category of the public sphere as the mediating concept which was missing in the *Dialectic of Enlightenment.*

The Disintegration of the Public Sphere

For purposes of clarification, let us briefly recapitulate the process of disintegration in the public sphere described by Habermas. This summary will be limited to the cultural

[1]Herbert Marcuse, "The Affirmative Character of Culture," *Negations* (Boston, 1968), pp. 88–133.

phenomena on which we will focus. The development can be expressed as a transition from cultural discourse (*Räsonnement*) to consumption. For the eighteenth and early nineteenth centuries the contents of culture, if not their form of distribution, are clearly separate from the market. As objects of discussion in a public sphere of responsible private citizens, they prepare the way for human self-determination and political emancipation. In contrast, the production and reception of culture since the late nineteenth century are not defined merely in formal terms by the capitalist market: culture has become a commodity and is consumed accordingly as leisure-time entertainment. Its goal is to reproduce labor power. Late capitalist mass culture differs from early bourgeois culture in its lack of rational discourse among the recipients. Where this rational discourse is continued in the mass media, it, too, takes on the character of a commodity.

Habermas considers the literary enlightenment and cultural emancipation of the masses for the most part a failure. Increased economic availability through lower book prices and higher wages has not made classical culture more accessible; it has merely offered the prerequisite for changed forms in which technological innovations and an expanded book market are employed in order to lower the level of cultural life. This applies not only to the literary market but, to an even greater extent, to the influence of electronic mass media, such as radio and television. These media speak directly to the consumer, as it were, by-passing the private sphere through which cultural reception was once mediated: "Publicly oriented inwardness has tended to yield to a reification of intimacy."[2] An image arises of a general and politically dangerous regression. Using the example of the press, Habermas shows the transition from a public organ concerned with formulating opinion to a primarily commercial apparatus that must align itself for the most part to the interest of its advertisers.

Habermas' presentation of disintegration within bourgeois culture does not differ fundamentally from Adorno's and Horkheimer's critique. It is no accident that Habermas refers to

---

[2] *Strukturwandel der Öffentlichkeit: Untersuchungen zu einer Kategorie der bürgerlichen Gesellschaft*, 2d ed. (Neuwied and Berlin, 1965), p. 189.

Adorno's famous essay "Über den Fetischcharakter in der Musik und die Regression des Hörens" (On the Fetish Character in Music and the Regression of Hearing")[3] and to the essays by Enzensberger which were influenced by Adorno. Mass culture in advanced capitalism is manipulated culture in which the masses have become objects. The affirmative character of bourgeois art has become complete: in the culture industry art serves at every level as an apology for the status quo. Here Horkheimer and Adorno, who were confronted with the America of the 1940s, were analyzing not so much the impact of the state as the power of private industry, whose commercial interests dominated the structure. This vehement protest against a form of culture totally transformed into a commodity appeals by contrast to bourgeois culture in the eighteenth and nineteenth centuries, one which was protected by autonomy even though it was accessible only to a minority. Faced with the choice between objectified and democratic culture, on the one hand and authentic but elitist culture on the other, Horkheimer and Adorno decisively support the latter, since for them emancipation cannot be expected from the realm of reification. "Even today the culture industry dresses works of art like political slogans and forces them upon a resistant public at reduced prices; they are as accessible for public enjoyment as a park."[4] Critical Theory mistrusts popularized tradition, as there is no longer a recognizable use value but only commodity fetishism. Habermas participates in this critique, because for him, too, culture legitimates itself as a medium of self-understanding and self-liberation. True to his point of departure, however, he cannot identify with the pessimism of Horkheimer and Adorno.

Noteworthy in Habermas' attempt to reformulate the critique of the older Frankfurt School is his effort to understand the dialectic of the Enlightenment sociohistorically—that is, by analyzing the contradictions in liberal capitalism. The weakest points in his investigation are those where he uncritically accepts Adorno's results and thereby makes himself into an advocate of

---

[3]Theodor W. Adorno, *Dissonanzen*, 5th ed. (Göttingen, 1972), pp. 9–45.
[4]Max Horkheimer and Theodor W. Adorno, *Dialectic of Enlightenment*, trans. John Cumming (New York, 1972), p. 160.

a cultural elitism which runs counter to his point of departure. Where in Horkheimer and Adorno *ratio* as instrumental reason comes to fruition in the alienation of advanced capitalism (the Lukácsian heritage of Critical Theory), it perforce denounces the tradition of the Enlightenment which is so indispensable for Habermas. In this respect, *Strukturwandel der Öffentlichkeit* must be seen as a critical response to the *Dialectic of Enlightenment*—based on a model of the liberal public sphere, Habermas examines the possibilities and limitations of political emancipation under conditions of advanced capitalism.

Habermas has been criticized, among other things, for idealizing the Enlightenment public sphere: failing to consider adequately its specific class character, the argument goes, he applies an abstract category of the public sphere to advanced capitalist conditions. Recourse to the Enlightenment thus hides the present class conflict and tries to reconstruct what has long since been lost. The liberal camp argues in a very similar manner: because Habermas constructs an ahistorical model from early bourgeois society, he misconstrues the conditions under which public opinion must function in an industrial or postindustrial mass democracy. This critique contains a kernel of truth. Habermas does indeed construct a model that has never existed in pure form. Such an ideal model is necessary for describing diachronic changes. The concept of structural disintegration, which constitutes the center of attention in the second part of Habermas' investigation, logically presumes a condition of standardized norms whose retrieval is desirable. Therefore, Habermas' model of public sphere has a double function. It provides a paradigm for analyzing historical change, while also serving as a normative category for political critique. In order to prevent a decline to a merely descriptive concept of public opinion, he insists on its emphatic use, although he admits the irreversibility of the historical processes involved.

This methodological critique of Habermas' model, while in part justified, focuses too much on peripheral weaknesses of the analysis. Not until we have realized that the double function of the model is for him unavoidable will fruitful critique be possible. In this context, central importance must be accorded to the chapter on Hegel and Marx, a section usually overlooked by his critics.

The Model of Classical Public Sphere

In order to present the logic of the investigation, we must outline the model of the public sphere which Habermas derived from the social and philosophical material of the eighteenth and early nineteenth century. The bourgeois public sphere, occasionally referred to by Habermas as classical, constituted itself in the seventeenth and eighteenth centuries as a sphere (*sui generis*) situated between the absolutistic state and bourgeois society—that is, the world of social labor and commodity trade. It consists of deliberating (*räsonierende*) private persons who critically negate political norms of the state and its monopoly on interpretation. The object of discourse is, on the one hand, questions of literature and art and, on the other, the theory and practice of absolutistic domination. Public opinion institutionalizes itself; its goal is to replace arbitrary secret politics with a form of domination that is legitimated by means of rational consensus among participating citizens. This model of the public sphere recognizes neither social differences nor privileges. Equality of the members and general accessibility are assumed, even if they cannot be realized in specific situations. The revolutionary potential of the model resides in the fact that it makes possible, even demands, its application to all social groups. The public sphere sees itself clearly distinguished both from the state and from the private domain. Whereas separation from the state is immediately understandable and is discerned early through the genesis of the public sphere (public opinion as the means of controlling government), separation of the public sphere and society remains latent and reveals itself only at that point where it becomes problematic through changes in the economic and social system. "The sociological premise is," according to a formulation of Wolfgang Jäger, "the existence of a society of small commodity producers, for only then is there a guarantee that all commodities... are exchanged at a value measured by the amount of work."[5] Active participation in the public sphere is based on property; the independent functioning of free compe-

[5] Wolfgang Jäger, *Öffentlichkeit und Parlamentarismus. Eine Kritik an Jürgen Habermas* (Stuttgart, 1973), p. 14.

tition, together with its balance of supply and demand, is always assumed as the natural order.

Here, then, are the points at which, according to Habermas, crises may arise. As soon as the development of capitalism causes economic contradictions to be reflected as social problems, difficulties arise for the classical model of the public sphere. The bourgeoisie, which has employed it as an instrument of political change (emancipation), now shows an inclination to adapt the public sphere to the changed circumstances, so that the contradiction between its own particular interests and the interests of the general society are disguised. Structural disintegration of the classic public sphere begins when the dividing line between the public sphere and the private domain (production and consumption) starts to waver. As soon as social conflicts of a developed class society are reflected as demands in the public realm, discourse loses its character of a discussion free of domination. "Laws which obviously have come about under the 'pressure of the street' can scarcely be understood as arising from the consensus of private individuals engaged in public discussion. They correspond in a more or less concealed manner to the compromise of conflicting private interests."[6] According to liberal theory, the market should regulate itself without the need for state intervention. There was no provision in this theory for social antagonisms arising from the capitalist mode of production which open the door to state intervention. "Interventionalism originates in the translation into politics of conflicts of interest which cannot be resolved within the private sphere itself."[7] Thus state and society penetrate each other increasingly and thereby destroy the basis of the liberal public sphere. This erosion of the classical public sphere begins, according to Habermas, after 1870, when liberal competitive capitalism gives way to the organized capitalism of cartels and trusts. Because, on the one hand, the state intervenes in the social system to resolve social conflicts and, on the other, various interest groups assert their demands in the public sphere, the classical function of

---

[6]Jürgen Habermas, "The Public Sphere: An Encyclopedia Article (1964)," *New German Critique*, no. 3 (Fall, 1974), p. 54.

[7]*Strukturwandel*, p. 158.

public opinion as the advocate of general interest is increasingly undermined. The persistence of a historical institution like Parliament can only disguise the fact that the structure of the public sphere has changed. As Habermas summarizes his critique: The structure represents no more than a sounding-board used to acclaim decisions that are no longer prepared by public discourse.

Habermas' disintegration thesis is not, as is sometimes assumed, an appendix to his theory, one that can be disregarded when the fundamental validity of the theory's truth is thrown into question. Its point of departure and the interest in positing a public sphere itself is precisely the problematic of political domination in advanced capitalism—that is, the depoliticization of the public, its manipulation by state administration and industrial public relations. Habermas' choice of the bourgeois public sphere as his frame of reference can be explained by the fact that the alternative proposed by Marx has not prevailed in the Western industrial nations. (Whether and to what extent it has materialized in the socialist countries after the October Revolution is never discussed by Habermas.) If the constitution of the liberal public sphere is connected to private property (the property holder as discoursing citizen), then the socialist public sphere must take as its starting point the socialization of the means of production. Continued political domination by one class in bourgeois society will dissolve, and the previously private world of production from which social conflicts arose will be subjected to public control. "The public sphere," as Habermas defines the changed relationship, "no longer mediates between a society of private property holders and the state, but rather the autonomous public as private people secures itself a sphere of personal freedom and tolerance in the systematic organization of a state absorbed into the society."[8] The private autonomy of the human being derives from the socialist public sphere, not the other way around. Habermas' Marxist critics link up to this socialist model—which represents for him only a theoretical alternative—by attempting to establish its actual existence.

[8] Ibid., p. 143.

The Liberal Critique

For Habermas' liberal critics the discussion of a socialist alternative model is equivalent to escaping into utopia. Peter
Glotz[9] and Wolfgang Jäger[10] agree that Habermas' theory does
not conform to reality and is therefore unable to do justice to the
contemporary form of mass democracy. Precisely the critical
comparison of this ideal type of the liberal sphere with its distortion in advanced capitalism provokes the objection of insufficient historical grounding. It is noteworthy that both critics try to
classify Habermas' theory as conservative or romantic and, thus,
to subvert its claim to rationality. They give us to understand
that Habermas' suggestions cannot contribute to improving
present circumstances because they rest on a historically insufficient material basis and, upon application, become stuck in a
purely utopian attitude. The connection of these arguments is
particularly important to Jäger. He bases his charge of a utopian
lack of specificity on Habermas' misrepresentation of historical
reality. This objection should be taken seriously, since Habermas' model must be able to claim a historical basis and not
merely present itself as an abstract ideal. Only with the aid of a
historical category can development and structural change be
described. For Habermas, the public sphere of the late
bourgeoisie should prove to be the historical result of inner contradictions present from the beginning in the bourgeois public
sphere.

Wolfgang Jäger

Jäger's historically oriented critique is aimed at proving that
Habermas incorrectly assessed the history and importance of the
English Parliament when he described the years 1832 to 1867 as
the high point of parliamentarianism and pointed to a decay
thereafter. In particular, Jäger argues that the alleged power of
public opinion assumed by Habermas in fact never existed as
such. Parliamentary politics were conducted not as rational consensus but on the basis of compromises adapted to interests. According to Jäger, public opinion served economic interests even

[9]Peter Glotz, *Buchkritik in deutschen Zeitungen* (Hamburg, 1968).
[10]*Öffentlichkeit und Parlamentarismus* (note 5, above).

during its classical period. Its institutions "helped serve the articulation of actual interests, be it those strata excluded de facto from parliamentary representation despite the right to vote or those excluded directly from the right to vote."[11] The alleged manipulation in contemporary parliamentarianism blossomed, as Jäger suggests, already in the mid-nineteenth century. Therefore, it is impossible to speak of a disintegration of the public sphere. If we follow Jäger, there has never existed a public sphere corresponding to Habermas' model: "If Habermas' statements about the bourgeois public sphere are examined for their historical content, there remain only a few substantiated theses."[12]

This critique clearly goes too far; no one expects of a model that it assimilate without contradiction all historical circumstances. Nevertheless, Jäger does touch on an unresolved problem. Habermas assumes that structural change in the public sphere is caused by the transition to organized capitalism. The conditions in England mentioned by Jäger—the massive interest lobbies in Parliament—contradict Habermas' theory, which claims that the liberal public sphere and its most important institutions remained strictly separate from the private domain of production. Jäger's arguments suggest the hypothesis that this structural change occurs as early as the phase of competitive capitalism. Habermas himself is contradictory on this point. Here he deals essentially with restrictions placed on classical theory by liberal critics such as John Stuart Mill and Tocqueville, as well as Marx's fundamental critique, yet these predate organized capitalism. Marx sees as early as the French Revolution of 1848, especially the June Revolt by the workers, the possibility of transforming the bourgeois public sphere for the benefit of the masses.[13] On the other hand, Tocqueville's reservations about domination by the masses crystallize in his analysis of liberal capitalist America.[14] From this one could conclude that the problem of the classical public sphere was not first caused by organized capitalism. Either the seeds of these difficulties are

---

[11] Ibid., p. 23.

[12] Ibid.

[13] Karl Marx, *The Eighteenth Brumaire of Louis Bonaparte* (New York, 1963).

[14] Alexis de Tocqueville, *Democracy in America*, trans. Henry Reeve, rev. Francis Bowen, ed. Phillips Bradley (New York, 1945).

contained from the beginning in the public sphere or, in order
to save the model, it is necessary to distinguish more precisely
between the precapitalist and liberal-capitalist phases. Jäger's objections point in this direction while accusing Habermas of constructing a historically untenable synthesis out of precapitalist
philosophy in Germany, English social history of the capitalist
period, and French political theory.[15] Within the framework of
Habermas' approach it is quite possible to support the thesis that
his projected model of public sphere is essentially rooted in precapitalist circumstances. It is in this sense that Annette
Leppert-Fögen reinterpreted Habermas' theory. Following
Hans Medick, she stressed the precapitalist character of classical
economic theory (Adam Smith): "the establishment of economic
liberalism did not come about as an apology for capitalism but
rather primarily in struggle against the feudal vestiges in a
commodity-producing society and against the mercantile politics
of the state."[16] The same can be said about the public sphere: it,
too, is primarily directed against absolutist political domination
and feudal social privileges. The social basis of this public sphere
is a community of small producers connected with each other by
fair trade. Leppert-Fögen makes this clear when she compares
the principle of openness and general accessibility in the public
sphere with the harmony between supply and demand.[17] In
both cases freedom from domination is the aim. Accepting this
reading, the problem of structural transformation appears in a
new light. As a concept of the petite bourgeoisie—that is, a transitional class between feudalism and capitalism, this theory became obsolete as soon as the inequality of property relations
became apparent in the Industrial Revolution. It is not in the
transition to organized capitalism, but rather in the split of the
middle class into the petite bourgeoisie and an economically
powerful bourgeoisie where the potential for crisis in the liberal
public sphere originate. This situation was reached in the 1840s,
as Marx demonstrated in his discussion of the 1848 Revolution
in *The Eighteenth Brumaire of Louis Bonaparte* (1852). As soon as

---

[15]Jäger, p. 42.
[16]Annette Leppert-Fögen, *Die deklassierte Klasse: Studien zur Geschichte und
Ideologie des Kleinbürgertums* (Frankfurt am Main, 1974), p. 107.
[17]Leppert-Fögen, p. 118.

the petite bourgeoisie finds itself confronted with a developed capitalist mode of production, to which it is not equal, it turns away from liberal theory and withdraws to a defensive middle class ideology, placing its own interests above those of the whole society and thereby undermining the foundations of the public sphere.

Peter Glotz

Whereas Jäger limits himself to a historical critique, Peter Glotz attempts to develop an alternative model for industrial society based on the essentials of this critique. His polemic against an alleged cultural elitism on Habermas' part seeks to smooth the way for an extended democratic public sphere. To achieve this he denies the disintegration of the public sphere. "Much has changed, but it is impossible to speak of 'disintegration.'"[18] The admitted changes are portrayed as a transformation that was basically progressive. Like Jäger, Glotz justifies his critique by pointing out the historical reality not covered by Habermas' theory. "The disintegration thesis," Glotz argues, "results from an idealization of circumstances in the period of bourgeois culture and from an empirically inadequate critique of mass communication."[19] Glotz rightly points out that the concept of disintegration is ambiguous and that Habermas approaches the position of conservative culture critics. For this reason he suggests that one speak of a restructuring of the literary-aesthetic elite. The point of this argument is to exonerate the public, since the intellectuals are now made responsible for the present unsatisfactory situation. The organization of the consciousness industry is no longer at fault for the separation of high culture and mass culture; rather, it is the intellectuals who refuse to engage in discussion with a broad public. Implicit in this criticism is the notion that the liberal public sphere is still basically intact and would function if literary intellectuals exploited the possibilities of modern mass communication. This argument, of course, ultimately dismisses the thesis of structural transformation. To admit that circumstances have changed means nothing more than that the specific conditions have be-

[18]Glotz, *Buchkritik*, p. 68.
[19]Ibid., p. 70.

come different, while the structural model remains operative. This tendency can be clearly recognized in the objections Glotz directs at Habermas. According to Glotz, the depoliticization of the German press is due not to its form of private ownership, but to the attitude of the editors. Also, Glotz sees in Habermas' view of mass culture (entertainment) an elitist prejudice that defies democratization and thus tends to undercut the development of the public sphere. Finally, Habermas is accused of a general hostility toward relaxation and entertainment, an attitude that, in Glotz's opinion, is not progressive but conservative.

Glotz concludes that the literary public sphere in Germany does not function adequately as a democratic institution because its administrators and representatives misunderstand their task and are biased with elitist conceptions. The material collected by Glotz demonstrates the correctness of this challenge. Yet it does not say much about the structure of the public sphere. Although Glotz does not do so consciously, he assumes that the classical model can still be achieved (the liberalist attitude), and focuses his polemic on establishing Habermas' empirical mistakes. Glotz wants to save the public sphere by disproving the signs of disintegration compiled by Habermas. The contradictory nature of Glotz's critique appears obvious when he tries to furnish a positive alternative model. For then it becomes clear that Glotz follows the liberal model of the public sphere. His critique of elitism postulates general accessibility, his definition of the literary critic emphasizes the importance of public discourse, and his communication plans for the press reflect once again the function of media for the self-determination of the public. Glotz is forced, however, to make a decisive concession that brings him close to elitist theories: Because the masses are no longer on an equal footing with the educated bourgeois public, the intellectuals must mediate between culture and an anonymous public—a hierarchy of good will, so to speak.

The liberal critique touches both historically and systematically on weak points in Habermas' theory of public sphere, and attempts to prove the failure of the whole theory by this insufficiency. In the final analysis, these objections are based on a disagreement with Habermas' concept of historical evolution. The sociohistorical process since the beginnings of capitalism should be read differently. Whereas Habermas' understanding of historical materialism conceives of a necessary transition from liberal to monopoly capitalism and, in the same way, deduces the problematic of the advanced bourgeois public sphere, his critics try to reinterpret the undeniable socioeconomic changes. Existing mass democracy is acknowledged positivistically as the logical and therefore inevitable outcome that we must accept. The liberal critic concedes to historical development an affirmative justification and denounces Critical Theory as utopian. This objection points to a fundamental dilemma in Habermas' theory. As a theory of bourgeois public sphere it must elevate one phase of the historical process to a norm in order to construct its pre- and post-history. But the liberal heritage of his theory (the concept of the bourgeois public sphere) in part turns against the theory when he limits his idea of post-history to this bourgeois stage and does not pursue the sublation of the bourgeois public sphere in a socialist one. Here Habermas chooses not to apply his analysis of Marx, but instead turns again to the classical concept of the public sphere to explain its faulty development in advanced capitalism. This is the Achilles heel of his theory, for this concept of the public sphere must then be abstractly opposed to historical development. This becomes evident in the objections offered by Niklas Luhmann.

Niklas Luhmann

Glotz and Jäger argue from an ideologically fixed position; their strategy is unmistakably aimed at characterizing Habermas' theory as "conservative" and "romantic" in order to discredit it politically. More fruitful and without doubt more influential for the further development of Habermas' theory is Luhmann's critique. Arguing from the standpoint of systems theory, he pursues the question of how and to what extent the concept and function of public opinion have changed. His premise agrees completely with Habermas. He, too, assumes an essential difference between the bourgeois public sphere and the present state of affairs. He proposes that those changes deduced from a perspective of intellectual history must have had social causes. "For sociology it is implausible that this disintegration can be interpreted as a self-explanatory, immanent, dialectical development of the mind; rather, it must be attributed to the improbability and unreliability of that complicated systems structure which upheld this belief and provided it with the necessary experiences."[20] Whereas Habermas insists that a collective social function must be found for public opinion (even in a Marxist model), Luhmann rejects this claim as an impossible solution for a society particularized into specialized systems. "The concept of public opinion," he argues against Habermas, "cannot simply be reproduced organizationally because organizations depend precisely on that segmenting of consciousness, and therefore they can realize neither these structural premises nor the corresponding experiences on which rests the supposition of a critical public opinion."[21] Thus Luhmann suggests not a returning to the Enlightenment but adapting the model to the particularized social system in industrial society as a means of renewing it.

Habermas actually never doubted the possibility of collective social communication. Luhmann, however, claims that under the conditions of an industrialized society, such an all-inclusive process of communication can take place only in special cases. The public sphere can no longer be recognized by its generality, rationality, and capability of consensus, "but by the form of the themes for political communication, by its suitability as a structure for the communication process."[22] In place of a general search for truth arises a pragmatic approach to how uncertainty can be resolved. Through public discussion the system's balance is sustained or reconstructed. According to Luhmann, then, a sociological analysis of public opinion must concern itself with the rules of attention and decision within a political system. Translated into everyday language, this means that public opinion grows around and follows "issues." The limited attention span of a public overburdened with problems produces a public sphere in which issues must be changed constantly just to maintain a discussion. What Habermas' model presupposes (the solution of problems by general consensus) is, according to Luhmann, no longer attainable. Luhmann stresses no less than Habermas that the public sphere in an advanced capitalist soci-

---

[20]Niklas Luhmann, "Öffentliche Meinung," in *Politische Vierteljahresschrift*, 11, no. 1 (1970), 2–28; the quotation is on p. 5.
[21]Ibid., p. 6.
[22]Ibid., p. 9.

ety can no longer function with the rules of the eighteenth century, for the particularization of the system into numerous specialized systems diminishes the efficacy of general opinion-building not produced in a specialized system. Habermas' problem of structural disintegration emerges for Luhmann as a question of how the public sphere can attain a new function after its liberal function has been exhausted.

Luhmann emphasizes the structure of "political communication through institutionalized themes."[23] In this situation, public opinion is dependent on the authority institutionalized in organizations—parties, bureaucracies, interest groups, etc. Even without assuming that mass communication is manipulated, one can easily recognize the advantage of these organizations in the production of public opinion. Luhmann himself has no illusions about this tendency: "The creation, use, and continuation of public opinion themes belong essentially to the domain of professional politicians specially groomed for the job."[24] The productive capacity of this public opinion as well as its importance for society lie in its integrating function: it connects the political system to other specialized systems in the society. "Public opinion . . . must be able to encompass the difference between politics and nonpolitics and, thus, also the relative remoteness and incomprehensibility of details in the process of political decision-making."[25] Luhmann's pragmatic assessment of the public sphere necessarily leads to a critique of Habermas' theory. The concept of the public sphere developed by Critical Theory depends, for Habermas, on the nominalization of the word "public," behind which he seeks a collective subject. Because systems theory, however, surrenders the traditional concept of domination and no longer assumes a collective subject, the insufficiency of public opinion—which Luhmann also admits—loses its strategic importance.

As in the case of Glotz and Jäger, there are fundamental theoretical differences hidden behind this discussion of the importance and function of the public sphere, but they can, at best, only be outlined. The concern here cannot be a general analysis

---

[23]Ibid., p. 18.
[24]Ibid., p. 23.
[25]Ibid., p. 26–27.

of the relationship between dialectical theory and systems theory; my remarks must be confined to the aspect of the public sphere. In his critique, Luhmann touches on essential premises of Habermas' position. Habermas' sociophilosophical thought is, according to Luhmann, still marked by presuppositions of the Enlightenment, considered by Luhmann as a naive antecedent of modern sociology. Habermas is also included when Luhmann writes in the essay "Soziologische Aufklärung" (Sociological Enlightenment): "That the individual, through self-reflection on his own, can find something common to all humanity, that he can reach a consensus, even truth, will not be plausible to sociologists."[26] The possibility, even the necessity of this reflection as a means of finding truth has been, under the title of knowledge constituting interest (*erkenntnisleitendes Interesse*), Habermas' central theme since 1965. Since Luhmann, as a sociologist, considers the social determination of the individual as the primary factor that will assert itself against consciousness in modern industrial society, he must necessarily reject a concept of the public sphere derived from the idea that collective identity could be constructed from consensus among individuals. The critical recourse to the Enlightenment implied in Habermas' theory is subjected by Luhmann to a historically argued ideological critique focusing on the increased complexity of modern society. Following in the steps of Max Weber and Emile Durkheim, Luhmann severs the connection to normative thought in early bourgeois social philosophy and subsequently finds himself in the position of describing the public sphere in advanced capitalism "without bias," as it were, and elucidating the limits of its capacity. The ideal of communication free of domination, which was contained in the liberal theory of the public sphere, appears to be historically superseded within the framework of this approach.

What appears fruitful to me in this criticism is that it questions, from a sociological perspective, the possibility of applying Habermas' theory, making visible the tension between normative discussion and historical explication. The price for this sociologically restricted argumentation is the loss of philosophical reflection. Theoretical thought is limited to the status quo

[26]Niklas Luhmann, *Soziologische Aufklärung*, 2d ed. (Opladen, 1971), p. 67.

and its systematic management. Luhmann defines enlightenment as a building of systems by which complexity is reduced. "Rationality in this world [can] only be furthered by the construction and stabilization of more encompassing and complex systems."[27] Because Luhmann values so little the changing potential of consciousness, the possibility of stimulating the emancipatory process through self-reflection is blocked. The path of history assumes just that rigidity which Critical Theory had attacked from its beginning. Therefore Habermas was right when he later criticized Luhmann's objectivism in systems theory as resulting in decisionism, since for Luhmann practical questions are explained by formal rules of behavior and can acquire no further legitimation. (Legitimation in substance must be illusory according to Luhmann). Enlightenment shrinks in systems theory to formal rationality because it throws overboard what for Habermas is the fundamental problem—that practical questions are capable of truth, that there are justifiable norms, that human self-determination is possible.

The Marxist Critique

As Habermas became the object of radical student criticism during the late 1960s, his theory of public sphere was increasingly condemned, although it had helped the student movement originally in defining its own position. This is not the place to retrace this development.[28] Our interest must be directed toward those counterarguments and alternative proposals which were advanced. It will be necessary to distinguish between critiques which continue the approach chosen by Habermas while radicalizing and thereby negating parts of his theory and those which identify Habermas as a representative of the Frankfurt School and thus of bourgeois ideology. Characteristic of the first position would be the investigation by Negt and Kluge, *Öffentlichkeit und Erfahrung* (The Public Sphere and Experience, 1972), in which acquaintance with Habermas' theory is explicitly presumed. Characteristic of the second position is Ulf

[27]Ibid., p. 80.
[28]See *Die Linke antwortet Jürgen Habermas*, ed. Oskar Negt (Frankfurt am Main, 1968). Includes essays by Wolfgang Abendroth, Peter Brückner, et al.

Milde's study in connection with a collective investigation on literature of the eighteenth century.[29] Although their objections coincide at certain spots, the goal and function of their respective arguments are significantly different. Whereas Negt and Kluge want to salvage the concept of the public sphere with their criticism, Milde's attack is tantamount to an ideological denunciation, which, by the way, corresponds in some ways to the liberal critique.

Ulf Milde

For Milde, Habermas is first and foremost an ideologue employing his categories and historical material to legitimate political and social objectives. Milde remarks: "Habermas proves himself a late bourgeois ideologue in that he must falsify the memories of heroic bourgeois illusions in order to extract from them what he wants."[30] To prove his thesis he claims that Habermas considers the principle of freedom from domination as the essential component of the public sphere. Because Habermas equates this element with the bourgeois public sphere, he becomes fixated on it. At this point the ideological critique proves to be a barrier to interpretation. In order to understand and assimilate Habermas' theory, Milde considers it in connection with the renewed scholarly interest in the Enlightenment. This interest must be seen as a symptom of the attempt by bourgeois intellectuals to criticize the restorative West German state. Because Milde includes Habermas in this group and attributes to him the same motives,[31] he misjudges the approach and also the goal of Habermas' theory. For the assumption that a space free of domination can be constituted within the bourgeois public sphere does not imply that this idea is inextricably tied to the bourgeois public sphere itself, but rather that this concept can only be recovered if the bourgeois public sphere is surmounted by a socialist one. The meaning of the disintegration thesis is that the liberal public sphere must conflict with bourgeois society as soon as the capitalist mode of production

---

[29]"'Bürgerliche Öffentlichkeit' als Modell der Literaturentwicklung des 18. Jahrhunderts," in Gert Mattenklott and Klaus R. Scherpe, *Westberliner Projekt: Grundkurs 18. Jahrhundert* (Kronberg, 1974), pp. 41-73.

[30]Ibid., p. 51.

[31]Ibid., pp. 46-47.

has triumphed. Habermas also does not maintain, as Milde claims,[32] that bourgeois property relations are unpolitical, but rather that liberal theory considers the realm of production and commodity exchange unpolitical and therefore becomes defensive as soon as social conflicts force their way into the public realm.

Not surprisingly, Milde considers the question of disintegration in the public sphere to be unproductive; that is, he fails to see that Habermas' theory must be read as a critique of the problems in advanced capitalism. Thus he closes off access to the historical sections of the investigation and draws problematical conclusions. Because Habermas links the idea of a nondistorted communication free of domination to the model of the liberal public sphere, Milde assumes that Habermas also considers bourgeois society free of domination and then critically objects that Habermas does not discuss antagonistic class relations. He overlooks the fact that Habermas accounts for the disintegration of the bourgeois public sphere from social conflicts generated by contradictions in the capitalist mode of production. In other words, Milde's critique focuses on the genesis of the bourgeois public sphere, and his arguments coincide for the most part with those of Jäger: insufficient historical specification, problematical synthesizing, incomplete development of the economic base.[33] When Milde suggests that the English bourgeois public sphere owes its strength "in fact to the maturity and variety of ideological and political class struggle within the most progressive nation in the European context,"[34] he touches on Habermas' problematical indecision whether the liberal public sphere established itself before or simultaneously with industrial capitalism.

In the final analysis, Milde's critique is directed against the tendency to qualify the orthodox interpretation of the relationship between base and superstructure in favor of an approach in which interaction (communicative action) is regarded as being

---

[32] Ibid., p. 52.
[33] Mildes' exegesis is not always immune to misunderstandings. For example, he assumes that for Habermas the bourgeois state derives from the functional transformation in the public sphere, whereas Habermas was concerned with demonstrating that the bourgeois public sphere constituted itself as an instrument of struggle for the bourgeoisie. Cf. Milde, pp. 54-55.
[34] Ibid., p. 57.

no less primarily important than work (goal-oriented behavior). Such an approach changes the relationship between economy and culture. Culture is no longer considered a simple variable, as in the orthodox concept, but rather an independent though interfering system. I understand the theory of the public sphere to be a first attempt to introduce a concept of communicative interaction within the notions of rational discourse (*Räsonnement*). The goal of the public sphere is intersubjective agreement on values and standards, which can then be used to resolve practical questions. What Habermas sees institutionalized in the public sphere—individuation, emancipation, extension of communication free of domination—appears in the 1968 essay "Technik und Wissenschaft als 'Ideologie'" (Technology and Science as "Ideology") under the category of "symbolically mediated interaction."[35] Since these deviations from orthodoxy are voiced in *Strukturwandel der Öffentlichkeit,* the reservations of the orthodox camp were to be expected.

Oskar Negt and Alexander Kluge

Two tendencies emerge in the study *Öffentlichkeit und Erfahrung* (1972): (a) critical analysis of the bourgeois public sphere based on Habermas but not relying unquestioningly on his categories and (b) the search for an alternative—that is, for a proletarian counterpublic sphere. The inherent connection between these two is especially important in the context of the form of mass culture in developed industrial societies. It is in this respect that the tradition of Critical Theory asserts itself; nor is it an accident that the study is dedicated to Adorno. Negt and Kluge use the framework of Habermas' disintegration theory but continue one step further and thereby turn critically against Habermas' model. They attack the idealist notion that the public sphere has at some point already taken substantial shape, and they exclude the possibility that the liberal-bourgeois public sphere could ever be revived in any form whatsoever. Habermas' ambivalence—his insistence on an emphatic concept of the public sphere in order to retain a regulative idea despite his insight into the irreversibility of structural transformations—

---

[35]Jürgen Habermas, "Technology and Science as 'Ideology,'" in his *Toward a Rational Society,* trans. Jeremy Shapiro (Boston, 1970), p. 93.

gives way to a clear and final negation. The resolution of crisis in late bourgeois society is sought in the proletarian public sphere. The bourgeois public sphere, Negt and Kluge argue, has only the appearance of being highly organized, functional, and efficient. However, "If one considers its true substance, then it is not at all unified but rather the cumulation of individual public spheres merely abstractly related to one another."[36] In other words, the self-image of the liberal public sphere followed by Habermas conceals the real structure, which is considerably more disjointed than bourgeois theory will admit. Negt and Kluge stress more strongly than Habermas that this bourgeois public sphere had an ideological character from the beginning, in that it negated its own material basis: the realm of production was excluded. Negt and Kluge resolve this tension between ideal claim and social reality, also recognized by Habermas, by contending that the capitalist bourgeoisie employed the public sphere in the nineteenth century primarily to serve its private, economic interests. The public sphere must conceal the fact that the state does not represent general interests but serves as an instrument of particular ones. From this apologetical framework, Negt and Kluge draw the not altogether convincing conclusion that the public sphere never really existed as a unified principle. What Habermas had described as an institution turns out to be a loose association of heterogenous organizations. Since Negt and Kluge do not sufficiently differentiate between levels of insitution and organization, the category of public sphere threatens to dissolve.

In place of a collective public sphere, Negt and Kluge identify a number of partial public spheres through which in each case particular social aspects are represented.[37] They distinguish first between constitutional public sphere (*Konstitutionsöffentlichkeit*) and public sphere as the organizational form of bourgeois society; in addition, they separate the public sphere as appearance of a collective synthesis from the forms of expression of certain use-value characteristics. By constitutional public sphere they mean the creation of a unified public principle by which all

---

[36]Negt and Kluge, *Öffentlichkeit und Erfahrung: Zur Organisationsanalyse von bürgerlicher und proletarischer Öffentlichkeit* (Frankfurt am Main, 1972), p. 15.
[37]Ibid., pp. 102 ff.

privileges and special rights are dissolved. In opposition to this is the bourgeois form of organization which prevents the principle of public sphere from prevailing against modes of private capitalist production. "The point is that the political public sphere should not exist."[38] The third point is closest to Habermas' intentions: Negt and Kluge introduce in the name of a collective social synthesis the existence of a common will, "of a meaningful coherence encompassing the whole world and the appearance of participation by all members of the society." Finally, the aspect of real use value coexists with this ideological construction so that actual human needs at least partially receive their due (emancipatory potential). The inner conflict of bourgeois society is characterized by contradictory aspects of the public sphere. Negt and Kluge assume that these contradictions are contained from the beginning within the structure of the public sphere. Therefore, they are less inclined to distinguish between a time of blossoming and a phase of disintegration. They employ the analytical sophistication of their arsenal of concepts in order to define possibilities and limits of the current actualization of the public sphere. The synthesis of the public sphere (Habermas' model) proves to be highly unstable. It is produced under changing conditions and then abandoned as soon as the social conditions change. "While the isolated phenomena of the contemporary public sphere are being criticized and this critical analysis is being prepared, the public sphere has already changed its costume."[39] The public sphere in advanced capitalism is abandoned as appearance without substance and a proletarian public sphere is postulated as the necessary alternative. Thus, in opposition to Habermas, they claim: "A counterpublic sphere, buttressed by ideas and discourse with enlightened content, is not capable of developing effective weapons against the coherence of appearance, public sphere and violence."[40]

This critique of the bourgeois public sphere owes more to Habermas than Negt and Kluge are aware. They analyze conceptually what Habermas, based on his model, has described as

[38]Ibid., p. 104.
[39]Ibid., p. 142.
[40]Ibid., p. 143.

the history of the public sphere. The results concur in the basics. Within the realm of media criticism *Öffentlichkeit und Erfahrung* undoubtedly has an advantage in that the study was completed ten years after *Strukturwandel der Öffentlichkeit:* by including the most recent developments in the media sector it is able to advance an important step beyond Habermas' results. Whereas Habermas' critique was concerned for the most part with content and response to programming, Negt and Kluge—in the footsteps of Brecht and Dieter Prokop[41]—deal critically with organization and the way in which it controls mass communication. The use and evaluation of available technology goes beyond the framework of the liberal public sphere and is therefore rejected by bourgeois theory as utopian. Negt and Kluge emphasize correctly that the problem cannot be solved with political controls (for example, equal representation on control commissions), but rather presupposes "massive changes in the mode of production in television and in its relationship to the audience."[42] Where Habermas, as an heir of the older Frankfurt School, once again calls on the bourgeois concept of culture to denounce mass culture, Negt and Kluge depend on the organization of social experience by the masses as the necessary condition for substantive change. In this way their critique points in a direction that was lacking in Habermas.

The media criticism in *Öffentlichkeit und Erfahrung* must be understood in connection with the concept of a proletarian counterpublic sphere. The proletarian public sphere is seen as the only chance of providing a historical grounding for social theory.[43] This is not the place to develop the concept in its entirety, so a few remarks must suffice. The proletarian public sphere is not identical with the labor movement and its organizations (parties, unions). To a great extent these have been subsumed, for historical reasons, under the bourgeois public sphere. The goal of the proletarian public sphere is for the masses as working people (not as a party) to constitute their own experience; in other words, for them to gain an autonomous sphere in which they can formulate their own needs. "The pro-

[41]Cf. Dieter Prokop, *Massenkultur und Spontaneität: Zur veränderten Warenform der Massenkommunikation im Spätkapitalismus* (Frankfurt am Main, 1974).
[42]*Öffentlichkeit und Erfahrung*, p. 180.
[43]Ibid., p. 143, n. 39.

letarian public sphere," as Negt and Kluge define it, "denotes not particular forms or contents but applies the Marxist method in a way that no source of social upheaval, no concrete interest remains excluded or unresolved, and it guarantees that the medium of this conversion and tranformation of interests is the whole framework of real production and socialization."[44] The proletariat is confronted then with the difficult and sometimes contradictory task of appropriating the bourgeois public sphere in order to prevent its misuse and with simultaneously constructing a counterpublic sphere. This new institution must not be understood as a mere organizational task, for example as the triumph of the workers over bourgeois society; rather, it must be grasped realistically as the expression of a qualitatively new framework of experience.

Habermas' refusal to discuss possibilities of a socialist public sphere in Western societies is directly tied to his notion that the proletariat as the "designated executor of a future socialist revolution" has dissolved in advanced capitalism.[45] In his view, revolutionary Marxist theory can no longer find its addressee in the proletariat. When he looks at the socialist world, it is also clear for him that Soviet Marxism has not been able to create a socialist society. Instead we find a political domination by functionaries, which under Stalin even became legalized terror in the hands of Party leadership. In this context the question arises how Negt and Kluge can project a notion of the proletarian public sphere without resorting to those very learning models of orthodox Marxism which were liquidated by Critical Theory. Because their description and evaluation of advanced capitalism generally agrees with Habermas, recourse to a concept of the proletariat is not without problems. On the one hand, we must define more carefully the proletariat and its class struggles in advanced capitalism while at the same time exploring the relationship between the political public sphere and the party organization—a central question for orthodoxy. The problem can be formulated as follows: can one even speak of the proletarian public sphere without presupposing a revolutionary pro-

[44]Ibid., p. 346.
[45]Jürgen Habermas, *Theory and Practice*, trans. John Viertel (Boston, 1973), p. 196.

letariat whose organization is to become the basis of this new public sphere? In order to develop the concept of the proletarian public sphere, Negt and Kluge proceed historically—that is, they elucidate through the history of the English labor movement possibilities, contradictions and limitations of the proletarian public sphere. In so doing, they reassert the existence of a class-conscious, struggling proletariat. Yet, in their conclusion they concede that this "proletariat" cannot necessarily be thought of as tangible: "'Proletarian' does not under all social conditions refer to a social substance."[46] To the extent that workers in advanced capitalism become appendages of commodity production, the "proletarian life context" can be defined only negatively as the blocking of needs, wishes, and hopes. Thus Negt and Kluge conclude that it is no longer necessary to organize real proletarian experience in advanced capitalism and that class struggle can no longer take the forms it did in the nineteenth century. To be sure, this qualitative difference is developed only in the form of criticism and analysis of historical class struggles in the early twentieth century. Using the example of Austromarxism, they demonstrate that the proletariat was unable to force its own organization on the bourgeoisie. The production process was excluded from the class struggle. Thus a political compromise was introduced that appeared progressive but that in the long run had to result in a defeat for the workers. Using the example of the German Communist Party (KPD) before 1933, Negt and Kluge show that separating the proletarian public sphere from the collective public sphere ultimately has catastrophic effects, for it leads to a separation from actual social reality. In their critique of the Communist parties which failed to resist Fascism, it soon becomes apparent that Negt and Kluge do not necessarily want to rely on party organization to revolutionize the proletariat. At the same time it is never made clear how the political struggle is to be organized. Thus a gap emerges between the earlier phases of class struggle and the current situation. For where Negt and Kluge reconstruct this earlier phase of class struggle, they are able to proceed from an organized labor movement, so that here the proletarian public sphere and the formal organizations of the proletariat (such as party and

[46]*Öffentlichkeit und Erfahrung*, p. 483.

union), although not actually the same, do at least overlap. Yet given that these organizations have been largely neutralized in Western capitalism through their integration into the late bourgeois public sphere, a contemporary proletarian public sphere has to be reformulated. Negt and Kluge acknowledge this and modify their concept of the proletariat accordingly. But they have yet to be successful in formulating the relationship between proletariat, public sphere, and class struggle in a way that makes visible a new political praxis.

The Public Sphere in Habermas' More Recent Theory

As far as I know, Habermas has never responded to criticisms of his theory of the public sphere. One can only speculate as to the reasons. Nevertheless, it is possible to draw some conclusions from circumstances both internal as well as external to the theory. First, the critique of Habermas' theory was formulated mainly in the 1970s, yet by this time the concept of the public sphere no longer had such central importance in his increasingly systematized theory. The attempt at a metacritique could not have followed directly from the older study, but would have necessitated reformulation of the problem in a new systematic context. Habermas' answer to his critics is contained in this theory itself, particularly in his analysis of crises in advanced capitalism, where the problems that were formerly characterized as disintegration of the classic public sphere reappear as crises of legitimation and motivation in the realm of the political and sociocultural system. Habermas seems basically to adhere to his earlier position, but he takes into account the critical objections to his construction of a historically ideal type. He chooses an approach derived from Niklas Luhmann's systems theory and on this basis demonstrates the crisis situation of advanced capitalism in a new light, which is also interesting for the concept of the public sphere.

The framework of this changed approach permits us to define more precisely the difference between Habermas and his critics. First, we see more clearly Habermas' ambivalent attitude toward the late bourgeois public sphere, his vacillation between a strict historical analysis and the use of this concept as a general model. In contrast to Negt and Kluge, the notion of an alternative public sphere is not open to Habermas. Constituting an autonomous proletarian public sphere that would actually dissolve the bourgeois public sphere is itself tied to an idea of fundamental social upheaval which, for Habermas, is no longer possible in advanced capitalism. Here he introduces three arguments to justify, his position: (1) the classical form of class struggle has become obsolete because of a growth in state intervention unforeseen by Marx; (2) because of the increasing interdependency of research and technology, the Marxist labor theory of value is inapplicable; (3) with the dissolution of liberal, competitive capitalism, the opposition between bourgeoisie and proletariat in its classical form has also dissolved.[47] Class struggle is replaced by the problem of legitimizing a system primarily interested in stabilizing itself. A substitute program is developed by which the system is obligated "to sustain the conditions of stability for a total system which can guarantee social security and opportunity for personal advancement and to prevent growth risks."[48]

The Scientization of Politics and Public Opinion

Even after completing *Strukturwandel der Öffentlichkeit* Habermas continued to examine the structure of the public sphere and its role for political participation by citizens. A first important step in reformulating the problem is the essay "The Scientization of Politics and Public Opinion" (1964), which critically presents Max Weber's model in which objectified administration and decisionistic politics are irreconcilably opposed. This technocratic model provides an appearance of cogent, objective logic without theoretically confronting the irrational side of political decision-making. Within the framework of this model, the function of public opinion is limited. Essential political decisions are withheld from discussion because they cannot be completely rationalized. For Weber and Joseph Schumpeter, the process of formulating political objectives in the public sphere is limited to acclamation. Public opinion leads here to the legitimation of elites and not to rationalization of domination. On the other

---

[47]Cf. Habermas, "Über einige Bedingungen der Revolutionierung spätkapitalistischer Gesellschaften," in his *Kultur und Kritik* (Frankfurt am Main, 1973), pp. 70 ff.
[48]Ibid., pp. 72-73.

hand, in the pragmatic model, as it was developed in the work of John Dewey, the relation between political decision-making and scientific research is mediated by public opinion. "Value beliefs" and scientific progress are joined unproblematically through public discourse. Regarding this model, in which the public sphere once again in its classical function, Habermas objects that because of the complexity of scientific theory and its technical consequences, scientific knowledge as well as social interests and values can no longer be mediated by common sense. Thus the pragmatic model is abandoned. At the same time, Habermas insists on the strategic role of public opinion, because, for the mediation of science and politics, it arises not externally but rather "immanently and necessarily from the requirements of the confrontation of technical knowledge and capacity with tradition-bound self-understanding."[49] This problem of mediation has two aspects. First, following his earlier study, Habermas asserts that the classical public sphere has disintegrated. Moreover, and this may be more important, the problem has become one of method: how can the rationality of scientific knowledge be introduced into the realm of practical life interest; in other words, how can instrumental rationality relate to practical interests? Habermas postulates an answer: "A scientized society would constitute inself as a rational one only to the extent that science and technology are mediated with the conduct of life through the minds of its citizens."[50] To be sure, there is no explanation of how such a mature society can arise. Habermas considers the conditions unfavorable in advanced capitalist countries, such as America. The aporia is both historical and theoretical. In attempting to get a grip on the theoretical vacuum by differentiating knowledge-constituting interests, Habermas prepares at the same time a more exact formulation of the historical problem.

Knowledge and Human Interests

In his inaugural address of 1965, Habermas undertook to separate technical, practical, and emancipatory cognitive inter-

---

[49]Habermas, "Scientization of Politics and Public Opinion," in *Toward a Rational Society*, p. 74.

[50]Ibid., pp. 79-80.

ests in order to refine, by means of both theory and method, the decisive problem for advanced capitalist society—the mediation of politics and science. At this stage the task of the public sphere can be defined as the linking of technical progress and sociocultural tradition through an emancipatory interest. The state of autonomy and responsibility (*Mündigkeit*) as a necessary, self-chosen goal of human action is, for Habermas, ultimately grounded in the structure of language, by which man is set off from nature. "Through its structure, autonomy and responsibility are posited for us."[51] The category of the public sphere is no longer exclusively historical but rather is derived from the quasi-transcendental principle of knowledge-constituting interests.

This derivation was not historically specified until the studies on advanced capitalism. In *Legitimation Crisis* (1973) the historical and sociological consequences are drawn from this transcendental principle of knowledge-constituting interests. Whereas in 1965 Habermas contended that "the knowledge-constitutive interests take form in the medium of work, language, and power,"[52] the later study develops these categories as partial systems within a total social system: work is formulated as an economic system, language as sociocultural and domination as political. The interaction between these partial systems not only determines the functioning of the whole but also characterizes the possible sources of crisis in advanced capitalist society. They emerge as crises in legitimation, motivation, and rationality. Within this systematic approach, which is more interested in synchronic than diachronic aspects, the crisis in advanced capitalism is interpreted in a new way. In order to demonstrate the impact of this approach, it will be necessary to look more closely at the character of such advanced capitalist crisis. Habermas considers advanced capitalist societies to be overlapping systems encompassing partial systems and engaged mainly in sustaining themselves and eliminating potential crises. To reach this goal, a large number of legitimating measures are necessary. According to Habermas, after the disintegration of

---

[51]Jürgen Habermas, *Knowledge and Human Interests*, trans. Jeremy Shapiro (Boston, 1971), p. 314.
[52]Ibid., p. 313.

precapitalist traditions, this can only be achieved by means of universalistic bourgeois ideology. Depleted as formal democracy, it provides the illusion of political participation without restricting government and administration in matters of content. At this point Habermas returns to the concept of the public sphere: "Structural alteration of the bourgeois public sphere provides for application of institutions and procedures that are democratic in form, while the citizenry, in the midst of an objectively political society, enjoy the status of passive citizens with only the right to withhold acclamation."[53] What Habermas had described in *Strukturwandel der Öffentlichkeit* as diffusion, as an intersecting of the state and private domains, as the transition to an objectified culture of consumption now appears as the shrunken basis of legitimation. Lack of participation is purchased with appropriate compensation in the domain of professional life, consumer possibilities, and social security. Habermas interprets the depoliticization of the population as the inner logic of a system in which a politically active citizenry is no longer desirable.

The classical public sphere was constituted in double form, literary and political. Therefore, its crisis in organized capitalism can be tied to the relationship between the sociocultural and political systems, while the relationship between the economic and political systems may be ignored for the moment. In the former case interaction arises in the exchange of social benefits from the state in the political system and mass loyalty in the sociocultural system. Disintegration of the public sphere can be defined in this context as a motivational crisis and as a legitimation crisis. The legitimation crisis arises from a dysfunction between the cultural and political systems. In Habermas' words, it results "from the fact that the fulfillment of state planning places in question the structure of the depoliticized public sphere and the formal democratic guarantee of private, autonomous control over the means of production."[54] The loyalty of the masses may no longer be presumed.

The legitimation crisis situated in the political system is op-

---

[53]Jürgen Habermas, *Legitimation Crisis,* trans. Thomas McCarthy (Boston, 1975), pp. 36–37.
[54]Ibid., p. 46. Translation modified.

posed to the motivation crisis in the sociocultural system. Motivation crises in advanced capitalism are caused by the depletion of cultural tradition and by the exhaustion of central components in bourgeois ideology which had continued to nourish liberal capitalism. If such a shrinkage of motivational factors occurs, the political system cannot count on necessary supports. Thus the bond between the literary and political public sphere is defined in advanced capitalism as a context of crisis-prone motivation: Because of the reduction of cultural tradition, political discourse loses its customary power.

The section on theorems of motivation crisis is essential for our analysis, for here Habermas attempts to develop this type of crisis both systematically and historically. He maintains that formal democratic systems are dependent on very specific marginal conditions in the culture which are historically unique and therefore not reproduceable within the system. The desired civic passivity rests on a tradition of the authoritarian state, for which the citizen is only an object of administration. Disintegration of the political public sphere proves to be regression to pre-bourgeois behavioral patterns or incomplete emancipation. The same applies to cultural values and socially determined moral norms. They, too, emerge from previous strata and are not immanently reproduceable in the system.

Traditional images of the world were abolished because of their incompatibility with the growth of instrumental rationality (Weber); simultaneously, the liberal ideology of achievement was increasingly eroded under conditions of organized capitalism, so that individual property finally lost its value. Thus structures become visible "that are unsuited to reproduce civil and familial-vocational privatism."[55] For Habermas, the new cultural patterns crystallize around scientism, post-auratic art, and a universalistic morality. Scientism creates an unstable situation because, on the one hand, it supports depoliticization with its illusion of pure objectivity, while, on the other, it contains critical elements that can be turned against technocracy. If the autonomy of the work of art is dissolved, a similar ambivalence arises. The grounding of art in politics as observed by Benjamin permits its instrumentalization both for propaganda and for

[55] Ibid., p. 84.

subversive countercultures. This evaluation contains a revision of the earlier thesis on disintegration of the literary public sphere, which had followed Horkheimer and Adorno. Obviously Habermas' new attitude on the functional transformation of modern art (loss of aura) was influenced by Benjamin.[56] But he follows his arguments only in describing the loss of aura (end of autonomy), without fully sharing Benjamin's hope for a revolutionary mass culture. From the argument between Adorno and Benjamin he draws the conclusion that "the divergence between the values offered by the sociocultural system and those demanded by the political and economic systems" is deepened.[57] That means motivation is diminished. The same tendency can be seen in the ethical realm, where the transition to a politically universal morality, presuming both generality of norms and autonomy of acting subjects, is contradicted by demands of the political and economic system in advanced capitalism. This happens because socializing processes no longer lead inevitably toward adaptation to social reality but rather increasingly exhibit unconventional results.

Legitimation and motivation crises are manifestations of what Habermas earlier referred to as disintegration of the public sphere. It was not seen simply as irreversible, but there was no ready alternative. The idea of a proletarian public sphere did not come under consideration for Habermas, because it cannot be developed without the notion of class struggle. With the transition from competitive to monopoly capitalism, however, the juxtaposition between the two was altered, so that the familiar forms of argumentation from the nineteenth century lost their significance. In his analysis of crises in advanced capitalism, Habermas continues discussion of the public sphere in the 1970s. He asks the question: Under what conditions and in what forms can a public sphere be constituted which hastens the process of human emancipation? Because language and communication (together with labor) are fundamental for Habermas, renewal of the public sphere is a central theme.

The discussion is carried out on two levels. It must be estab-

---

[56]Cf. Jürgen Habermas, "Consciousness-Raising or Redemptive Criticism—The Contemporaneity of Walter Benjamin," trans. Philip Brewster and Carl Howard Buchner, *New German Critique*, no. 17, (Spring 1979), pp. 30-59.

[57]*Legitimation Crisis*, p. 86.

lished theoretically that political questions can be determined not only decisionistically, but rationally as well, by means of a shared search for truth. Habermas adheres strictly to this presupposition against the decisionistic model. He argues that practical discourse has always imputed an ideal speech situation "that, on the strength of its formal properties, allows consensus only on generalizable interests."[58] On the level of historical interpretation it would be a matter of proving how and to what extent the structurally crisis-ridden situation can be overcome. Habermas offers no clear answer. If in this context he refers once again to the *Dialectic of Enlightenment* and to Adorno's *Minima Moralia,* his intent is to show that Horkheimer's and Adorno's pessimistic exposition does not offer a solution to the problem. Rather than capitulating, Habermas urges at least a critique of theories that consider the goal of a shared search for truth obsolete. This is especially directed toward Luhmann's theory, which had dismissed Habermas' theory as antiquated. For Luhmann, popular participation in administrative decisions is possible but not sensible, as it involves too much frustration. Habermas' argument with Luhmann remains in the realm of theory and never proceeds to a concrete appraisal of the possibility for a public sphere within and beyond an advanced capitalist society. Discussion of alternative concepts (Frieder Naschold, Claus Offe, Fritz W. Scharpf) does not go beyond hypothetical considerations. Habermas is aware of this dilemma and honest enough to articulate it in the concluding section. In Luhmann's theory the interest in reason is particularized; enlightenment (in Kant's sense) as a common goal of mankind is abandoned. Habermas is not prepared to accept this approach and thereby to forsake his concept of the public sphere. He equally rejects the path back to an orthodox Marxism. "Both ways," he concludes, "are unfeasible for a praxis that is bound to a rational will and does not avoid demands for justification but aspires to theoretical clarity about those things we do not know."[59] *Legitimation Crisis* ends with a rhetorical appeal not to abandon the idea of a society free of domination. This demand implies the necessity of a functioning public sphere in which political deci-

---

[58]Ibid., p. 110.
[59]Ibid., p. 143. Translation modified.

sions are discussed and rationally explained. To this extent Habermas still adheres to the model he established in *Struktur-wandel der Öffentlichkeit*.

In *Legitimation Crisis* Habermas basically limits himself to a defensive strategy—that is, he upholds fundamental positions of Critical Theory by metacritically subverting counterpositions. In *Zur Rekonstruktion des Historischen Materialismus* (On the Reconstruction of Historical Materialism, 1976), however, he presents the beginnings of a new theory of the public sphere (without, to be sure, actually employing the term). It is not accidental that these suggestions follow from his criticism of Niklas Luhmann, which should at least be outlined here. The dialogue between Luhmann and Habermas focused on minimal presuppositions: the question, namely, whether there can be a collective identity in addition to the individual one; in other words, whether inter-subjectivity is essential for constituting society. Luhmann rejects this necessity emphatically: the modern social system no longer needs collective identity, because integration is achieved on the level of system and not on that of normative regulation. Thus self-reflection within the populace becomes superfluous for the functioning of the system. As Luhmann maintains, "social evolution has proceeded beyond the point where it makes sense to relate social relations to people."[60] The achievement of identity, the capacity to define through reflection the relation between oneself and one's environment, can be managed just as well by the system. A partial system can be specialized for this task. Habermas correctly objects to the interpretive suggestion that it completes the dehumanization of society by turning all subjects "into mere environments for the system." Habermas charac-terizes the result of systems theory in the following manner: "Disclaiming any unity of system beyond that produced by normative integration means that cultural tradition can be manipulated according to control needs, that history can be neutralized. . . . Historical consciousness is immobilized in favor of self-objectification."[61] Habermas adheres to the postulate of

[60]Quoted in Habermas, *Zur Rekonstruktion des Historischen Materialismus* (Frankfurt am Main, 1976), p. 113.
[61]Ibid., pp. 113-14.

human self-determination, and that means, as opposed to Luhmann, that social integration cannot be achieved simply through
integration of the system. Significantly, Habermas at this point
resorts to the *Dialectic of Enlightenment* in order to articulate the
continuity of his critical approach as well as the differences in
possible solutions. He renews the polemic against atrophy and
ossification of the subject as the central objection of Critical
Theory toward modern, rationalism. Yet this position is modified
to the extent that both the autonomy of nature and of the system's structure is conceded.[62] For this reason Horkheimer's and
Adorno's solution is not revitalized, nor is Marx's approach,
which linked problems of system integration and social integration by analyzing the commodity in *Capital.* Here Habermas
notes: "Today an analogous attempt at cutting through theoretical connections in the system to structures of intersubjectivity
would hardly be promising."[63]

Having opposed systems theory while assimilating its prob-
lematization of the Marxist tradition, Habermas then outlines a
theory of collective identity which includes fundamental elements of the public sphere theory, although not within the old
framework (the liberal public sphere). Among these elements
are the categories of generality, equal opportunity, and universality of norms. The future society is expressly defined as a
"world society"; its goals include democratization and politicization of its members (both constant themes of Habermas). It is
noteworthy that Habermas now seems dissatisfied with these
concepts, as they do not appear well suited for characterizing the
specific nature of the postulated collective identity. In contrast to
the traditional concept of politics anchored in institutions,
Habermas stresses the subpolitical character and informal structure of the new collective identity. He mentions grass-roots
interest groups [*Bürgerinitiative*] as an example of this public
sphere, for their mark of distinction is that they bypass official
channels of communication and standard mechanisms of political decision-making. "The concept of democratization does not
really describe this phenomenon, because such interest groups

[62]Ibid., p. 114.
[63]Ibid., p. 115.

rarely extend the margins of effective participation in political decision-making. Their real accomplishment lies in changing the interpretations of publicly recognized needs."[64] It is precisely under the conditions of a fully differentiated social system in which traditional values and norms have been liquidated or have lost their influential power that Habermas now postulates the validity of a universalistic morality emerging from the fundamental norms of rational speech. This morality, however, is not deduced according to the form of metaphysical moral systems; on the contrary, it represents an open, emendable system which can be developed further through collective learning processes. These norms are constructed from identity projections. They "cannot claim the status of scientific theories; they resemble, rather, practical hypotheses whose success or failure depends on their ability to structure a populace's understanding of itself and its world."[65] Habermas argues, against systems theory, that there is more to be done than simply solving social tasks through planning. This potential collective identity is neither exclusively oriented toward traditional values nor exclusively a projection of planning perspectives. Rather, says Habermas, it develops without goal-directed, organized action; it comes from the communication of participating subjects. Habermas is careful to make clear that neither the state nor the party organizations can seriously stimulate this communication. Thus he states: "If a collective identity would emerge in complex societies, it would have a form of community identity hardly prejudiced in content and independent of well-defined organizations. The members would develop their identity-related knowledge about competing identity projections discursively and experimentally, that is, while critically recalling tradition and through the inspiration of science, philosophy, and art."[66] To translate this formulation into the language of politics, Habermas is thinking of counterpublic spheres which are situated beside and among partial social systems and which provide for their subjects a critical distance to the total system and its integrating mechanism.

[64]Ibid., pp. 116–17.
[65]Ibid., p. 118.
[66]Ibid., p. 121.

In conclusion we should consider the current status of the discussion in connection with the theoretical as well as the political development. The turn which is manifested in Habermas' writings after *Legitimation Crisis* (1973) is evidently grounded in his political experience with grass roots interest groups in West Germany, which have organized independently of existing parties and unions in the struggle against state intervention in the citizen's quality of life. Their partial successes have demonstrated that the thesis of individual passivity in advanced capitalism, as developed by Critical Theory, is only partially correct. Applying these experiences to his theory undoubtedly brings Habermas closer to the notions of Negt and Kluge. The structure of the early liberal public sphere as an ideal pattern is finally abandoned. A populist concept takes its place, recalling in some ways the proletarian public sphere. In agreement with his earlier theory, however, Habermas avoids any tie between this new public sphere and historical classes, as is the case for Negt and Kluge despite their objections to orthodoxy. This does not seem to me to be only a disadvantage. Unlike Negt and Kluge, Habermas is able to escape the danger of romanticizing the counterpublic sphere. (An interpretation romanticizes if it generally and ahistorically imputes the possibility, if not the actualization, of an experience of total solidarity within the proletariat as the oppressed class.) The opposition of bourgeois and proletarian public sphere suggest the opposition of society and community. Habermas avoids such a transfiguration of historical formations, which he does not find useful for the current situation. This opposition of liberal and proletarian public spheres might sound like Ferdinand Tönnies' juxtaposition of society and community. Fortunately, Habermas avoids such an idealization of historical formations—which would be less than useful for the definition of the present situation—by taking up the discussion with Luhmann's systems theory.

It would be difficult to argue that this discussion has found a satisfactory conclusion. Habermas' populist concept is still relatively vague and requires specification. That could come about if the idea of collective identity is analyzed against the background of the social structures it seeks to affect. How and why does a collective identity arise in advanced capitalist societies against the expectations of systems theory? How does it relate (as a new public sphere) to traditional classes and their conflicts? In what way does a new social and political praxis emerge from aesthetic experimentation after the end of the autonomous work of art, as Habermas expects? Such questions, as yet unanswered by Habermas, should indicate the direction of future debate.

INDEX

Index

Index

Index

Library of Congress Cataloging in Publication Data

Hohendahl, Peter Uwe,
   The institution of criticism.

   Essays translated from German.
   Includes index.
   Contents: Introduction—Literary criticism and
the public sphere—The end of an institution?—[etc.]
    1. Criticism—Addresses, essays, lectures. I. Title.
PN85.H6   801'.95'09   81-15188
ISBN 0-8014-1325-7   AACR2